The Idea of
Higher Education

SRHE and Open University Press Imprint
General Editor: Heather Eggins

The Idea of
Higher Education

Ronald Barnett

The Society for Research into Higher Education
& Open University Press

Published by SRHE and
Open University Press
Celtic Court
22 Ballmoor
Buckingham
MK18 1XW

and

1900 Frost Road, Suite 101
Bristol, PA 19007, USA

First published 1990
Reprinted 1994,1997

British Library Cataloguing in Publication Data

Barnett, Ronald
  The idea of higher education.
  1. Great Britain. Higher education. Theories
  I. Title
  378.001

  ISBN 0-335-09421-X
  ISBN 0-335-09420-1 pbk

Library of Congress Cataloging-in-Publication Data

Barnett, Ronald, 1947–
    The idea of higher education / Ronald Barnett.
      p. cm.
    Includes bibliographical references.
    ISBN 0-335-09421-X – ISBN 0-335-09420-1
(pbk.)
      1. Education, Higher–Aims and objectives.   2. Education, Higher–
Philosophy.   I. Title
  LB2322.B37   1990
  378'.01—dc20   89-48476 CIP

Typeset by Rowland Phototypesetting Limited
Bury St Edmunds, Suffolk
Printed in Great Britain by St Edmundsbury Press Limited
Bury St Edmunds, Suffolk

For my mother

Contents

Acknowledgements

It gives me much pleasure to acknowledge my debt to several friends. Tony Becher, Roy Niblett, David Watson, Kenneth Wilson and John Wyatt responded to my request to read the manuscript with generous diligence. Their perceptive comments gave me much to reflect on in subsequent redraftings, although it should not be assumed that they will subscribe to everything in the finished work; I know that they will not. Robert Murray performed a similar task but, even more, supported the idea of this book from its inception, helping to see it through to publication.

The appearance of this book also owes much to Terry Moore who, over several years, was my supervisor for two research theses in the University of London. Not only did that period see the thinking behind this book begin to take shape, as I was encouraged to develop my own ideas; it was also an open learning experience much akin to that argued for here. I am pleased to record my appreciation of the assistance I have received from my employer, the Council for National Academic Awards: to sabbatical leave has been added more intangible backing for these extramural efforts. Finally, the support given to me by my wife, Upma Barnett, has been prodigious: my energy level has been maintained by her continuing interest and the manuscript has benefited considerably from her professional editorial skills. I accept, of course, entire responsibility for any inaccuracies and omissions that remain.

Introduction

The aim of this book is quite simple. Its focus is higher education, and its purpose is to ask: What is it all about?

The introduction could be left there, but the reader may like to know something about the general approach taken. First, this work is essentially conceptual in nature, for I attempt to explain what is meant by 'higher education'. The strategy adopted, though, is far from being confined to a philosophical analysis, for the book takes its bearings partly from what is actually happening in the world of higher education; and it goes on to make some definite proposals.

The second point is double-barrelled. On the one hand, I shall claim that the general analysis I offer of 'higher education' does reflect our common understanding of the term. On the other hand, I am not suggesting that the implications that I go on to draw from that general conception, or the specific proposals I make, are normally accepted or are much to be found in place in the curriculum in higher education institutions. Indeed, that is part of the purpose of the book – to recover our hidden understandings of the term and to show what it would mean for our aims and practices if we were to take 'higher education' seriously. This is not, though, a how-to-do-it manual. There are plenty of those available. While there are curricular examples to be found here, and illustrations of how the argument connects with current debates, the approach is unashamedly about how we understand higher education rather than how we practise it.

A book which tries to theorize about higher education may today seem a luxury or an anachronism, depending on one's point of view. Both lecturers and students have more than enough problems simply in getting through the day. As the resources available to higher education (including staff time) have to be used more economically, as institutions are being restructured, and as students focus their energies on gaining a good degree in order to secure a well-paid career, the idea of reflecting about the aims of higher education may seem self-indulgent. But it is precisely because there is little reflection of this kind that the attempt to work out an integrated view of higher education is needed now.

There is a further motivation behind this book. Not only is higher education facing pressing problems of funding, structure, resources and numbers of students, but it is also undergoing a fundamental shift in its relationship to society. Higher education is securing more funding from industry and other independent sources; it is offering more consultancy and other services to the marketplace; and its research profile is more geared to the needs of private sponsors. Most recent of all, the curriculum itself has begun to undergo a remarkable change. In the UK, under the influence of governmental and industrial agencies, the curriculum is being shifted ever more towards developing enterprise, competence and industry-related skills in the student body.

These are striking developments but, in reality, they are just symptoms of a much more profound problem facing higher education across the Western world. There are certain features which collectively affect the deep structure of, and possibilities open to, higher education. As a result, the historical conception of higher education as standing for intrinsically worthwhile ends – essentially, the idea of a liberal higher education – is being lost from sight. The question, therefore, I want to address is: Can the idea of a liberal higher education be recovered, and be implemented? I shall try to show that it can.

The argument is in three stages. First, I try to show (Chapter 2) that, in its various formulations through history, the idea of higher education has contained – as I term it – an emancipatory element. The idea of higher education promises a freeing of the mind, but also looks beyond to bringing about a new level of self-empowerment in the individual student.

However, as we see in the second stage of the book, this emancipatory concept of higher education is faced with a double undermining. On the one hand, liberal higher education has rested on the assumption that objective knowledge and truth are attainable. But this assumption has recently been put in doubt with modern developments in philosophy, such as relativism, critical theory and post-structuralism. This amounts to an epistemological undermining of higher education.

The liberal idea of higher education rests on the additional assumption that higher education is offered in institutional settings relatively independent of narrow social interests. This axiom, too, has been undermined. First, higher education has become a pivotal institution in the apparatus of the modern state and, secondly, the academic community has grown in size and influence to such an extent that it has become a pseudo-class in its own right, exerting its own partial claims on the curriculum. So higher education has also suffered a sociological undermining.

In the final section, I try to show, in the face of this double undermining (epistemological and sociological), that it is possible to reinstate a liberal higher education in such a way as to do justice to its emancipatory promise. Attention has to be paid both to the content of the curriculum and to its educational processes. Specifically, I propose four strategies: critical self-reflection by the student; open learning, including group activities; elements of interdisciplinarity being introduced to open up the student's programme of studies; and a particular place being given to philosophical and sociological perspectives, in casting light on the student's core curriculum. If these four strategies are taken on board together, a liberal higher education with genuine emancipatory potential can be realized, even against the double undermining which confronts it.

The argument can be set down simply enough but, if it is to be substantiated, it has to be set within a justificatory framework. That framework needs to be established because, at present, there is no recognized way of conducting a serious educational discussion of higher education, at least in the UK. In what follows, between exposing the double undermining and constructing a new conception (in the final section), there is, therefore, an intermediate section. Key concepts – culture, rationality, research and academic freedom – are analysed, so building the structure on which rest the proposals of the final section. The argument moves on two levels, therefore. There is a specific argument, and it is set out in a theoretical framework which is constructed at the same time.

Because the argument of the book is mainly conceptual in character, the idea of higher education developed here – if it has any validity – should have a value not confined to any one country. The argument is certainly connected with the way things are in the world, but its empirical location is that of the modern industrial state in general. Also, the theoretical resources for the book have been drawn widely from several countries of that kind. Particularly in the USA, but also in Europe, I have turned to writers working in philosophy and in social theory, as well as in the field of education. Admittedly, the examples of changes in the curriculum that I identify are taken mainly from the UK, because I am most familiar with its developments. But the examples are intended to fill out an argument which is independent of the UK.

It will be obvious from these introductory notes that the first half of the book has a predominantly theoretical flavour, as the basic argument is established. As the book goes on, though, the discussion becomes more focused on curricular matters. And the final chapters contain my practical suggestions. Some readers may wish to avoid the base-building of the earlier chapters and turn directly to the second half of the book. I hope that such readers will dip into the first half at some stage, for it provides the foundations of the proposals that emerge later on.

Talk of a theoretical framework should not deter the prospective reader, for the book has been written with different audiences in mind.

In the first place, it is addressed to individuals active in higher education, including the institutional leader, lecturer, administrator and student. The real test of the validity of this book is whether those engaged at the sharp end can recognize in the argument at least something of their educational aspirations, if not their actual practices.

Secondly, I hope that this book will interest different groups of scholars. These include, obviously, the growing number of those who are involved in research and scholarship devoted to higher education itself. Another group consists of those who are interested in the philosophy of education, for the approach I have taken may be helpful in giving philosophy of education a new sense of direction. Finally, those doing work in social theory, epistemology and critical theory may find some interest in this work. Their contemporary debates have certainly helped my own thinking, and it is just possible that this work may have a reciprocal interest in showing how their insights can be extended to higher education.

Above all, this book has been written for anyone who cares about higher education.

Part 1

Higher Education –
Educationally Speaking

1

The Missing Element

The paradox of higher education

Higher education is facing many difficulties in the modern world. Some even believe that these difficulties constitute a crisis (Scott 1984; Reeves 1988). I agree, but there is a particular crisis facing higher education which has been largely overlooked. It is a crisis to do with the way in which we understand higher education, the fundamental principles on which the idea of higher education has traditionally stood, and the way in which those principles are being undermined.

It is worth reminding ourselves that, in one sense at least, higher education is far from being an institution undergoing fundamental difficulties. Higher education, if only in terms of the number of people who are involved in it, is a growing institution. Even if its income has dropped in real terms over recent years, when seen historically it is a marginal decrease. Higher education continues to attract more people than ever before: in 1987–8 in the UK, there were 667 000 full-time and part-time students engaged on degree courses taught by about 50 000 staff.[1]* Allowing for research staff and students, we can estimate that there are around 750 000 people involved in higher education. And the total budget to finance the whole enterprise in the UK is of the order of £4 billion. Proportionately, in other advanced countries, higher education is even larger.

In any estimation, then, higher education is big business. It is a major institution of modern society. And yet for all its size, its costs and the increasing concern over its performance, there is very little attempt to stand back and ask in any serious way what it is all for.

Higher education in the UK is marked by the absence of any systematic effort to understand itself, at least from an educational point of view. We have an economics of higher education, we have a developing understanding of student learning – particularly from a psychological perspective – and we have a number of other approaches which I shall touch on in this book. But, astonishing as it may seem, we have no theoretical framework in which we can talk

---

* Superscript numerals refer to numbered notes at the end of the book.

about higher education *educationally*. Put simply, we have no modern educational theory of higher education.

This is a paradoxical situation. One of the distinguishing features of higher education is that it is concerned with the development of elaborate conceptual structures, or *theories*. And yet, in the UK at least, it has no theory of itself. It is as if, within higher education, it is worthwhile to develop an informed perception of anything except higher education itself. When it comes to understanding itself, higher education fails to practise what it preaches.

This missing element has not gone unnoticed. As Roy Niblett once observed:

> For every book on the philosophy of higher education, it may well be that there are six on its planning, five on its administration, four on the methodology of teaching its subjects, and three even on its curriculum.[2]

That was written in 1979. Since then, admittedly, the position has begun to change. A number of books have been published in the UK on the aims, values and goals of higher education. In addition to those by Scott and Reeves, others by Allen, Nuttgens and Birch have appeared.[3] But it is fair to say that we are still short of a properly worked-out examination of the meaning of 'higher education'.

It might be thought that this suggestion is exaggerated. Are we not confronted with a surfeit of debate and polemic over higher education in a way that would have been scarcely imaginable a generation ago? But, in the public debate over higher education, what we see is mostly an exchange over the size or the cost of the higher education system. Justifications for changes to the system are couched in terms of economic need or individual rights to access; in other words, a primary belief in the value of higher education to the national economy *or* in higher education as a vehicle for improving life chances. Consequently, in the public debate, the contestants' volleys pass each other by because the parties are defending different interests.

However, underneath the rhetoric, both the contesting groups – those who are concerned about the contribution of higher education to the economy, and those who argue for its expansion on account of the supposed latent demand – share something fundamental in common. Both viewpoints are instrumental in orientation. They look to the wider social outcomes of higher education, and in particular to its social benefits. This, as Kenneth Minogue observed in his book on *The Concept of a University* (1973), is a 'functionalist' view of higher education. It is an approach which is dominant in public debates on higher education; and it is a view that this book sets out to dispute.[4]

There are a number of elements to the functionalist view: it is not so much a particular view as a general perspective. It includes the tendency to understand higher education in terms of the values and goals of the wider society, and the drive to evaluate the effectiveness of higher education in terms of its demonstrable impact on the wealth-generating capacity of society. As a result, the costs of higher education and its contribution to the economy through supplying qualified personnel come to the fore. These kinds of claims should not be taken lightly. Higher education owes its size and influence to its host society which

underwrites its bills. The problem is that issues of this type exert a disproportionate influence, in two senses. First, even as reflecting the interests of the
wider society, they reflect a narrow set of interests. Higher education comes to
be judged almost entirely by its direct contribution to UK Inc. Secondly, and
more significantly, the functionalist approach neglects the *intrinsic* character of
higher education.

There is, then, little serious attention paid to higher education *as* higher
education, not only in public discourse but also by the academic world itself.
This missing reflection on higher education is evident not only among
academics who study education in general, but even among those who study
higher education itself. There are, though, three qualifications to this
generalization.

First, there *is* a modern literature in the UK, albeit small and irregular,
focused on what might loosely be termed 'the idea of higher education'. I have
already referred to certain books which have something of a reflective character,
exploring the aims and values of higher education; and there have been a limited
number of others (the most significant of which is the collection of essays on the
political philosophy of higher education edited by Montefiore, *Neutrality and
Impartiality: The University and Political Commitment*, 1975). There are two things to
be said about all these books, however. None offers any serious consideration of
the notion of 'higher education' as such. Most of them, after all, bear the phrase
'the university' in their titles, rather than 'higher education'. The other point
is that all the books I have so far mentioned have been written by authors who
are not themselves professionally employed as academic educationalists.[5]
Extraordinarily, it appears that if there is to be a literature on higher education
from an educational point of view, it is unlikely to emerge from that branch of
the academic community which is paid to study education.

Admittedly, there have been some contributions from within the fold –
departments and institutes of education – and this is the second qualification to
the earlier generalization. Some books, though not many, on the philosophy or
the sociology of education, contain the occasional reflective passage on higher
education; White's (1982) book on *The Aims of Education Restated* is an example.
And there has been the occasional article in the academic literature and
elsewhere. Here, two observations are worth making. So far as general educational books are concerned, there is little recognition that higher education
might pose conceptual problems of its own, and even less acknowledgement that
higher education might offer the chance of attaining some aims which are not
normally achievable elsewhere in the educational system. And so far as the more
specialist articles are concerned, the problem is just that: they are relatively
inaccessible, and have appeared too much at random to generate a real
debate.

That leads to the third and last qualification. There is a debate on the aims of
higher education, but it is conducted largely outside the UK, particularly –
though not only – in the USA. There, we find a book called simply *On the
Philosophy of Higher Education* (Brubacher 1978). It was so successful that a
second edition appeared. Another, less scholarly, work carries the title *On the*

Meaning of Higher Education; additional American titles could easily be identified.[6]

The point of mentioning these books – and others could be cited from Sweden, Canada and Australia[7] – is to indicate that a serious debate about the aims and values of higher education *is* possible. Indeed, it is not only possible, but also vital, if the principles for which higher education has always stood are to be maintained in a viable form in modern society.

The specialness of higher education

The reader may not yet be convinced that higher education needs any special consideration. After all, would that kind of exercise not promote undesirable divisions between the different sectors of the education system? There are two immediate answers. First, showing that higher education can realize educational aims of its own need not imply any undesirable division from other parts of the educational system. Recognizing distinctiveness need not in itself lead to separation. The second response is simply to reiterate that, as a matter of fact, the considerable educational literature on aims and values and the accompanying educational debates have largely focused their attention on schooling, with a consequent neglect of higher education. There are, though, some more positive points to be made about the specialness of higher education.

The objection that higher education deserves no particular *educational* attention on its own account rests on the assumption that higher education is a sub-species of education and that whatever is said in general about education must hold for higher education. I want, though, to make the reverse argument. Far from the idea of higher education being a sub-set of general educational ideas, the concept of education is itself part of the concept of higher education. It follows that the concept of higher education is not exhausted by talk of 'education'.

The explanation for this state of affairs is partly to be found in the term 'higher education' itself. It is not 'further education': it is not simply more of what has gone before. Rather, the term is a reference to a level of individual development over and above that normally implied by the term 'education'. There is, therefore, a conceptual distinction between the two processes actually built into our language. As a description of educational processes, 'higher education' allows for processes of education – as normally conceived – either as having taken place earlier or as taking place at the present time. But, crucially, it indicates that additional processes are taking place, bringing about in the individual student a special level of personal development.

The term 'higher education' is, as a moment's reflection will show, just part of an extensive language generated by this particular educational enterprise. The words student, lecture, tutorial, seminar, degree (bachelor, master, doctor), course, interdisciplinarity, academic freedom, research and academic community are not just elements of a language game. They are the carriers of, and symbolize, a set of traditions with medieval origins and having a wide international currency. They are testimony to intentions, embodied in special institutions, regarding educational processes which reflect certain kinds of values and are designed to have particular kinds of outcome.

Higher education is, then, more than just a sub-set of the education system. There are certain values and aims which are intrinsic to educational processes and which warrant the description 'higher education'. The term 'higher education' is, to employ a distinction made by Peters, as much an achievement term as a task term.[8] It refers to continuing sets of activities which have their own coherence and purpose (the task element). But those processes have to fulfil certain criteria in order to justify the description 'higher education' (the achievement element). There is a conceptual difference between primary and higher education, a difference which is not just a matter of the ages of those undergoing the associated educational processes. Setting out the criteria associated with processes of higher education is one of the tasks of this book.

Before beginning to pin down the nature of higher education, it is worth identifying some social factors which also mark out the idea of higher education as worthy of attention in its own right.

First, until relatively recently, higher education in the UK was provided almost entirely by universities.[9] However, the last 25 years have seen first the establishment and then the development of a system of higher education in non-university institutions, principally the polytechnics, but also a large number (over 100) of other institutes and colleges of higher education. In terms simply of the numbers of undergraduates, the polytechnics and colleges sector now caters for about 40 per cent of students on undergraduate and postgraduate courses.[10]

As a result, higher education is now offered by a diverse range of institutions, with their own ethos and mission. There is a wide interpretation as to what counts as a valid programme of studies for higher education. Credit transfer, part-time courses, professional education, discipline-based, interdisciplinary, open learning, experience-based learning: these are just some of the kinds of programmes on offer. This proliferation of varying models of higher education prompts us towards an examination of the concept of higher education, in terms of the various justifications on offer. 'Higher education', we can say, is a contested concept.[11] But a more unsettling issue arises: given this range of views and practices on offer under the heading 'higher education', is there anything that they have in common by virtue of which they warrant the same description?

A second matter is easily overlooked. The immediate clients of the system are adult and attend voluntarily; more than a third are over 21, and an increasing proportion are over 25.[12] We talk of 'students' rather than 'pupils'. Though not unique to higher education, these aspects may have implications for our understanding of 'authority'. For example, the students' maturity may affect the justifiable control that they might enjoy over the direction, pacing, evaluation and assessment of their own learning.

A third point which helps to bring out the special nature of higher education is that, institutionally, it clearly stands in a close relationship with research. The question then arises: Is there a *conceptual* relationship between the two? Some have argued that there is. On this view, all bona fide institutions of higher education ought to be involved in research. Others have seen little and even no place for research. Research, therefore, presents particular problems in the conceptual geography of higher education.

A final matter underlining the particular character of higher education is connected with its relationship with the wider society. The education system of a modern society can be understood as an institution whose functions include its capacity to reproduce its host society, both economically and culturally. Higher education, while it does have these reproducing functions, also has added functions by virtue of its relationship with knowledge. Because it is connected with not only the transmission of knowledge, but also its advancement through research, higher education has the task of legitimating society's cognitive structures. Modern society is founded on knowledge (Bell 1976), but some kinds of knowledge receive higher marks than others. Higher education is inevitably bound up in all of this, in developing competencies in the valued corpuses of knowledge, and in imparting an evaluation of the different forms of knowledge that are available. Astrology and witchcraft are not allowed in at all. The humanities are tolerated, but only just: they are increasingly obliged to prove their worth. Certainly, what counts as bona fide knowledge (as we shall see) is a philosophical problem which bears directly on our understanding of higher education. But it is also a sociological matter, for the post-industrial society looks to higher education to safeguard and promote the required kinds of knowledge.

There are, then, a set of educational and social considerations which justify the attempt to provide an educational account of higher education in its own right. Higher education poses special problems of its own, which a general account of education (from nursery and primary school onwards) is most unlikely to meet. It deserves special treatment simply because it is special.

The value background of higher education

There are other points which fill out the context in which an educational theory of higher education has to be situated. These arise from the undermining of the value background of higher education.[13]

What is meant by 'the value background of higher education'? By that term, I mean the cluster of aims, values and general ideas which have been traditionally associated with higher education, and which have commanded a relatively wide consensus in their support. They would include something like the following:

1. The pursuit of truth and objective knowledge.
2. Research.
3. Liberal education.
4. Institutional autonomy.
5. Academic freedom.
6. A neutral and open forum for debate.

7. Rationality.
8. The development of the student's critical abilities.
9. The development of the student's autonomy.
10. The student's character formation.
11. Providing a critical centre within society.
12. Preserving society's intellectual culture.

In setting these themes down, I am not suggesting that they constitute the only aims of higher education, or that they have each always received unanimity of support. Clearly, neither such claim would be true. They do not include any aims which link with the function of higher education to meet the needs for professional competence in the labour market. So the list fails to contain aims which would be thought by many to be necessary, if higher education is to fulfil its place in modern society. Equally, it poses a number of conceptual issues, such as the relationship between research and higher education – a matter, as we have seen, of some controversy.

Simply as it stands, though, this list of ideas reminds us that higher education has been regarded as an institution with a particular set of linked and intrinsic aims, however indefinite and ill-defined they may be. Higher education is not normally in the business of running casinos or selling soap-flakes.[14] It has its own *raison d'être*.

How does this claim square with the earlier observation that higher education is a contested concept, with all kinds of institutional arrangements and educational processes and practices being conducted under its banner? The answer is that the two propositions work at different conceptual levels. It is entirely possible for higher education to command a consensus as to the general character of the enterprise, while the realization of the general aims takes a wide range of specific forms. For example, the idea of higher education as a process which develops the critical abilities of students manifestly has widespread support. It is the kind of statement which is increasingly appearing in government statements[15] and in the views of employers and professional bodies, in describing the desired abilities of graduates, as well as being common in vice-chancellors' addresses on graduation day. But what actually counts as being critical can take all sorts of forms: Is it a matter of better managerial competence, being critical of out-of-date practices, or is it a matter of attending to underlying value systems and implications of professional actions, say on the environment?

In other words, it is possible for there to be wide agreement on the general aims of higher education, while institutions which bear the title *institution of higher education* vary considerably in their individual character.

In this book, I shall examine many of the ideas that appear in the above list. Here, I want to make just two observations.

First, embedded in our shared ideas and our public discourse about higher education, there is a set of interlinked ideas, something of the sort implied by the list. As a test, we might try the following thought experiment. Suppose we were to show that list to a number of reasonably well-informed people and ask them which social institution the ideas describe. Could those aims taken together be said to be descriptive of any other institution, even any other part of the educational system? The answer, surely, is no. In other words, what is extraordinary – perhaps without our realizing it – is the shared understanding there is, in our language and public discourse, about higher education.

The second, and more serious, point arising from those ideas taken together concerns their current acceptability. The shorthand for those ideas is 'liberal education', but the idea of liberal higher education has almost become a relic of past discourse. Hardly anyone today would admit to being a liberal in educational matters: it is no longer fashionable. And with good reason. Liberal education is associated with 'knowledge for its own sake'; but the thrust of present developments is entirely the other way. Skills useful in employment, technically useful knowledge, 'competence', 'enterprise': this is the discourse of today. And the new discourse reflects parallel developments in the curriculum. It is one of the tasks of this book to rehabilitate the traditional value background of higher education, and to reassert the claims of a liberal higher education, though in a modern form.

The double undermining of higher education

There are two principal areas in which liberal higher education is under particular attack, and their identification will form themes for the discussions throughout this book.

Traditionally, higher education has been founded on two axioms. First, there is a realm of objective knowledge and there are recognized truths – to which students are to be introduced, and about which they are expected to be able to demonstrate some assurance. This is the epistemological axiom. Secondly, the sociological axiom: objective knowledge is most effectively maintained and disseminated in institutions which are relatively autonomous and in which members of the academic community can enjoy comparative freedom. However, both of these axioms are under attack or are in doubt. In other words, higher education is facing not a single but a double undermining. The evidence for these claims will be the subject of later chapters, but it may help to sketch out some of the general features of this double undermining.

Consider, first, the epistemological undermining. Higher education is, in any conception, intimately connected with knowledge. The relationship is conceptual: a process is not entitled to be termed a process of higher education unless the student is having some kind of encounter with knowledge. But higher education is not concerned with just any kind of 'knowledge'. Traditionally, it has been concerned with systematic, elaborated, conceptual frameworks, worked up over time in an academic literature. The shorthand way of referring to knowledge of this kind is 'objective knowledge' (Popper 1975). Where it is lacking, it is difficult for new domains of knowledge and their proponents to gain admission to institutions of higher education. It has been the absence of a research base in support of new kinds of courses – such as food sciences, paramedical areas and sports science – which has prolonged their acceptance as bona fide courses of higher education.

So the idea of objective knowledge is central to higher education. But from various theoretical quarters – philosophy of science, sociology of knowledge, epistemology, critical theory and post-structuralism – the ideas of objective knowledge and truth have come under a massive assault. What, if anything, is to replace objective knowledge is unclear. Pragmatism, relativism, 'metacriticism' and even 'anything goes' are all proposed. The very diversity of the alternative options is testimony to the collapse of some of our basic epistemological tenets. As one commentator has observed, 'From a post-modern perspective, the central characteristic of modernism, in a philosophical sense, is ... that objective truth is assumed to be in principle unobtainable'; and that means even our observations about knowledge and truth.[16]

Turn now to the sociological undermining. Consider, for example, the relationship between higher education and the wider society that we touched on in the previous section. Particularly, but not only, in the UK, higher education has enjoyed a large measure of autonomy, ever since its medieval origins. But that relationship has developed considerable tensions, as higher education has been swept up by the state. As signs of this shifting relationship between the state and higher education, the concepts of academic freedom, neutrality and autonomy have come to the fore as deserving attention.[17]

The effect of this is apparent in the way in which higher education supplies highly qualified personnel for the modern industrial society. Students are increasingly required to undergo programmes of study which are organized to fulfil particular objectives and are designed within a restricted subject area or epistemic field. Restricted programmes of study ('courses', as they are appropriately known) are admittedly also to be found elsewhere in the educational system, particularly in the post-school sectors. There is, though, a particular problem so far as higher education is concerned. From Newman's thoughts on *The Idea of the University* in the mid-nineteenth century, higher education has promised, more than any other part of the education system, the prospect of a liberal education. One of the key ideas within the admittedly complex notion of a liberal education is that students should have an unrestricted access to knowledge.[18] As students, they should feel that the whole world of knowledge is open to them. But higher education in modern society seems designed to prevent such an open-ended relationship between the student and knowledge.

The point can be pushed further. There is a general recognition that the process of higher education should not be confined to the development of skills and understanding which are narrow in their scope and application. The 1963 Robbins Report on Higher Education is sometimes said to be the last important statement of a liberal higher education. Whatever the correctness of this view, Robbins certainly saw higher education in more than just instrumental terms. The Report talks, for example, of the general powers of the mind (1963: 6). We might wonder if such a vague phrase has any cash value; but we do not have to get into the murky waters of its definition before we accept that the specialization of modern courses of higher education renders problematic the fulfilment of any general educational aims.

An additional notion in the idea of liberal education is that education is worthwhile in itself – 'knowledge as its own end', as Newman put it.[19] Again, though, the growth of higher education has been accompanied by the development of courses which are explicitly vocational or professional. Is this compatible with the image of novitiate scholars acquiring objective knowledge in the company of a community of scholars disinterestedly pursuing truth? If the image is outdated, what do we replace it with, which does justice to the place of higher education in the modern world, but also has some kind of allegiance to its intrinsic values?

Here, I am just sketching the background to this inquiry, identifying some of the key features to be explored. Enough has been said to show the size of the task of establishing an educational theory of higher education. The double undermining – epistemological and sociological – of the value background constitutes an attack on the legitimacy of higher education. It is far from clear whether the values and aspirations for which higher education has traditionally stood can be maintained. And, if they cannot, it is even less clear what is to replace them. Higher education is, therefore, facing literally a legitimation crisis: its legitimacy is in doubt. Against that background, how are we to understand higher education in the modern world? Can we give a general description of it in educational terms which would command a consensus of assent from those who work in higher education?

Filling the vacuum

We have seen that there is little sense of educational direction about higher education. Some views about the aims of higher education can be detected in its historical traditions and in the seminal works on the topic (as we shall see in the next chapter). But there is nothing of a worked-out kind, which does justice both to recent debates about the nature of knowledge and to the place of higher education in modern society.

One of the problems here is that our views about higher education may be ideologically contaminated. This possibility has only to be acknowledged *as* a possibility. For if it is possible that any general set of aims for higher education may be ideological, can we seriously proceed with our search for aims in higher education? If we do proceed, how is the enterprise to avoid running into the sands? Surely, any set of aims that emerges will be open to the charge, 'That is just your view, representing your interests and values.'

This is a substantial problem which any educational theory has to face. There is no way of forming a pure idea of higher education, free of all suppositions and interests. I accept that I am approaching the task with a set of conceptual spectacles and wishing to defend certain kinds of values. These will emerge as we proceed. Nevertheless, what is on offer here is not simply an ideological view, imposed by fiat, for it is accompanied by an argument which the reader will be free to agree with or reject. The counter – that is merely your view – is, therefore, an evasion: it avoids confronting the content of the argument.

Where, then, do we make a start? Clearly, because we have neither well-formulated aims for higher education to hand, nor a recognized framework for theorizing *educationally* about higher education, the task has to be a pulling-up-by-the-bootstraps operation. In order to produce an overarching description of higher education we have, at the same time, to construct the framework in which we can conduct that theoretical inquiry.

What is to be the shape of that theoretical framework? We are not devoid of pointers. To begin with, we have to confront the double undermining of higher education. Because there are fundamental problems arising from our contemporary understanding of the nature of knowledge, we have to embrace debates in epistemology. Again, because issues arise from the place of higher education as a pivotal institution in the modern world, we are also obliged to take account of relevant debates in sociology.

Reflecting earlier observations, we will also need to pay some attention to what might be termed the social theory of higher education. The application of the concept of ideology to higher education is perhaps the dominant example; but many of the central concepts associated with higher education fall into this wide realm of inquiry, overlapping both social philosophy and sociology. The ideas of academic freedom, of academic autonomy, of 'the academic community', and even the notion of research, all fall into this domain.

Earlier, we noticed that higher education as a social practice has its own language, with terms like student, tutor, 'reading for a degree', and so on. This might suggest that we should also employ the techniques of conceptual analysis, uncovering the inner assumptions and beliefs of this form of life. But we have seen that higher education cannot be properly understood apart from its place as a key institution within modern society. That being so, analytical conceptual analysis cannot by itself deliver an educational theory of higher education which in any way confronts the social and ideological complexities of the situation in which higher education is placed. Nevertheless, the language is a pointer to the practices, assumptions and traditions which make up higher education. We cannot, therefore, ignore it in our search for an educational understanding of higher education.

The following six elements, then, suggest themselves as forming the framework for an educational inquiry into higher education:

1. The value background of higher education, its central aims and concerns, as found in its historical origins and in the seminal writings on the matter (Newman onwards).
2. The implicit assumptions in our commonsense language of higher education (as revealed in such terms as lecture, tutorial, reading for a degree, academic freedom, research).
3. The concept of higher education itself. What is conceptually distinct about higher education? What is *higher* about higher education?
4. The epistemological problem core. How are we to understand knowledge

and truth in the context of higher education? Can we assume that what is on offer constitutes 'objective knowledge' and, if we cannot, what are the implications for the way in which we present knowledge to students?

5. The sociological problem core. If higher education as a social institution is becoming increasingly incorporated into the institutions of the modern state, what are the implications for academic autonomy and academic freedom?

6. The ideology of higher education – at the levels of aims, processes and functions. Is higher education necessarily ideological? If so, how can we – with any legitimacy – understand and conduct the processes that we term 'higher education'?

These six elements constitute the framework of any adequate attempt to sketch out a specific theory of higher education. They form, in other words, the outline of the general framework we have to adopt if *any* educational theory of higher education that emerges is going to be adequate at the levels both of theory and practice.

There are, here, two senses of 'educational theory'. The first is the general framework, the skeleton of which has just been outlined. It is a framework which gives meaning to, and makes possible, our theorizing about higher education. As the theoretical framework in which we can seriously theorize about higher education, it can justifiably carry the title '*the* theory of higher education'.

This is not, though, a theoretical programme in the worst sense of simply producing academic armchair accounts. For such theoretical efforts, if vigorously pursued, are likely to generate specific accounts of higher education which offer an overarching view of what *ought* to go on under the banner of 'higher education'. This, then, is the second sense of educational theory: specific sets of aims emerging from within the general theoretical framework.

Educational accounts of this specific kind would contain a recommendatory element (Moore 1977). This is because the components of the general framework are such, including a sensitivity to tacit values, to traditional values, to ideological components and to social possibilities, that specific prescriptions are very likely to suggest themselves. In other words, specific theories may emerge from the general theoretical framework; and those specific theories will actually inform and guide our practices in higher education.

In this book, I want to attempt both tasks: to develop and to exploit the general theoretical framework I have outlined, and to produce a particular theory of higher education with a practical intent.[20] If it is to be adequate in both respects, the theory which emerges can be tested against two questions. How are we to conceive of our practices within higher education? And what criteria do our educational processes need to satisfy in order to justify the appellation '*higher* education'? If a specific theory of higher education cannot supply clear answers to these questions, it would not be a real educational theory at all. For it would fail to answer the question, what are we to do?

We shall begin by identifying the dominant values inherent in higher education, as found in its Greek and medieval origins and in some of the seminal writings on the topic (element 1 in the theoretical framework sketched earlier);

that exploration will also reveal some clues as to the substance of the concept of higher education itself (element 3). The following two sections will focus on what I have called the epistemological and the sociological undermining of higher education (elements 4 and 5). We will then look at certain key concepts, namely academic freedom, rationality, culture and research. And on the basis of these investigations, we can turn to working out a particular theory of higher education. Throughout the whole inquiry, we shall also need to take account of both the language of higher education (element 2) and the various ways in which higher education is ideological in character (element 6).

An inquiry along these lines should provide us with 'a progressive research programme'. The phrase was coined by the philosopher of science, Imre Lakatos, in developing a sophisticated version of Popper's 'falsification' account of the progress of scientific theories. Lakatos suggested that theories that do not withstand the severest critical tests should not be lightly discarded, but should be seen as part of a larger theoretical complex which, through time, can be seen as progressive, in the sense of generating more and more interesting theoretical problems.[21] I hope that the theoretical framework I will be using will be progressive in just that sense.

In the end, the specific theory of higher education that I shall develop will be debatable: it will be *a* theory of higher education. At the same time, I would hope that the theoretical framework in which it is situated and which will also be developed in this book will be seen as progressive, in that it generates a wide range of interesting theoretical problems and points to a number of useful resources which others may feel able to use. I hope, of course, that the particular view of higher education for which I argue will be recognized as adequate to the problems I raise. But, if I have at least formulated a progressive research programme that assists the task of thinking educationally about higher education, the inquiry will have been worthwhile.

2

A Contested Concept?

Introduction

The idea of higher education has a history. It has developed over time, emerging from its institutional forms in classical Greece and in the Middle Ages, to be articulated in written form in successive versions in the nineteenth and twentieth centuries. While there are definite links between the successive formulations of the idea, each version has to be understood in its own age. And over the last 150 years, there have been, at any one time, not just one idea on offer, but a number of conceptions of higher education, often set up as rivals to each other. In each case, we can see different configurations of social interests and values.

The question then arises: Is 'higher education' a single, albeit contested, concept? Or is it a number of different concepts, with little if anything in common? Is it a term which is used in distinct language games, representative of rival ideologies? When we look at it in depth, does the idea of a single idea of higher education vanish before us?[1]

I want to argue to the contrary. Certainly, as we shall see, the idea of higher education has undergone considerable development and, indeed, change. But I want to show also that despite appearances to the contrary, there turns out to be a high level of agreement over the conceptual core of higher education; that is, over what counts *as* higher education.

In this chapter, therefore, I want to engage in what we might term conceptual archaeology. I shall look at some of the main historical stages, and extract the key elements, of the idea of higher education. But this will not be conceptual history for its own sake. For, in recovering the key elements of the idea, we will be reminding ourselves of what the idea of higher education is, or might be, now.

In an age when our current concept of higher education has been so enfeebled that it has almost been lost from view, it is important to realize that higher education has stood for notions of substance. Our idea of higher education is largely buried in the past, but it need not remain there. It can and should be reconstituted, so that it gives our current practice of higher education a sense of being linked with a historical tradition – which it has largely lost – and a view of the way forward.

Before we start this part of the inquiry, let me deflect two possible criticisms:

that the material that follows is unduly selective, and that it runs together discussion of *ideas* on higher education with observations on the different forms its *organization* has taken. Both charges are accurate. But there is a mitigating plea.

My concern here is the idea of higher education, and I try to show that there are certain elements of continuity across the centuries. I turn, therefore, to authors who most sharply help to demonstrate this continuity. I identify institutional forms where the idea is contained in the institutional form itself, and where no obvious articulate writer is available. I also touch on historical and institutional matters in order to place a writer in the context of his age. Certainly, other individuals and other institutional forms could have been examined as part of the continuity which I draw out.[2] But I am not trying to be comprehensive; only making a point.

The Greek idea of higher education

Higher education, as a distinct social institution, has medieval origins; but it would be a mistake to begin any historical overview there. Although the Greeks did not have the large-scale communities of students and teachers that we associate with higher education, they certainly possessed *an* idea of higher education. Indeed, their lack of a complex institutional apparatus is an advantage; for there we can see the idea of higher education in a relatively pure form.

The Greek idea of higher education is clearly represented in Plato's dialogues. The dialogues of most help here are those concerned with the guardians and the lengthy preparation that they were to undergo to fit them for their role as leaders of the community. But of more interest are the dialogues as a whole, for dialogue itself is central to Plato's idea of higher education. The key elements in Plato's idea of higher education are these:

1. *A sense that what ordinarily counts as knowledge is contaminated.* Plato presents the allegory of the cave, in which prisoners are kept, and whose knowledge of the world is merely the shadowy appearances on the wall before them. Not having access to the outside world, the images they see constitute their only knowledge, which they take to be actual knowledge.[3] The allegory illustrates the view that our conventional views of the world, which we call knowledge, are epiphenomena: they are the product of other events in the world, the way in which we are situated in relation to those events, and the way in which those events appear to us, given our circumstances and the conceptual tools at our disposal.

2. *It is possible to see through the conventional knowledge of appearances to a new realm of unchanging 'knowledge'*, though to achieve it 'the entire soul must be turned away from this changing world' and embark on 'the ascent to see things in the upper world . . . into the region of the intelligible'.[4]

3. *The way forward lies in criticism of conventional knowledge through a process of dialogue involving the learner.* Only in 'the discourse of reason' can fundamental

assumptions be uncovered and questioned,[5] although that competence was, for Plato, only acquired after a long and arduous developmental process around the age of 30–35. The process was to be accomplished through a method of open, critical dialogue. Certainly, there were differences between masters and pupils in their possession of insight and understanding. The pupil, though, learned not through the master's didactic instruction, but through the pupil's own mastering of the 'technique of asking and answering questions'.[6] And it is this process which is exemplified by Plato's dialogues themselves.

4. *In this process, the student critically examines the knowledge acquired.* In modern terminology, we could call it a reflexive process. However, the Greeks were clear that this kind of education was not just a matter of cognitive development. For them, it provided a broader process of development in which individuals realized their own good or potential. The process of dialogue was not just an effective technique, therefore. It was deliberately and explicitly value-laden.

5. *This conception of education was connected with the idea of freedom in two distinct senses.* First, there were to be no limits in principle to the range and form of a critical inquiry. 'The philosopher, with his passion for wisdom, will be one who pursues all wisdom, not only some part of it.'[7] Secondly, through the exercise of critical reason, the student could free himself from the constraints of the world of appearances and attain a new life of independence.

In setting out this Platonic model of education, we do not have to accept it in its entirety. For our purposes, we can ignore Plato's metaphysical epistemology of a world of unchanging forms;[8] and we can also question the notion of approaching middle age as the time of one's life when that kind of knowledge is most likely to be possible. However, the five central points picked out above can be prised from their Greek inheritance. Indeed, they will recur as themes in the rest of this book, and will emerge as key elements in developing a modern idea of higher education.

The medieval idea of higher education

Although Plato's education of the guardians took place in a specialized institution (the Academy), the modern institution of higher learning – the university – has its origin in medieval times. The actual details are obscure and need not concern us here. Institutions which we can recognize as embryonic universities were founded in the late eleventh century onwards, with Bologna in 1088, Paris about 1119, and Oxford between 1167 and 1185.[9]

Cambridge saw its beginnings in 1209, following a riot in Oxford between the students and the townspeople, which caused a group of students to flee for their safety. The point has more than historical interest, because it indicates that tensions between institutions of higher learning and the host society have a long tradition, and are arguably a generic feature of higher education. If the relationship between higher education and society becomes too cosy, it is time to enquire whether the institutions of higher learning have forgotten their tra-. ditional role.

What then were the essential features of the idea of the medieval university? To begin with, medieval universities were democratic in two senses. First, they were open to all: each foundation constituted a *studium generale*. Secondly, the members constituting the guild of students and masters were joint participants in the enterprise, whatever their specific level of competence. Soon after their earliest beginnings, the universities were seen to warrant an independence from the rest of society. Each university was permitted by its ecclesiastical masters to become a *universitas*, with its members forming, literally, a self-governing community of scholars.[10] This independence was legitimized and protected by a papal or imperial bull. The corporate aspect of the groups of scholars was reinforced by the later founding of the separate colleges within the university, for the residential character they brought to university life ensured the continuing close association of the scholars.

Although the objects of study were strictly controlled – essentially the study of texts – there was an underlying axiom that what counted as knowledge required continual reassertion and demonstration. One of the key methods for this purpose lay in the use of structured discussions, or disputations as they were termed.

The student's advancing competence was recognized by the award of a degree, which could only be granted by other scholars. The degree was universally recognized, and it carried the right to teach in all centres of learning (the *ius ubique docendi*). However, there was no requirement to complete the degree, for the educational process was considered worthwhile as such.

In this brief overview, several dominant themes emerge as constitutive of the medieval idea of higher education. They include a participative approach to learning and inquiry, a collaborative form of internal government, institutional autonomy, institutions being open to allcomers, and a belief in the value of study in itself tempered by a critical discourse. Any modern theory of higher education will need to pick up these themes, and they will recur in the discussion that follows.

Newman's *Idea of a University*

In England, Oxford and Cambridge monopolized higher learning for nearly 700 years, until the establishment in 1828 of a non-conformist university college in Gower Street in London. This was followed by more conventional religious foundations in the Strand (King's College 1829) and in Durham (1832). In turn, efforts were made later to found a new Catholic University of Ireland, and so on 5 April 1851, John Newman – a former fellow of Oriel College who had been converted to Rome in 1845 – was invited to help in its formation and shortly after to accept the office of Rector. Newman set out his ideas in a series of *Discourses on the Scope and Nature of University Education*, which began in Dublin in May 1852.

In the end, Newman was unable to put his ideas into effect, and resigned the rectorship in 1858; but his ideas still contain much of value in understanding higher education. Those ideas, however, need to be seen in part as a response to the growing impact on education and knowledge of the developing industrial society. Consequently, we see in Newman's writings many of the themes which have characterized debates over higher education ever since.

In the first place, Newman considered that a university education should be 'liberal', by which he meant primarily that the knowledge it imparted should be 'its own end'.[11] Another view of Newman's – which today we would also want to include under the notion of a liberal education – was that learning should form 'a connected view or grasp of things'[12] or, as he describes it, a 'philosophical' acquisition of knowledge.[13] In both senses, Newman was attempting to keep the emerging industrial society at arm's length. On the one hand, Newman was carving out an idea of higher education grounded in something more than its being 'useful'; on the other hand, he also held to a conception of knowledge unconfined to 'the particular' which the increasing fragmentation of work, even professional work, seemed to him to be bringing. In order to be able to offer this larger view, the university had to take a generous approach to the domains of knowledge that it embraced. Accordingly, the university 'teaches *all* knowledge by teaching all branches of knowledge.'[14]

This conception of knowledge had implications for the curriculum. The breadth of understanding that Newman sought called for an active learning process 'which grasps what it perceives through the senses; which takes a view of things; which sees more than the senses convey; which reasons upon what it sees'.[15] And, as a model for the approach to learning, Newman drew attention to the 'sort of *self-education* in the academic institutions of Protestant England'.[16]

While, therefore, the 'object [of a university education was] nothing more or less than intellectual excellence',[17] it rested on an integration of experience and reason and required an act of reflection upon that experience and reason. In this act of reflection, it was important for the student to retain a proper conception of the relation of the parts to the whole: 'the mind never views any part of the extended subject-matter of knowledge without recollecting it is but a part'.[18]

Newman's idea of a university lay, then, in a continuing process of intellectual reflection on what had already been perceived. In his own words, 'if we would improve the intellect, first of all we must ascend; we cannot gain real knowledge on a level . . . in every case, to commend it is to mount above it'.[19] (The closeness between this view and Plato's conception of 'the upward ascent' is striking.) In other words, higher education is literally that: it is a higher form of understanding, gained through self-reflection on what is taken for knowledge.

What, for Newman, was the point of this kind of university education? In the first place, it offered 'an intellectual enlargement' or 'an expansion of the mind'.[20] Secondly, it was intended to produce 'the formation of a character',[21] namely those aspects of a person's character that were developed by 'the cultivation of the mind'.[22]

Newman, however, had an even more fundamental aim in mind, an aim made possible by the process of reflection upon knowledge and understanding.

As he put it, its purpose was 'to open the mind, to correct it, to refine it, to enable it to know, and to digest, master, rule, and use its knowledge, to give it power over its own faculties, application, flexibility, method, critical exactness . . .'.[23] The effect, as he put it, would be like 'a prisoner, who having been accustomed to wear manacles or fetters, suddenly finds his arms and legs free.'[24] (Again, the parallels between this image and Plato's allegory of the cave are unmistakable.) What Newman was offering us, then, is a particularly radical conception of liberal education. It was liberal not only in relation to the range of potential subject matter or the teaching and learning methods, but also, and more importantly, it was liberal in terms of its effects on the individual. The general effect of such a university education was an intellectual self-empowerment.

Karl Jaspers and *The Idea of the University*

Although Karl Jaspers' book *The Idea of the University* was first published in 1946, it was a revised version of an earlier work published in 1923. The dates are important because, in both cases, Jaspers was giving a succinct statement of the idea of the university in the aftermath of a world war which had threatened the values represented by the university. The writing is informed by a sense that the university, through the fragmentation of knowledge and its emphasis on useful knowledge, had underwritten nationalism and the new technological age. Against that background, Jaspers saw the possibility of the university playing a role in the reconstruction of a more humane society, but based on a more unitary and purposeful conception of knowledge. To a certain extent, the book is wrapped up in a European philosophical outlook, and is both idealist and existentialist in orientation. And it reflects the tension acutely felt within Germany between the state (and nationalism) and the university. Nevertheless, Jaspers' idea of the university contains many points of continuing relevance.

Jaspers considered that the modern university had four main functions: research, teaching, a professional education, and the transmission of a particular kind of culture.[25] Even so, the essence of the university remained that of a community of scholars and students seeking knowledge and truth. As a philosopher, Jaspers could not remain content with that kind of traditional formulation: he felt bound to offer an account of what seeking knowledge and truth meant. He was arguably the first theorist of the university to confront the knowledge base of the university and to provide an appropriate theory of knowledge or, in short, an epistemology.

Jaspers was particularly conscious of the theoretical difficulties of securing reliable knowledge. Although it might be 'universally valid',[26] knowledge is not absolutely objective, for what counts as knowledge is the product of a particular method chosen by the investigator, and which involves 'a framework of assumptions which we know to be only relatively valid'.[27] From where, then, does its 'universal validity' derive? Jaspers was clear that 'consensus is the mark of universal validity'.[28] What counts as truth is therefore the present point in a dialogue intended to reach a consensus.[29]

In parallel with Newman, Jaspers considered that the different disciplines constituted a single cosmos of knowledge, and so the university could not arbitrarily restrict the range of knowledge in which it was interested. But Jaspers recognized that the disciplines had become so fragmented that they constituted separate cultures of their own; the split between the sciences and the humanities was especially problematic. Jaspers also observed that the pursuit of 'universally valid' knowledge was more difficult as a result of the increasing tension between the university and the modern state. Academic freedom was therefore necessary, if the essential tasks of the university were to be safeguarded.

Knowledge could be pursued as a narrow enterprise, focused only on the world of appearances. But it can also, Jaspers reminded us, be pursued with a broader sense of rationality, of the value and power of the creativity of the human mind. This kind of 'purposive reason' can give 'meaning and vitality' to the inquiry into knowledge.[30] The life of inquiry into truth is none other than research. There was, therefore, for Jaspers, a necessary relationship between teaching and learning on the one hand, and research on the other.

From this epistemology and sociology of knowledge, Jaspers drew certain implications for the university curriculum. First, students must be allowed to be personally active in academic inquiry, and this in turn implies that they must have academic freedom in order to be able to learn in that way. Secondly, the importance of the student's own active inquiry (or 'research') is bound up with Jaspers' view of the nature of the individual's encounter with knowledge. *Higher* learning implies more than the mere acquisition of knowledge. It requires a sceptical and questioning attitude to that which is encountered as knowledge. Thirdly, and connected with the different realms of knowledge being ultimately complementary to each other, there needs to be an interdisciplinary approach to knowledge.

Higher education could never, for Jaspers, just rely on the individual student's approach to knowledge, however critical. For the search for truth and the critical outlook depended on interpersonal communication. And the form of communication required was essentially Socratic dialogue in which the participants 'stand on the same level'. It is a dialogue in which neither imposes a view on the other: 'both are meant to be free'.[31]

We can see, in conclusion, that Jaspers' idea of the university was not simply an idea of the university as such. It was intimately connected with larger views both about what it meant to be a person in modern society, and about the proper development of modern society itself. At the level of the individual, the educational process typical of the university cannot just be confined to the acquisition of knowledge, or the preparation for professional life. Understood properly, it is a 'formative process aiming at meaningful freedom', producing the 'transformation of the whole man'.[32] This is a transformation, though, produced essentially by the student acting upon himself. It is a process of self-formation through 'self-criticism'[33] in which the learner is 'referred back to himself for all his decisions'.[34] At the level of society itself, 'criticism is a necessary condition of life'.[35]

Is the idea of higher education ideological?

The four sets of ideas just outlined have to be understood in terms of their own history and culture and the social interests they represent. The education of the Greek philosopher-kings, the formation of a clerkly stratum in medieval Europe, the response of the university in the nineteenth century to industrial society, and the contribution that the university could make to social reconstruction following the twentieth-century world wars: contrasting historical contexts such as these are bound to generate a view of the university which is each partly culturally specific.

Looked at in this way, it may seem that the idea of higher education cannot be pinned down, that it is in reality no single idea but a number of different ideas reflecting the age in which they are formed. That conclusion would be premature. For what is striking about the different conceptions is their degree of consensus. We can readily see that there are certain recurring themes, such as knowledge, truth, reason, wholeness, dialogue and criticism.

We can, though, be more definite. We can say that there is a general allegiance to the university having as its dominant idea a community of individuals collaborating in a particular form of life, namely an inquiry into knowledge and truth. It is, however, an inquiry which is sensitive to the interconnectedness of different domains of knowledge, and the difficulties of obtaining real knowledge. Accordingly, the inquiry should be conducted in a critical spirit, having as an outcome new ways of perceiving the familiar. A fundamental condition of the process of higher education is a lessening of the taken-for-grantedness of the individual's hold on the world. It is in this sense that higher education essentially embodies a liberal outlook or, as we might say today, an emancipatory concept of education.[36]

That liberal conception of higher education has, as we have seen, undergone a succession of redefinitions, each redefinition meeting a particular set of challenging social and epistemological circumstances. Today, a new set of social and epistemological circumstances faces the emancipatory conception of higher education, and a redefinition is required to make it once again relevant to the modern age.

It could be argued that the attempt is flawed from the start. The different formulations on offer, it might be said, not merely represent a response to the exigencies of the time, but reflect certain social interests which the particular variant of the idea was intended to defend. On this reading, the various forms that the idea of higher education has taken on are simply shifting ideologies. For example, Plato's ideas, with their imagery of prisoners being led into the light, can be seen as an ideological justification of rule by the guardians. Newman's conception, in turn, can be said to be a thinly disguised apologia for an education for a leisured class faced with the claims of a vocational education for the emerging bourgeoisie.

Coming more up to date, compare the concentration on English and literary criticism in Leavis' idea of higher education (1969), himself a dominant figure in literary criticism; and the way in which the architectural historian, Nuttgens

(1988), singles out design as deserving a special place in the curriculum. It seems as if social ideologies in the early formulations of the idea of higher education have been replaced by disciplinary ideologies. They have, though, a single hidden code: 'be like me'.

At this point, the suggestion forms again that the idea of higher education is a contested concept and that it has no conceptual core of its own. The legitimacy of that reading, which sees the differences between the various conceptions of higher education not just as random happenings but as being related to social interests, is not lightly to be denied. However, it is possible to have it both ways, both that in its various formulations, higher education has acted as an ideological carrier,[37] and that there is in the archaeology of both the concept and the practice of higher education a continuing emancipatory conception of higher education.

The claim that higher education as a practice is potentially ideological is not new. It was made with particular force by the radical student movement of the late 1960s and early 1970s. At this point, we should resume our overview of the history of the idea of higher education.

The counter course conception of higher education

The 1960s saw an exponential expansion of higher education across the Western world.[38] During this period, the various functions that the university was called upon to offer were considerably expanded, especially in scientific, technological and military research and development, and in providing an underpinning for social policy, but also more widely, for example in legitimizing the claims of emerging professions by offering a graduate-entry stream.

In the UK, the consequent expansion of the system was achieved partly through the founding of a number of new universities, but also through the establishment of a new *public* sector comprising polytechnics and colleges of higher education. These latter institutions were to be 'comprehensive' and 'socially responsive', underlining the service functions which the expanded higher education system was being asked to perform.[39] Internationally, it was a period in which the 'multiversity' was firmly established as institutions grew in size to accommodate the new functions.

It was partly in the context of this expansion that the radical student movement of the late 1960s took off across the Western world. Far from being grateful for the system's expansion, the radical movement viewed it as providing an underpinning for the modern technological society. Higher education, from the radical perspective, was not a neutral force in society, but sustained a technological rationality which represented a form of societal domination.[40] The students sought critically to evaluate their educational experience, and to understand the ways in which, as reflections of the wider interests of state capitalism, their curricula constituted a form of ideological repression. Alternative forms of 'liberating' educational experience were offered, to assist the development of a counter-culture within society.[41] More obvious still, the movement looked to direct action beyond the confines of the campus. (The titles of the books containing their thoughts are significant in themselves: for example, in the USA, *University in Revolt* and *The University and Revolution*; and in the UK, *Student Power* and *Counter Course*.[42])

The analysis and the programme of the radical movement have not received the examination they deserve. I want to make just two points, the first on the theoretical analysis, and the second on what might be termed the practical analysis, offered by the movement.

On the theoretical level, the analysis offered claimed not only that higher education was ideological in character, but also that it was bound to be so. A position of neutrality was simply not available to higher education within the modern state. The analysis then went on to draw the additional conclusion that higher education should declare itself in support of certain social and political interests, movements and policies, and against others. On the practical level, the movement believed that ideas and knowledge were of secondary importance (part of the superstructure of capitalist society rather than the base, in Marxist terminology), and that higher education should focus its energies directly on action. 'Student power' became a popular phrase; institutions of higher education were, accordingly, to become revolutionary bases for transforming society.[43]

In effect, the movement was saying that, as an institution, higher education had not lived up to the promise of higher education as an idea. Objective knowledge, the life of reason, the full development of students, and the emancipatory character of higher education were being given mere lip service: in practice, they were not on offer in any serious sense. This basic analysis at least had plausibility, even if it was exaggerated. The problem lay rather with the remedies the movement offered. First, we were being asked to accept one ideology (its version of Marxism, and its view of the new kind of society) in exchange for another. Secondly, in collapsing together theory and practice, the movement would have had the effect of reducing rather than expanding the room for debate, for the exercise of reason and for the pursuit of truth.

The disappearance of the idea of higher education

The final stage in the idea of higher education is the current phase, characterized by a sharp change in attitude on the part of the state. Having expanded the system very rapidly and dramatically, it came to have doubts about both the economic value of higher education and, in the wake of the radical movement, its wider social value. The state turned to maximizing its investment in higher education, a move reflected in changes to the national systems through which higher education is delivered and its associated vocabulary. There is a new emphasis on value-for-money, accountability, planning, efficiency, good management, resource allocation, unit costs, performance indicators and selectivity, and there are reduced opportunities for tenure. Subjects within the curriculum are favoured to the extent that they make a clear contribution to the economy: the sciences and technological subjects are supported, even though they do not always find it easy to recruit students; the humanities and social science subjects try to prove their worth, by developing skills-oriented courses.

But if it is an age in which closer attention is being paid to the inner processes of higher education, it is also – as we have seen – an era strangely devoid of public debate about the wider aims of higher education. In a climate faced with economic contraction, and the threat to staff posts and even to institutions themselves, it is not surprising if the focus of attention has shifted from ends to means. The result is that, over time, the idea of higher education itself shrinks. The concept of the 'multiversity' is testimony to the increasing incoherence of institutions of higher education: with their competing missions of service, scholarship, military and commercial research, access and income generation, they have no single sense of direction. In so far as there is a publicly acknowledged agenda, it is formed around the problems of ensuring that as many students graduate and pass into employment as economically as possible. Any attempt to ask what it is all for is likely to appear at best an inconvenience and at worst an irrelevance.

A pure inquiry?

The modern higher education system stands, then, in the dock, accused and surely convicted of being an educational practice without an educational theory of itself. Where can we turn to recover an educational theory that is adequate to the place of higher education in the modern world?

One way, as I have shown, is to return to the seminal thinkers and the key institutional embodiments of the idea of higher education, throughout its history. Another way is simply to turn to the last period of fundamental thinking about higher education in the UK, at the time of the student protest movement.

The radical movement marks one boundary of modern discourse about the idea of higher education. Its fundamental analysis – that the idea of higher education has been undermined epistemologically and sociologically – was and is correct. Both objective knowledge and academic autonomy, the two underpinnings of liberal higher education, are not available in modern society. It is the movement's conclusions about knowledge and higher education in the service of the new society to come that are objectionable to liberal thought. The other boundary of modern discourse on higher education is marked by Kenneth Minogue's book *The Concept of the University* (1973), which provides a critique of the radical movement. Minogue's thesis is important because it is the sole modern British attempt to offer an epistemological justification of the university.

Minogue argues that academic inquiry is not concerned with matters of practicality. Secondly, academic inquiry is a continuing process: it has no obvious end-point. Thirdly, it is an *intellectual* process. Fourthly, it consists of continuing reinterpretations of what we already know, so that gradually we come to see the world in quite a new way. Fifthly, those who conduct this inquiry (academics) are assisted in this process by the presence of those (students) who are encountering it for the first time. Finally, the interactions between academics and students take the form of a Socratic dialogue. On this view of academic inquiry, there is 'a certain crudeness about distinguishing the work of universities into teaching and research'.[44]

Minogue acknowledges that this distinctive character of academic inquiry has not always been upheld, for the university has long been subject to attempts to assimilate it into society. This dynamic rests, he suggests, on the mistaken view that what counts as knowledge in society and what counts as knowledge in the university are essentially the same kind of entity. There is an underlying view of knowledge, termed Monism by Minogue, which assumes 'that there is a single world of facts for man to use'.[45] Against this, Minogue offers a dualistic model, in which 'there is a consistent difference in the kind of meaning that is found in academic discourse, by contrast with that found in the world at large'.[46]

Examples of Monism that Minogue identifies are the view that quality journalism is a form (albeit inferior) of academic inquiry, and the belief that the university ought to concern itself with important matters of social policy and welfare, providing, for example, cures for cancer and remedies for overpopulation. Because, by his definition, academic inquiry is not intended to provide solutions to social problems, this conception of the university is, for Minogue, profoundly mistaken.

Among other threats to the dualism of the academic and the practical worlds, Minogue cites the student protest movement, ideologies in general, and Marxism in particular. These he considers to be especially dangerous, because they offer an aggressive form of Monism. Not only do they want to run together the theoretical and the practical worlds but, in this version of Monism, 'theory must always be . . . a reflection of practice . . .'.[47]

That is Minogue's argument: how might it be appraised? First, as Minogue himself accepts, the university – ever since its medieval origins – has failed to realize the ideal of academics conducting an inquiry after truth, subject to the rules of rational, open debate. The idea has been subverted within universities, sometimes embarrassingly so. Equally, there has always been, and increasingly so, traffic between higher education and the outside world, both in ideas and in people. Journalism, of the kind found in the 'quality press', is just one such field of interchange between the two. The kind of tight distinction that Minogue is pressing between the character of the knowledge available within and outside the world simply cannot be sustained.

Minogue is, in effect, claiming a privileged status for the truth claims that typify academic discourse. But this view could only be maintained at the price of a neglect of the debates over knowledge in modern social theory and epistemology. There, to put it briefly, the key message has been that there are no guarantees of objective knowledge. In other words, despite its attempt to offer an account of academic inquiry, Minogue's thesis betrays an epistemological naivity.

The second difficulty with Minogue's view of the university derives from the scant attention he pays to the actual relationship between institutions of higher education and their host society. Nor is there any indication of the extent to which non-academic interests have seeped into the educational processes in higher education. We are offered an assumption that a pure Socratic dialogue is still available in modern academe, and that problems of academic freedom, academic autonomy, ideology and academic self-interest need not detain us. As a result, Minogue's account has a sociological thinness with respect both to the relationship between institutions of higher education and the wider society, and to the ways in which the academic community sustains, develops and transmits knowledge.

We can summarize the Minogue versus radicals debate in this way. The strengths of one are the weaknesses of the other. The radical movement was strong in its analysis of the social and epistemological problems facing higher education, but was weak in its characterization of the academic process. Minogue has given us a strong theory of academic inquiry, but has surely provided a misleading reading of the relationships between higher education and society.

Both conceptions focused on the relationship between the university and the wider society, in particular the allegedly ideological nature of higher education, but they differed over the character of that relationship and the resulting implications. The radical movement faced with directness the relationship between higher education and society, and sought to show that higher education was an ideological force, both as an institution and in the character of the knowledge it purveyed. In turn, it offered an uncompromising Marxist ideology of its own, believing that the only acceptable institution of higher education was one which explicitly acted as a revolutionary base for overturning modern capitalist society.

Minogue, on the other hand, anxious not to surrender higher education to any ideology, carves out a theory of academic inquiry as a bulwark against contamination from any source. Given such a view of higher education, with its own internal strength, it is not surprising to find Minogue discounting the possibility of non-educational and non-academic influences contaminating actual practice in higher education. But this is to claim a social and cognitive purity for higher education that it does not, and never did, possess.[48]

Conclusion

The idea of higher education has undergone a historical development of its own and a range of formulations have been offered. But what is striking is the consensus, from Plato to the twentieth century, over the core of themes and values for which it has stood. Together, these themes and values constitute what can be termed an emancipatory conception of higher education. However, that idea has suffered an undermining from two sources. There is the problem of objective knowledge – the epistemological undermining; and there is the problem deriving from the place of higher education within the modern state – the sociological undermining.

The tasks facing us then are these. Can we couple Minogue's theory of academic inquiry – essentially the idea of Socratic dialogue – with the social and epistemological realism of the radical movement? Can we generate an educational account of higher education which is non-ideological in theoretical terms and feasible in practical terms? Is it possible to reconcile the traditional emancipatory value-background of higher education with the double undermining it faces? The argument here is that it is indeed possible to achieve these conceptual goals. However, we shall have to switch our attention away from 'the university' (which is an institutional embodiment of the idea) to the idea of higher education itself. Minogue is right: we need a theory of academic discourse; but we also need to add to it a theory of the student's educational development, a theory which does justice to those processes of *higher* education.

Before we do that, however, we should be a little clearer about the extent of the double undermining confronting the idea of higher education, and it is to that which we now turn.

Part 2

The Epistemological Undermining of
Higher Education

3

Witchcraft, Astrology and Knowledge Policies

Introduction

Is there any good reason for not including witchcraft and astrology in courses in higher education? On the other hand, can we give any rational justification as forms of *knowledge* for the presence of fine art, music, physiotherapy, legal studies, business studies, chiropractic and theology? What is it that the second group of disciplines have that the first pair do not? I am not going to answer this question directly, but it is not just put rhetorically. It is a serious question; and if it were to be taken up without presuppositions, we might find that there is no single characteristic that the second group of disciplines share which the first pair do not. There may turn out to be no logical distinction between them after all.[1]

Without pursuing the matter in detail, we can note the following features of these clusterings of 'knowledge'. All are related to activities in the world, and those activities require a combination of theoretical and practical understanding. Indeed, on any objective appraisal, witchcraft and astrology might be found to have a higher theoretical component than some of the other disciplines mentioned;[2] after all, they have a conceptual framework, and their adherents entertain claims about the external world in a way that the practising artist or musician would hesitate from claiming. Astrology and witchcraft may even emerge as having a richer conceptual structure than legal studies, despite the latter having been part of the Western university for nearly 1000 years.

That, though, is not the case I want to make. I raise the question to illustrate that any justification that applies to the clusterings of knowledge found in our higher education curricula is likely also to apply to orderings of knowledge not found within the academic community. Any waverers on this point need only to recall – as the recent entry of chiropractic shows[3] – that our ideas as to what counts as a bona fide form of knowledge, suitable for inclusion in higher education, have been changing continually. For the most part, the process has been one of widening, albeit usually grudgingly, to accept the newcomer. Gradually, over the last 100 years, the natural sciences, engineering, the social sciences and, more recently, professional studies of various kinds have been admitted. Often, though, admission came only after a long struggle to gain approval, and some institutions of higher education took longer than others (Oxbridge acquiescing normally some time after others had done so[4]). In each case, part of the argument of the opponents was that *this* kind of subject is simply not a legitimate subject for the academic community to study. Each contending new subject was, in turn, felt not to constitute a serious branch of knowledge.

Against that background, although we might have a nagging sense that astrology and witchcraft are different in some way, can we be certain that they are? I repeat: I only raise the issue to illustrate the point that the basis on which the various forms of knowledge are declared admissible and acceptable to higher education are far from clear. There is no articulated account of knowledge to hand which a majority of academics would be able to elaborate and which would command a consensus of support.

What is it 'to know'?

Knowledge is itself the subject of study within the academic community, in the branch of philosophy known as epistemology. In addition, philosophy of education as a sub-set of philosophy has itself understandably paid attention to epistemology. Other branches of intellectual thought – such as critical theory, the sociology of knowledge and post-structuralism – have also reflected on what passes for knowledge. From all this, have there emerged any accounts of knowledge which can help us in understanding higher education (from a 'knowledge' point of view)? If higher education is in part founded on an interest in knowledge, and if knowledge has been the object of study in various inquiries, then those inquiries should surely be able to shed some light on understanding what higher education is up to?

The short answer is yes, but it is far from being a straightforward connection. There are two main problems in trying to take on board mainstream epistemology in understanding our 'knowledge' policies in higher education.[5] First, a major part of epistemology has been largely formal in character, attempting to elucidate what is meant in logical terms by such formulations as 'I know that x'. This debate, having been conducted at such a high level of generality, has little to offer in helping to distinguish 'real' bodies of knowledge from the sham.

It is said, for example, that to justify a claim 'to know', a speaker has to have the right to make the claim in question.[6] But this tells us nothing about the criteria which have to be met in order to justify such a claim. Further, epistemology has often depicted an imaginary single knower as its focus, undervaluing the point that knowledge is in an important sense a clustering of ideas, concepts and theories that stands independently to some extent of the individual.[7] In short, while much of the mainstream of epistemological inquiry may assist in helping us to understand something of the language of 'knowing', it can shed no light on the substantive issues as to: What is to count as knowledge? How wide is the field of bona fide knowledge? How different are the various forms of knowledge? What criteria, if any, should count in determining whether a form of knowledge is suitable for admission to higher education?

The second problem in trying to draw on epistemology to understand our knowledge practices in higher education is that where epistemology has had anything substantive to say about knowledge as such, it has done so by taking science to be the epitome of what counts as knowledge. Either it has deliberately confined its attentions to science, declaring that any other form of a claim to knowledge is spurious; or it has been prepared to come to some kind of view on other knowledge claims, on the assumption that science provides the standard and all that is in question is the extent to which other contenders match up as pseudo-sciences. This was notoriously part of the ensignia of the logical positivism of the 1930s.[8] But its representatives are also to be found in more recent times: two modern representatives of this approach to knowledge are Ernest Gellner and Karl Popper.

The shadow of scientific knowledge

Much of Gellner's work has provided us with an anthropological perspective on the thought and belief patterns of modern society, comparing them with those of the primitive mind. In that endeavour, he has not shrunk from turning his attentions to intellectual belief systems, including science and philosophy. Gellner claims that modern philosophy (especially in the hands of the later Wittgenstein) has naively presented us with a picture of different forms of life, of equal cognitive status.[9] For Gellner, this perspective underestimates the degree to which modern society is characterized by a particular cognitive framework, that of science. In a telling giveaway phrase, he sees 'the central question of modern anthropology (the characterization of the savage mind) and the central question of modern philosophy (the characterization or delimitation of science) [as] but the obverse of each other'.[10]

On this view, science receives high – indeed, the highest – marks as a form of knowledge. The corollary is that other possible forms of knowledge are downgraded; indeed, they are seen as not even real forms of knowledge at all. Non-scientific forms of thought 'contain claims, assertions, which *sound* cognitive . . . but it is somehow understood that they are not fully serious, not commensurate or continuous with real knowledge'.[11] Clearly, if higher education were seriously to take that stance on board in determining its knowledge policies, much of it would be put out of business.

Popper's approach, on the surface, is considerably more tolerant towards non-scientific forms of thought, and looks much more promising as an epistemology for higher education. As is well known, Popper has a definite view of the form that serious knowledge claims should take: they are founded on the method of conjecture and refutation, in which specific theories are formulated and are subject to critical evaluation.[12] But this method, 'the method of problem solving', is, as he sees it, not at all confined solely to science, but is also the way in which inquiry proceeds in other areas of human understanding, including the arts and the humanities.[13]

The Popperian epistemology is founded on a sense of an external world, against which we match our theories, in an attempt to bring the two ever closer together. This produces discrete problems and definite solutions; but *contra* Popper, we should note that very often there are neither discrete problems nor definite solutions. Consider, for example, the cases of professional knowledge being advanced through improved professional *practice*; of interpersonal under-standing and empathy being essential elements of thinking in literature; of genre and alternative theoretical traditions and approaches in the humanities and in the social sciences which do not compete against but co-exist alongside each other; of critical self-reflection as a method of evaluation of theories in social and psychological inquiry; and of the immediate (that is, unmediated) insight and knowledge that comes in the performing arts. Although it can be stretched in an attempt to cover such cases, the Popperian view is surely in some difficulty in these domains. This is partly because, in human affairs, we are happy to develop all kinds of response (depending on our aims and values). Partly, though, we are not solving problems; we are trying to do things more imaginatively, creatively and interestingly.

That much might be conceded on the Popperian epistemology. But then, it might be added, we need to distinguish those instances of the use of imagination or creativity which lead us towards truth from those which do not. We need, in other words, a criterion by which knowledge claims can be assessed. One criterion suggested by Popper is that of the impact on our critical discussions. Real understanding advances the argument through the presentation 'of some new evidence'. But very often, we can observe, understanding advances in other ways. Sharper insight, improved performance, conceptual enlargement, more acute value judgement, or deeper self-understanding: any of these can constitute an advancement in understanding.

What Popper is holding out to us, then, and what we should resist falling for, is a model of advancement characteristic of a single form of thought. We should beware of resorting to labelling; Popper was always keen to distance himself from 'Positivism', for example.[14] Nevertheless, Popper's epistemology amounts to a scientific imperialism. In his own words, 'epistemology I take to be the study of *scientific* knowledge' (his emphasis).[15] To accede to the Popperian strategy, then, would leave us acting as collaborators in a form of closure; of neglecting the inherent worth of other ways of gaining knowledge.

Popper's epistemology has, though, come under attack even as an account of scientific progress. Kuhn (1970) has offered us a view of science which sees it as less linear, and less coherent. Feyerabend has gone even further in pointing up the shortcomings in scientific progress, from a rationalist perspective.[16] Both have emphasized that science has made progress precisely because scientists have not been bound by the extreme canons of logic and methodology which Popper has outlined.

Before moving on from Popper, we should not leave the impression that he has had nothing to say to us, as we try to understand the manifold activities which make up our knowledge practices in higher education. There are actually several elements which provide a positive contribution towards our quest. Implicit in Popper's view of science – and non-science, for that matter – is the sense of an interpersonal exchange, taking place within a form of life with its own traditions, where the participants are seriously trying to make progress. These three elements – intersubjectivity, a specific framework of ways of going on, and a commitment to progress – can be found in other contemporary writers. They are part of an emerging consensus about what it means to be involved in the knowledge enterprise.

Epistemologies as selectors

Before we say more about that consensus, what general observations can we draw from our discussion?

What counts as knowledge does so by virtue of criteria held separately. Whether we allow our conception of knowledge to embrace the immediate awareness of her own limbs that a ballet dancer has, or to include the ethical considerations that are part of the professional's interactions with his client, is not a matter which is determinable in any absolute way. In the past, philosophers have sought to identify and indeed prescribe general rules to demarcate 'real' knowledge from make-believe knowledge. But the attempt has foundered. For any set of such general rules is itself based on presuppositions, that such-and-such form of knowledge is supremely valid. Questions can then, in turn, be raised about the legitimacy of the rules and the presuppositions that we are being offered.[17]

Demarcation criteria, in short, tell us more about the rule-setters than about the forms of knowledge to which they are applied. Those who are wedded to a particular form of thought are unlikely, we can surmise, to frame criteria which would have the effect of excluding their own favoured knowledge form from the arena. Rules for classifying forms of knowledge, especially those which result in admission and rejection, may look harmless enough on the surface. We may find, though, that in reality they are ideologies, serving hidden social interests and fundamental conceptions of man and society. (Is man as knower funda- mentally a technologist, interacting with and manipulating the natural environ- ment, or an imaginative creator of artistic artefacts, or perhaps an empathic social being in communication with recognized 'others'?)

Epistemologies which serve as selectors, ruling this form of knowledge in and that form out, have therefore two characteristics which indicate their unsuit- ability as an underpinning for our knowledge policies in higher education.

Firstly, institutions of higher education in principle offer the prospect of an open inquiry after truth. This means that no serious contender for knowledge can be ruled out in advance and kept outside the discourse of the academic community.[18] Instead, it must be allowed in to state its claims, for it has a right to be heard. The problem with selector epistemologies is that they determine in advance what shall be allowed to join the discourse. They prejudge the issue. Alternative viewpoints are denied a hearing. (Consider, for example, the difficulty that alternative medicine has to be taken seriously. Part of the problem is that it is not even granted a fair opportunity to state its case; it is declared inadmissible, and considered not to amount to real medical knowledge, without a hearing. That is why the admission of chiropractic, albeit to the public sector of UK higher education, is so signal a development.)

Secondly, selector epistemologies are far from being the open supremely rational viewpoints they take themselves to be. A selector epistemology is none other than an evaluation of forms of life, declaring that this rather than that is the preferred form of life. Some time ago, in his book *Education*, Spencer (1929) asked the question: 'Which knowledge is of most worth?' But the answer cannot be supplied in some kind of academic quarantine. It has to reflect wider allegiances to the kind of society we want or can envisage or can feel slipping away. So we find, for example, Leavis' (1969) impassioned plea for the maintenance of a strong English school in the university as a defence against the 'technologico-Benthamite' tendencies of the age, as he saw it. Epistemologies (in their widest sense) cannot be taken at their face value purely as a technical account of knowledge.[19] Any attempt to offer us a classification of knowledge begs the question: Why this view of society, rather than any other? Selector epistemologies cannot, therefore, provide us with any sure ground on which to base our knowledge policies in higher education.[20]

Broadening the base

We appear to have run into an impasse. Any attempt to lay down rules as to what is to count as real, bona fide knowledge as opposed to make-believe, shadow knowledge is open to the charge of acting as judge before the hearing has got under way. Is there, then, any rational basis for deciding what is legitimate and what is not? Is everything to be allowed in? Are witchcraft and astrology suitable candidates after all? Is there a middle way between being overly restrictive and being too liberal in the application of rules for distinguishing putative knowledge forms?

The reader will have sensed how tendentious is the term 'knowledge'. Its application is never simply a neutral description: the mere application of the term is to offer an evaluation. In being applied to a form of awareness, the term 'knowledge' evaluates that realm of awareness as coming up to some standard or other; and in so doing, it places a positive evaluation on it. Or if the evaluation leads to a withholding of the appellation 'knowledge', the form of awareness is actually disparaged (as not really amounting to knowledge). In the post-industrial society, formalized knowledge is crucial (Bell 1976); and so the use of the term is bound to act as a form of praise – or disparagement.

There is a double-bind here. Because there are no presuppositionless or value-neutral criteria of knowledge, we seem to be obliged to possess criteria and values before we begin to apply the term 'knowledge'; before, that is to say, some forms of awareness are ruled in and some are ruled out. But this is to commit ourselves to a prior theory of knowledge, this presupposing just that which is in question. On the other hand, if we decline to prejudge in this way, we end up by not being able to discriminate at all. This is an uncomfortable situation. We are not in a position to state unequivocally that a form of awareness *is* a form of knowledge; but nor do we want to stand idly by, unable to say anything of substance. Faced with the prospect of being asked to admit a prospective field of knowledge to the academic community (say, occupational therapy), or of having to justify as a form of knowledge the retention of a problematic knowledge area (say, philosophy), we seem to be impotent. Clear, uncontroversial answers are simply unavailable.[21]

There is a real problem here. Our age is characterized by rapidly shifting conceptions of knowledge, with candidates for inclusion vying with possible victims of expulsion. Most notably, in the technological, computer-oriented society, we are encountering a renewed 'crisis in the humanities'. Are the humanities only to be saved by demonstrating their affinity with information technology, or can they demonstrate their own legitimacy as forms of knowledge?[22]

The general problem before us is the difficulty of giving any secure grounding to our attempts to get to grips with knowledge within the academic community. It is both a matter of exclusion (why not admit transcendental meditation?) and inclusion (are there good grounds for retaining the study of poetry?). It is an issue that strikes at the heart of the higher education enterprise: What is to be taught? Can we provide some general epistemological (as distinct from a political or self-interested) justification?

This is not just an issue concerning higher education. It is an issue drawn from the centre of philosophical debate about the character of modern society, for which the problem of knowledge is central. The difficulties and doubts about the possibility of grounding knowledge are, in part, a reflection of the more general problem of legitimating modern society itself.[23]

Philosophers and theorists who have wrestled with the problem of knowledge, recognizing the inadequacy of justifications which give special privilege to science, have moved in two directions. The first camp have tried to find ways of broadening the base of forms of human experience deserving the title 'knowledge'. They have retained the basic conception of demarcating knowledge from non-knowledge, but within 'knowledge' have sought to give legitimacy to non-scientific forms of inquiry. The second camp have suggested that the search for rules of demarcation is spurious, that no valid distinctions can be made, and that a thousand flowers should be allowed to bloom.

The problem that the first path leads to is that, no matter where the demarcation line is drawn, there will always come along another candidate for which the rules just laid down do not seem to cater. For example, Paul Hirst supplied in the 1960s what seemed to many a comprehensive account of, and justification for, the inclusion of forms of thought in the educational curriculum. On his account, seven forms of human thought had developed, and were legitimately seen as forms of knowledge, because they had their own concepts, their own conceptual structure and their own tests for truth. The seven forms of knowledge picked out – mathematics, physical sciences, human sciences, history, religion, literature and the fine arts, philosophy – seemed catholic enough (Hirst 1974: 46). Hirst's account appeared to offer an apologia for the

entire school curriculum. But its comprehensiveness was deceptive. For ultimately, it contained the view that all knowledge was propositional in character,
'involving the use of (public) symbols and the making of judgements' (ibid.:
103).

Knowledge in action

Hirst's approach reflects a tendency by some philosophers to take a dismissive
attitude to any claim to knowledge that is not based on formal spoken
language.[24] In contrast to such knowledge – *knowing that* such and such is the
case – we might be tempted to employ the expression 'knowing-how'. But
knowing-how to do something (Ryle 1949) is but a sub-set of the much wider
area of human awareness which we can term 'non-propositional knowledge'
(Hampshire 1970). For example, the gymnast's ability *to know where* the bar is,
while performing a somersault on the bar, and *to know how* to complete the
somersault with style and in keeping to the music, is much more than 'mere
know-how'.[25] If, in the context of higher education, this is thought to contain too
little cognitive demand, consider another example. A student hears an unfamiliar piece of music, but is able to place it as being Russian, and assesses it
correctly as having been composed by Rachmaninov. Notice that this kind of
knowledge is independent of any formal musical understanding, and even of the
history of music. It is an immediate knowledge of musical sounds.

Let us move to a more intricate integration of theoretical knowledge and
non-propositional knowledge by looking at the surgeon's abilities in performing
an operation. Anatomical drawings in medical textbooks are themselves mere
representations;[26] and each patient's anatomy will have its own characteristics.
The surgeon will, therefore, have to perform an intricate interplay between his
formal knowledge (knowing-that), his past experience and the present patient
before him. The 'recognizing', of this valve, artery or organ, has to be in part a
non-verbal ability, for the object is itself non-verbal. This knowledge is then
itself integrated with the surgeon's skills in performing the operation. In turn,
that may well require the use of complex technology. What we have here is a mix
of all kinds of knowledge, a mix in which propositional knowledge plays a part
certainly – but only a part.

In fact, if philosophers had not held propositional knowledge, expressible in
the written language, in such high regard, and had paid more attention to
knowledge captured in action, in performance, in practice and in sheer experience, we might surely have found that non-propositional knowledge is no less
complex than propositional knowledge. And it is just that kind of knowledge which arguably has formed the basis for many of the developments in
curricula in higher education over the past 20 years. Not just courses in which
professional bodies have an interest, and in which the interplay between the
professional and the client plays a significant part (such as social work and
nursing), but other more performance-based subjects have found their way into
the curriculum (such as graphic design and sports science). At the moment, we

have no satisfactory way of legitimating these new forms of knowledge *as* forms of knowledge. Stuart Hampshire's comment, made two decades ago, that 'the opposition between thought and action has been wholly confused' is, sadly, still largely true.[27]

The point in drawing attention to the different kinds of knowing-how which have been accepted as suitable matters for study has been to demonstrate how what counts as acceptable 'knowledge' seems continually to elude the analytical frameworks which philosophers offer. Every time they widen the scope of acceptable forms of knowledge, other contenders work their way into the academic community, surreptitiously. Hirst, admittedly, has recently modified his position, now accepting that professional practice is not just a matter of the application of theoretical knowledge, but has its own 'practical principles' written into it (Hirst 1983). This still has the whiff of propositional knowledge, for even these practical principles are construed as being susceptible to oral and written articulation, so that the best examples can be disseminated to the trainee professionals. Hirst's move is, perhaps, a case of too little, too late. But the essential point here is that the philosophers' project of identifying criteria which absolutely separate legitimate from non-legitimate knowledge is bound to failure.

Epistemological egalitarianism

It is not just that, sooner or later, a form of knowledge will arrive which is accepted by some part of the academic community, but which lies outside the criteria. It is, as we commented earlier, that there are no absolute criteria available. The decision to place the criteria here rather than there is a matter of judgement, and the judgement reflects prior values. There are those who value the aesthetic, or the religious, or the physical, or the interpersonal, or the professional forms of human life and their associated forms of awareness; and they will all wish to accord those forms of awareness the title of 'knowledge'. Those who do not hold those values will deny that the title can legitimately be extended in such a way.

If, then, there are no absolute criteria available for distinguishing real from sham knowledge, how is knowledge to be conceived? Are the different forms of knowledge just so many language games,[28] there being no way of evaluating them in any comparative fashion? Are we really denied the possibility of saying anything in general about these forms of life? This certainly seems to be the message of European post-structuralism (Foucault 1974; Lyotard 1984), as well as American pragmatism (Rorty 1980; Feyerabend 1987). But if so, we seem to be arriving at a situation in which decisions to include *and* to expel forms of academic discourse (for example, should sociology remain?) are just a matter of fiat. That would mean that, in the end, the composition of the academic community would be governed by the interests of the big and powerful battalions.[29] Bergendal's gloomy judgement that the one-dimensional curriculum[30] is about to arrive may be over-pessimistic; but the signs are

ominous. Will there be any departments of philosophy in the UK in the year 2000? There is a cognitive drift of the higher education curriculum which amounts to a tendency to abandon those subjects unconnected with science, technology, computers and the dominant professional bodies. It may come to that anyway, but do we have any arguments against it?[31]

One feature of the philosophical situation now emerging is that even science itself offers no firm foundation on which to build the knowledge practices of society. The presence of tacit knowledge undermining the assumption that scientific claims are entirely susceptible to verification (Polanyi 1966); the argument that Galileo and others achieved their success and scientific progress deliberately through non-rational means (Feyerabend 1978; 1982); the depiction of science as a non-cumulative form of inquiry, but as subject to revolutions where incommensurable paradigms are pitched against each other (Kuhn 1970); the view that science develops not through consensus, but through conflict, splintering and incoherence (Lyotard 1984); and the insight that science has its own inbuilt 'constitutive interest' in technical control (Habermas 1978): modern theories of science of this kind are inevitably bringing about a re-evaluation of the substance and status of scientific knowledge. Even if it is to remain as the dominant example of legitimate knowledge, science cannot any longer be taken for granted as the disinterested, supremely rational form of knowledge it has traditionally claimed to be.

These theoretical developments have not had the effect of disparaging science as a form of knowledge. That, in any case, would have been entirely inappropriate: in the modern society, science is bound to remain a dominant, if not *the* dominant, form of knowledge. Instead, what has occurred is a greater appreciation of science as the dynamic discourse of a social community, with its own traditions, squabbles, rivalries and interests.[32] In this way, science is coming to be seen not as a discourse completely distinct in every sense from all other forms of discourse oriented towards knowledge, but as akin to them in many ways.

A new framework

We have seen that epistemologists who have provided a framework for making sense of the many claims to knowledge in the modern world have tended to specify criteria to separate 'real' knowledge from the spurious; or they have realized the futility of the task and have left us without any way of distinguishing one from the other. Perhaps a thousand flowers should be allowed to bloom; but, unfortunately, there are those who cannot sort flowers from weeds. The arch-apostle of this anarchic way of thinking, Paul Feyerabend, is at least consistent here: for him, there is no virtue in wanting to stick to reason and truth. For those of us, though, who hanker after some kind of elemental framework on which to base our knowledge policies, it is difficult to see how that outlook could underpin any human institution.

It appears, however, that the situation is not quite as bleak as it may seem. It may be possible, after all, to glimpse a framework which is sufficiently flexible

not to rule out specific forms of human inquiry, but is substantial enough to provide some means of discriminating between all possible contenders to the title of 'knowledge'. Many of the ingredients of the framework have already presented themselves in our discussion.

First, we have a sense of forms of knowledge, not as inert corpuses of knowledge lying 'out there' in some ethereal realm but, rather, as dynamic discourses. Certainly, in its dominant form – that of the natural sciences – knowledge refers to an external world; but that should not allow us to overlook the internal character of all inquiry. Each form of knowledge has the form it has as the result not just of personal human, but also of interpersonal, endeavour. Knowledge, as Berger and Luckmann (1971) observed, is socially constructed. (This is not to say it is *only* a social construction; it cannot be dismissed by the relativist simply as the expression of opinion of a particular group, bent on imposing their own view on others.)

We earlier recalled that one of the philosophers' stock examples for epistemological analysis is 'I know that *x*'. This hypothetical example overlooks the interpersonal character of knowledge.[33] However, buried in the example is a further important feature of knowledge. It is – and this is the second aspect of knowledge I want to draw out – that knowledge is in part a matter of individual participation, of involvement, of interaction. Knowledge consists in part of knowledge claims which in turn can be examined by others. But anyone making a knowledge claim, in any real sense, has to be personally committed to the claim. Without the commitment, there is an element of insincerity or disengagement.[34] Whether, in practice, we actually do encourage our students to have a personal stake in the knowledge claims they entertain, or whether we promote a passive uninvolved stance by them, are, of course, further issues which our academic institutions should be addressing.[35]

This leads us to another important feature, which is that knowledge-oriented activities produce a developmental process on the part of those engaged on them. If students are really involved in what they are doing, if they are prepared to commit themselves to the intellectual positions they take up, they will experience a process of personal development.[36] The notion of 'maturity' hardly does justice to this developmental process. Probably the nearest term for it is the German *Bildung*, which formed an integral part of the idealists' vocabulary in founding the nineteenth-century German universities.[37] The term also recalls the Greek sense of knowledge acquisition leading to a higher state of personal well-being. Theory was never, on this view, solely theoretical; it offered personal transcendence.

We have now alighted on a fourth aspect of knowledge, that of values. The developmental process we envisage knowledge offering the student will depend on the kind of human development we want to see. If we see knowledge as factual, external to human interests, and employed primarily to exert power and control over the natural environment; or if we see knowledge as a means of interpersonal communication; or if we see knowledge as a vehicle for critical self-understanding: in each case, the value we put on knowledge will profoundly influence the experience that we offer students in encountering and

participating in knowledge. In short, knowledge acquisition cannot be a value-free process; values are inescapably involved.[38] The point, though, is surely not sufficiently acknowledged within higher education. Consequently, the higher education community consistently evades its responsibility to declare the particular values that underpin its activities.

Social interaction, personal commitment, the development of the mind, and value-implicated, then, are the four key elements which appear to be common to any knowledge-oriented activity.[39] However, this set of elements by itself is not adequate to act usefully as a discriminator between serious and non-serious knowledge. Yes, philosophy might be retained; but arguably witchcraft still sneaks in too. Is there any way of legitimating our knowledge practices which neither is so open that in effect 'anything goes',[40] nor is so restrictive that potentially valuable forms of thought are denied admission?

Knowledge as conversation

I want to suggest that a fifth criterion is not far from hand which will have the desired effect. It is simply that of openness. Admittedly, within the academic community, knowledge has splintered into many different domains, to which staff give their allegiance; and the openness of these domains is inevitably limited. Nevertheless, in principle, each of them is open at various levels. Obviously, for propositionally based domains, specific findings are challenge-able. So are the concepts and theories within which the findings are offered. On occasions, too, the dominant paradigm of the discipline – its framework of assumptions, practices, truth criteria, fundamental perspectives and orien-tation – may come in for critical scrutiny. And on even rarer occasions, the entire apparatus of the discipline as a whole may be questioned.[41]

An academic discipline is in principle transparent: at any time, its findings, concepts and so forth may be 'seen through', uncovering an improved percep-tion of the world. If we now put this criterion of openness alongside the four we have already identified, what seems to be emerging is that bona fide knowledge activities have something of the character of a conversation (Bernstein 1983: 223). For in a genuine conversation, in which the parties are seriously trying to sustain *and advance* their mutual understanding, we find the five elements of interaction, personal commitment, the development of the mind, a value-commitment and a measure of openness.

Seeing knowledge activities in this way as a kind of conversation does indeed begin to offer a means of legitimating what is going on, in epistemological terms, in higher education. To return to our opening question, fine art, music, physiotherapy, business studies, legal studies, chiropractic and theology are justified in their presence among the curricula of higher education because they are able and willing to sustain a conversation, having the characteristics just identified. These particular knowledge practices are very different: the charac-ter of their own internal conversations varies considerably. That is testimony to the openness of the framework just sketched out. But that should not be taken to

imply the framework is unduly permissive. The framework is certainly not going to allow all comers into the academic world: it is a selector, which not all candidates will necessarily pass.

It is, though, a flexible framework, offering a general account of very different disciplinary cultures. This flexibility comes about through the framework being addressed not to the content of a knowledge corpus but to the process of gaining knowledge. It does not, for example, specify that the conversation of the discipline has to be conducted in a written language. The worlds of the performing arts and of professional practice do not have to be translated into a theoretical language before their place in higher education can be justified. Within this framework, it is quite possible for the lecturer as an artist or a professional lawyer (say) to offer a practice rather than a proposition to the student. And the conversation is continued and expanded through responses in the form of alternative practices or performances.[42] The point is that it is always possible to counterpoise an alternative way of doing things. It remains open for the teacher to say: 'Have you thought of this?' – the 'this' being followed not by a proposition but by an action.

There are those, not only of a Marxist persuasion, for whom the practical success of a form of discourse is a required test of its admissibility.[43] While the framework I am proposing allows for the possibility of a knowledge form advancing through action, it does not require that that be an outcome. It is agnostic on the matter. A prescription of that kind should be avoided if the academic community is to retain any pretence at openness; for it ends up prejudging the acceptability of a discourse. It is, in the end, another form of closure.

Alternative perspectives

In drawing this chapter to a close, there is an aspect of openness implicit in the framework I have outlined which deserves to be brought out more fully. As we saw, it is always possible, in principle, in a genuinely open form of awareness, for the participants to reflect on and evaluate the form of awareness itself. In practice, this happens infrequently. Whereas it seems almost to be a way of life (literally) in some of the social sciences, its occurrence is much more scarce in the natural sciences. Even so, it can and does happen there too; and some believe that we are on the verge of such a major reappraisal within natural science itself (Lyotard 1984). The point, though, is that in theory it is always possible for this kind of reflexive or self-referring inquiry to break out at any time.

It follows that a higher education – to be worthy of the title – will encourage the student to develop a competent awareness of alternative ways of seeing things, or of doing things. By 'competent awareness', I mean that the student is not just aware in some abstract way that things – concepts, theories, traditions, actions, principles – could be different, but is actually able to demonstrate an ability to work with those alternative ways of going on. Without such a flexibility of response on the part of the student, the programme of studies becomes a mere training in technique – whether of the scientist, the philosopher, the artist or the architect.

Returning, then, to the opening question of this chapter, we can say that the inclusion of a form of human awareness within the higher education curriculum is justified if it offers the range of personal response sketched out here. It may be that any objective appraisal of witchcraft and astrology would testify that they satisfy these criteria; that must remain an open question for others. More importantly, though, it might turn out that while the forms of thought that have found their way into the higher education system have the potential to offer these elements of personal development, it might also transpire that some of the courses on offer fail to take full advantage of that developmental potential. Instead of the encounter with knowledge being seen as an exciting experience, with the student encouraged to be an active participator, collaborator, and possibly contributor, the process would surely be found to fall short of the ideal more often than we would wish.

4

The Truth, the Whole Truth . . .

Introduction

Modern epistemology has given up the search for ultimate foundations of knowledge (Rorty 1980). It is acknowledged that there are as many putative forms of knowledge as there are forms of life; but it is also accepted that there is no set of criteria that enables us absolutely to sort out real from make-believe knowledge. And yet the hope dies hard. We still retain the vocabulary of such an aspiration. Two such terms are *objectivity* and *truth*: they are often heard in the language of the academic community, and they serve as symbols of the knowledge on offer in higher education. The two terms do seem to point to some kind of safeguard, to standards that bona fide knowledge claims should meet.

Part of the argument that follows may seem unduly remote from day-to-day issues of higher education. But this philosophical part of our inquiry is vital. First, because higher education is founded on the beliefs that objectivity and truth are attainable; and if those beliefs are suspect, they need to be exposed. Secondly, because if objectivity and truth can no longer be taken on trust, then we may have radically to rethink our practices in higher education. A philosophical inquiry of this kind can and should have practical implications.

Objectivity

Knowledge claims are said to be objective when they are felt to be free of personal or social bias. Objectivity is contrasted both with 'that's only your view' and with 'that's only the view of your social class (or sex or whatever)'. Where there is objectivity, there is no contamination or distortion. The ascription of objectivity is an accolade: it stamps the hallmark of purity on the knowledge claim. How is such an achievement possible?

Independence theses

Accounts of objectivity fall into three kinds. First, there are *independence theses*. These cluster around the view that it is possible to gain objective knowledge in virtue of its independence from possible sources of contamination. Various strategies are enlisted in aid of this aspiration, each relying on some kind of methodological instrument to secure the end. One strategy relies on the use of logical criteria, such as refutation (Popper 1975), truth criteria (Hirst 1974) and general fundamental logical concepts (Lukes 1973). Unfortunately, the firmness of these underpinnings are illusory. From within both epistemology and the sociology of knowledge, what appear to be fundamental (logical concepts or truth criteria) either turn out to be forever changing or to be purely formal and empty of substance.[1]

A second approach in securing independent objectivity calls on disciplinary procedures to guarantee objectivity.[2] The difficulty here is that, on investigation, there appears to be no definite set of procedures which all members of the discipline follow all the time.[3] Indeed, if the work of Feyerabend can serve as a guide, even in the field of physical sciences, scientific progress could not have been achieved very often if scientists had actually adhered to the normal procedures.

Thirdly, it is suggested that 'facts' offer a basis on which to found a source of independent objectivity. 'Facts', however, are fools' gold. In the end, there are no facts, in the sense in which discussion has been completely exhausted. For it is always possible to ask: 'But is that so?' At one and the same time, 'facts' are both descriptions of the world and claims about the description itself. They not only say this is how the world is; they make the further assertion that the claim is true.[4] They do this by implying that the first claim (that x is the case) is obvious, and that only an idiot would think otherwise. The apparent obviousness of the particular features of the world in question assumes that we have direct access to the world, to be able to see the world as it really is. But even the simplest perceptions are, in the epistemological jargon, theory-laden. So we cannot get behind our 'facts' in any kind of presuppositionless way to see the world in its pure state.

'Facts', then, constitute a nasty piece of bluff. They are a bluff because they prejudge just what is in question – our success in gaining secure knowledge of the world. And they are nasty, because the label 'fact' serves to warn off further debate. The vocabulary of facts is therefore anathema to a genuine higher education where intellectual options must always remain open.

As the final version of independent objectivity, we find the notion of 'givenness'. R. S. Peters, who shows a fondness for the idea of givenness, points, by way of example, to 'such things as the phenomena coordinated by the law of gravitation [and] the heat of the fire'.[5] But scientific theories change: the law of gravitation had no meaning in a heliocentric universe, and has limited meaning in a post-Einstein world. At the same time, what appears as 'the heat of the fire' is far from given: the Indian fire-walking mystic and the Eskimo will have quite different senses of it. 'Givenness' cannot, then, provide any guarantee of objectivity; what appears at first sight to be 'given' is so in virtue of our conceptual and experiential apparatus. That can and does change.

Dependence theses

Whereas independence theses of objectivity claim that it is possible to have more or less direct access to the world provided that the correct method is chosen, dependence theses recognize that complete independence of all intervening factors is not possible. Instead, they are based on the assumption that objective knowledge is available via some particular medium. Three forms of dependence thesis stand out.

First, in its structural form, the world is believed to be revealed through an immutable, inescapable, structured framework of experience. It has been offered in various guises; conceptual (Kant), psychological (Piaget, Chomsky) and sociological (Parsons' functionalism, Marxism and structuralism itself). We need only to note this form of dependence thesis. For if true, it is largely irrelevant to educational theory, depicting as it does an immutable structure of experience, while education – especially higher education – is in part a developmental or changing process within the individual. Higher education also looks to interventions in the developmental process, and to personal responsibility on the part of both teacher and student. Again, these developmental concepts fit uneasily with the idea of an unchanging structure. We can conclude, therefore, that structural theses of objectivity have little to say to us, in understanding the acquisition of knowledge in the context of higher education.[6]

A second line of defence taken by the dependence thesis of objectivity recognizes that knowledge claims are themselves social activities, and are connected with wider social institutions and settings. On this view, producing, sustaining and justifying knowledge claims are not just the actions of individuals, but are caught up in a web of social relationships and social interests. If, though, forms of knowledge have the general character of social activities, the way in which they are at the same time objective in character requires some explanation.

One line, in bringing objectivity and the social character of knowledge together, takes the path of arguing that it is precisely through interpersonal interaction that objectivity is obtained. Yes, it is accepted, knowledge springs from our social interests and interactions; but we are not consigned, as a result, to prejudice and bias. In the hands of one advocate, D. W. Hamlyn, this line of thinking takes the following course: our 'forms of life' generate our concepts, and – just because they are anchored in our forms of life – produce our 'intersubjective agreement'. In turn, intersubjective agreement makes possible the formation of truth and, as such, 'provides the basis of objectivity'.[7] This argument runs epistemology and sociology together; unfortunately, it rides neither horse successfully. Sociologically, it does not go far enough; philosophically, it goes too far.

Sociologically, it is not sufficiently sensitive to different forms of life. Forms of life are not given; they constitute, on the contrary, a problem.[8] It is not just that we live in a pluralist, multi-ethnic, class society, with different life orientations across the many groups that constitute society. Even within a small arena like higher education, fundamental choices have to be made. The design of the higher education curriculum represents the choice of values and a view of the kind of life the graduate should be able to lead. It could be performing ably in a professional sphere, or earning a high income, or demonstrating a capacity for intellectual thought and endeavour in a disciplinary field, or widening and empowering the life of the mind. Each of these is a form of life held in high or low esteem, depending on one's values. Sociologically, then, Hamlyn's argument can be met by the response: Whose 'intersubjectivity' is supposed to provide the basis of objectivity?

Yet, for the sake of higher education, there is a further consideration. If higher education is to mean anything, part of its meaning must surely look to students taking up a critical stance towards the knowledge claims they encounter. But this point can be generalized to counter Hamlyn's argument. In higher education, where in principle nothing can be taken for granted, forms of life cannot be taken as self-justifying. The different practices which constitute higher education – for example, forms of thought themselves – must be potentially subject to critical scrutiny, with their social location and conceptual presuppositions seen through. It is part of the essence of higher education to present alternative forms of life – the student needs to be able to form a view of the forms of thought encountered on the course, to be able to 'place' them. The law graduate will be able to bring the perspectives of sociology and moral philosophy to bear on sentencing policy; the medical graduate will be able – even if unwilling – to see the doctor's activities as a manager of scarce resources, and be able to evaluate different treatments dispassionately through a range of performance indicators. In short, the student should be able to leave the course having some sense of other viewpoints, of other forms of life, and that his chosen profession or discipline could be other than it is.

Philosophically, too, Hamlyn's argument neglects key distinctions. For example, the argument misses the point that intersubjectivity occurs at different levels of interaction – intersubjectivity at the level of concepts is different from intersubjectivity at the level of theories. Dispute may break out at the different levels: there might be agreement at the level of basic concepts in a form of thought, but not at the level of theories, or evidence, or practices, or principles. Consequently, nothing much is served by talking generally about 'intersubjectivity'. What appears on the surface to be a general consensus within a domain of thought may hide deep conflict. Consider ethnomethodology and functionalism as rival accounts of doing sociology; or holistic and mainstream approaches to medical practice. Or even more radically, there may be theories which seek to evaluate or offer a perspective on a discipline as a whole (such as critical theory's account of science, seeing it as based on fundamental human interests of power and control). In all these senses, our students deserve to be fully exposed to a form of thought, warts and all, even if the sense of objectivity slips somewhat as a result.

An alternative way of seeing objectivity as social in character comes from David Bloor. Whereas Hamlyn wants to keep the objective and social characteristics of thought at arm's length from each other, Bloor deliberately runs them together. For Bloor, objectivity is none other than 'institutionalized belief'.[9] This formulation may seem odd and even heretical: it seems to lack precisely that firmness, stability and certainty which objectivity promises. Bloor argues to the contrary. Those knowledge claims which are felt to be objective have the necessary firmness and stability precisely because they are institutionalized beliefs.

By way of a case study, Bloor turns to mathematics. After all, if his account has plausibility there, if mathematics can be shown to have an inescapable social component, then surely all 'objective' forms of thought can be seen in a similar light. Bloor takes an uncompromising line on the matter. Mathematics, for Bloor, is actually about society: 'the reality that it appears to be about represents a transfigured understanding of the social labour that has been invested in it'. Concepts and theories have the status of objectivity because they have become firmly embedded in a culture. Their firmness is not illusory: 'they cannot be changed by whim or caprice'.[10] Their objectivity is real because they are social entities: they are socially structured and sustained, and are resistant to change.

While Bloor brings society and objectivity together, it is still a rather passive relationship that we are offered. If we turn, though, from a conventional sociology of knowledge approach to a post-marxian account, we find the society–objectivity relationship much more active. Jurgen Habermas (1978: 28), for instance, has argued that 'The nature that surrounds us constitutes itself as objective nature for us only in being mediated by the subjective nature of man through processes of social labour.' In other words, objectivity is just as much a hallmark of our interactions with our environment as it is a stamp of approval on our knowledge claims. Here, objectivity represents the necessary structure of experience deriving from our fundamental human interests and activities.

What can we make of all these differing accounts of objectivity? The first point is quite simple. Because these different accounts exist, we cannot try to legitimize our knowledge activities in higher education by pretending, in any facile way, that they offer objectivity. 'Objectivity' is itself a contested concept: calling 'objectivity' in aid is liable to beg more questions than it answers.

Secondly, as our comments on the independence theses and on Hamlyn's form of the dependence thesis have shown, affixing the label of objectivity to a form of knowledge does not absolve the inquirer from asking: What interests are served by this form of knowledge? Knowledge forms may be 'objective', but their presuppositions, and inner interests and values, can still be explored. Fundamental inquiry of this kind should never be closed off. The accounts of Bloor and Habermas at least leave open this possibility. They show that the idea of objectivity can be deployed without it acting as a barrier to investigation of the deep structure of a form of thought. Is this, though, how we generally view our forms of knowledge in higher education? Do we not, all too often, by describing them as objective, forestall any such inquiry? Do we not pretend that our bodies of knowledge possess a purity they do not contain?

Third world theses

The dependence and independence theses of objectivity have in view the knower and the known, and offer various accounts of that relationship. They look to two worlds, the external world (world I) and human consciousness (world II), and claim that it is possible that a reliable relationship can hold between them.[11] Third world theses, on the other hand, argue that this whole way of conceiving of objectivity is wrong. As the term implies, for third world theses, objectivity resides in an altogether different world.

The most detailed modern version of a third world thesis has been developed by Karl Popper. (Among others, F. R. Leavis offers a corresponding viewpoint in his writings on higher education.[12]) Popper develops his idea of a third world partly against 'the commonsense view of knowledge', that 'there was only one kind of knowledge – knowledge possessed by a knowing subject'.[13]

For Popper, this third world of objective knowledge is characterized by the following features:

1. 'Apart from valid and simple proofs', it does not provide objective certainty.
2. It is the site of rational criticism in the attempt to find the most satisfactory theories to answer our problems.
3. The third world can act on world II, and through world II upon world I; but the reverse is not possible.
4. The citizens of world III (our theories) are to be understood by examining *them* and not their sources or origins.
5. The theories which inhabit the third world are not confined to mathematical theories or theories of the physical sciences; they may be theories or conjectures about human activities, including works of art.

In developing a theory of higher education, this is a powerful theory. Indeed, 'examples of objective knowledge are theories published in journals and books and stored in libraries'.[14] Given the special place that the library has in institutions of higher education (lists are available showing the pecking order of university libraries in numbers of volumes), and given, too, the language of higher education (we talk of *reading* for a degree, of booklists and bibliographies), Popper's theory begins to seem like an epistemological justification for the traditional practices and beliefs of higher education. Popper's theory might well be termed a librarian's philosophy of higher education.

There are, though, a number of problems with the third world approach to objectivity. First, there is no room in this world for knowing-how. We saw, in the last chapter, that many – if not all – of the components of knowing-how are non-propositional. Often, the most appropriate response to an example of knowing-how is not a verbalized theory but an alternative example of knowing-how: the artist or the doctor shows the student another way of going on. That cannot be captured in any adequate way in books.

Secondly, the theory hypostatizes a third world free of cognitive pollution. The theory denies the legitimacy of questions as to the origins or causes of theories.[15] This is none other than 'objectivity' serving again to close off debate.

But even in the field of mathematics, it is perfectly possible (as we saw from Bloor) to ask intelligible questions about the sources of its theories; and some of them may be sociological, rather than a matter of scientific methodology. It may be that such inquiries into origins will not tell us much about the truth of theories, but they may well shed some further light. There are other questions to be asked about a theory apart from its formal truth. We might, for example, wish to ask of a claim about the safety of nuclear power: Whose interests are being served by making the claim? It follows that world II (human consciousness, in the form of our values) can affect world III (objective knowledge), and to deny it is to reduce the scope for rational debate.

It might be countered that Popper's theory could be modified to take these arguments on board, that the world of objective knowledge can include knowing-how (for example, it can be captured on videotape), and the links between the three worlds could allow exchange in both directions. We could make those changes, but still hold on to the sense of a world of objective knowledge apart from the human mind and the physical world. This is, though, to miss the point.

The point is that the human mind is inextricably part of objective knowledge; it cannot be excluded. The contents of the library books are in themselves simply printers' marks on a page. They only have meaning when they are interpreted by a human mind. There is no single interpretation of a book which counts as objective knowledge, with all other interpretations consigned to the wastepaper basket. Certainly, some interpretations are more significant than others; recognizing the presence of the active human mind does not necessarily lead us into naive relativism.[16] What gives some interpretations added significance is agreement by other minds. An inescapable element in the formation of objective knowledge, therefore (if we must retain the term), is the presence not just of mind, but of minds.

This is crucially important for any well-founded theory of higher education. For despite Popper's disavowal of human learning as a matter of filling a kind of bucket,[17] and his insistence that individuals must be free to identify and to solve their own problems, his theory of objective knowledge can all too easily lead in the other direction. Instead of promoting an engaged, independent mind, actively involved in its own development, the idea that objective knowledge is independent of 'knowing subjects' and resides in a separate world, outside the human mind, can offer a prop for passive learning experiences, where the student is introduced to and expected to assimilate the seminal works in different subjects.

So far as higher education is concerned, we can put the point directly. It is the life of the mind (Popper's world II) which is of the essence, and not the non-corporeal realm of world III. What is at stake in higher education is: What kind of development do we hope to see taking place in the mind of the student? To conceive of objective knowledge as residing in some other world is pernicious. For it is all too easy to avoid asking: What kind of encounter with knowledge (in all its manifestations) do we want to bring about for students? I suggested earlier that Popper's theory could be termed a librarian's theory of knowledge; it might help to keep librarians in business. Another way of describing it, though, is as a researcher's theory of knowledge. It reflects the interests and activities of those who engage in writing books and journal articles *and* who see academic debate in those media as the epitome of academic life.

This is not to say that those values are illegitimate. Indeed, they could be said to be fundamental to the interests of the academic community, concerned as it must be with the establishment and formulation of new knowledge and understanding. But that set of concerns is distinct from those embodied in the concept of higher education, which is primarily a matter of the developmental process offered to students. The distinction reminds us that academics can legitimately have very different attitudes towards objective knowledge. Being a matter essentially of the student's human development, higher education has a primary interest in knowledge in so far as it promotes that development. Journals in the library and researchers' debates may be a necessary condition of that development taking place, but they are not the foremost concerns of the teacher *qua* teacher. For that role centres around galvanizing, ordering, orienting and provoking the mind of the student.

Truth

The centrality of truth

Perhaps the key concept frequently called up to legitimize our knowledge activities in higher education is that of *truth*. Almost everyone in the academic community is agreed on its importance; it appears central to the academic form of life. Truth does indeed matter; its centrality is no illusion. It is not just an element in academics' language games; it is integral to their form of life. We can see why, if we reflect on the form of discourse of the academic community. It is an elaborated discourse, built upon sophisticated disciplinary languages allowing all sorts of fine discriminations.[18] But unlike talk about cricket, it is not just a technical discourse about a particular set of human experiences. It is a discourse with a special orientation, namely towards truth. It engages with currently contending truths, and offers a commentary on them or attempts to dislodge them or even go beyond them.

What gives a truth-oriented discourse its special character is the determination of the participants in the discussion to get somewhere, by advancing the discussion (Rorty 1980). Admittedly, what counts as advancing the discussion varies across the disciplines. And not every academic is actively engaged on its advancement; some are quite happy to be interested eavesdroppers. As a general rule, though, the discourse of the academic life has this dominant characteristic of leading onwards, of progression, of refinement.

'Truth', therefore, is not to be mocked. Its centrality is quite legitimate. It is not surprising, therefore, if the idea of truth is not far below the surface of the curricula our students experience (and it often breaks through). Teachers wish to impart or direct students towards the truth, even if they also encourage students to have a sense of its provisional status. But what do teachers understand by 'the truth'? Despite its centrality to academic discourse, academics seldom give it any explicit attention. That task is left to the philosophers. But again, just as with objectivity, the matter cannot be left only to the philosophers, for they cannot agree over the nature of truth. At the same time, every teacher in higher education will have – normally tacitly held – a vague idea of truth which will enter into the way in which the curriculum is arranged and experienced by the student.

Passive reflections

The most widely held view is based on the correspondence theory of truth, which is that 'true' propositions give a precisely accurate picture of that part of the world which they describe. The world is reflected in and by the true proposition: there is a direct correspondence between them. One implication of this theory is that the mind plays very little part in the process. The mind is simply a passive mirror, an intermediary between the world and the proposition which the world somehow generates. There is clearly a passive image of man at work under this theory of truth.[19] As *a* theory of truth, it could be, and is, argued on its merits by the philosophers.[20] But the problem for us here is that it enters surreptitiously into the way we organize the curriculum for our students. Particularly in the teaching of the natural sciences, but also in some professionally directed courses, there is a tendency to believe that the world takes such-and-such a form, that our bodies of knowledge contain truths with increasing 'verisimilitude', and that the role of the student lies in assimilating and reproducing the current set of truths. Yes, it is normally acknowledged that the current set of truths may change tomorrow, but still, once established (if only for the time being) by the academic community, they stand independently of the human mind, and need only to be passively assimilated.[21]

If this seems exaggerated, recall the language of higher education, in which we find as terms in common use 'the transmission of knowledge', 'facts' and 'things which the students must know'. Not far beneath the surface of such terms is the assumption that there is one world and one legitimate form of adaptation to it. This is false. As we saw earlier, so-called facts are theory-laden: we do not have the independent access to the world that the correspondence theory of truth implies.[22] Secondly, the world can be represented in an infinite number of ways. Our current orderings are those of Western intellectuals in the late twentieth century; they have been, could be now, and will be quite different. Unfortunately, what counts as truth all too often takes on the form of holy writ just because it carries the label 'truth'. But, even in empirical science – allegedly the most open field of knowledge – 'the suspicion arises that [the] alleged success (of a theory felt to be true) is due to the fact that the theory . . . [has] turned into rigid ideology'.[23] Consequently, we assume that what counts as true *is* true, and any counter opinion begins with suspicion and even hostility hanging around its neck.[24]

As a basis for our practices in higher education, therefore, the correspondence theory of truth is doubly pernicious. It overlooks the manifold ways in which what counts as truth is negotiated, presenting it instead as something which is given. And it reduces severely the role of the individual as an active member of a community with the capacity for redefining 'truth'. The better kinds of student experience have certainly not been limited in this way. It is not unknown for individual students actually to make (and be encouraged to make) a definite contribution to knowledge as undergraduates; examples are known of young undergraduates having their own scholarly papers published in research journals. Increasingly, too, the use of open learning is promoting a more active role on the part of students. The curricular effects, then, of the correspondence theory can be overcome. But we do not have to stick with the theory, in any case.

Hanging together

The other two dominant theories of truth, the coherence theory and the pragmatist theory, are also to be seen at work in higher education at the chalkface (or visual display unit). Both, at least, have the merit of allowing for a more active role on the part of the student; neither prompts the passive assimilation of established truths. Each, though, has its own weaknesses.

On the coherence theory, as its name implies, the truth of a proposition is a matter of the way in which it hangs together with other propositions of the same kind. This clearly has some plausibility: if a proposition were widely out of keeping with the set of accepted truths in the same domain, it would be understandable if our initial reaction assumed that the new theory was at fault rather than its established rivals. Kuhn has suggested that the scientific community does, indeed, tend to react in that way, assuming the conventional paradigm is 'true' and putting the extra burden of proof onto the new contender. With coherence, then, goes conservatism of approach.[25] The academic mind is reluctant to take on board new perspectives unless forced to do so. But that kind of conservatism must be anathema to any genuine higher education. What we want to generate there is not a desire for coherence, but a readiness to tolerate, and even search for, *incoherence*.[26] The idea of 'higher' in 'higher education' implies a willingness to go beyond the given (whether conceptually, theoretically or performatively), and not be bound by it.

Truth that works

The third of the dominant philosophical theories of truth is the pragmatist theory. This looks to the use-value of propositions: indicators of effective use are 'satisfactory results in experience'; or 'ideas that have a value for concrete life'.[27] Arguably, it is this theory of truth that is gaining most ground in higher education, and not only in curricula that are explicitly designed to produce graduates for the professions.

As curricula in general are turned more towards the world of work, and as undergraduates are expected to acquire transferable skills with general utility in the wider society, knowledge is valued accordingly. Logically, there is a gap here: the truth value of propositions, or practical principles, or theories should not be affected by such considerations. But it appears that that is what is happening in practice. Whether in the field of agricultural technology or in fashion design, whether in management studies or in pharmaceutics, correctness comes increasingly to be determined by social, technical and economic feasibility, or, quite simply, by what can be achieved in the world. As Lyotard (1984: 46) tellingly puts it, 'the technical criterion, introduced on a massive scale into scientific knowledge, cannot fail to influence the truth criterion'.

The pragmatist theory of truth cannot simply be dismissed. That we are able to rely on a truth claim, to make reliable predictions, and to perform our social and technical routines: these are surely indications that we have arrived at something we can call truth. But our ability to perform is not absolute. It is coloured by interests and resources at play in the world; in other words, power and control. So if we are tempted to look to use-value as a standard of truth, the rejoinder is always open: Whose use is in question?

The pragmatist theory of truth is, it will be apparent, a potential weapon in the hands of those who would use 'truth' to their own ends. The modern university has seen this kind of infiltration from governments of the left and the right, e.g. Soviet Lysenkoism in the 1930s, and the creation of university chairs in Germany in the 1930s to promote Nazi sociological, biological and psychological doctrines. In both cases, what counted as the truth reflected 'satisfactory results in experience' for their supporters.[28]

The conservatism of truth

What can we draw from this discussion? First, as with objectivity, there are on offer alternative philosophical theories of truth, so there is no single general idea of truth which we can pull off the shelf to prop up our claims to truth in higher education. Secondly, each of the available alternatives offers useful insights into truth, but each has its drawbacks simply because it is limited in scope. In so far as any curriculum in higher education is founded primarily (albeit unknowingly) on any one of these theories, nothing other than a skewed educational experience will result.

In establishing philosophical foundations for higher education, there is a general problem underlying all the main theories of truth we have looked at. It is that the role of the student is severely reduced. We saw this to be the case particularly with the correspondence theory, but it is also evident in the coherence and the pragmatist theories. Admittedly, the pragmatist theory embraces an active image of man as truth seeker, but it tends in practice to limit truth to serving particular interests. As a result, under all three conceptions of truth, the role of the student is limited essentially to rehearsing truths already established by the academic community.

Is this, perhaps, not inevitable? Is it not the role of the student, as an initiate into academic discourse, to be prepared to take on, to understand and to show some competence in handling the truths of established academics? Some of the things that have already been said about the conversational nature of academic discourse and about the opportunities for student independence that are a hallmark of higher education, will have suggested the answer. Students can be, are and should be seen as partners in the discourse of academics. But, in establishing that position, let us draw together with these concluding reflections on truth the earlier discussion on objectivity.

Beyond objectivity and truth

Negotiations

Objectivity is normally felt to be a good thing; something worth maintaining in the academic world. Suppose we question this assumption. What is wrong with subjectivity? To many, the question will seem heretical. But recall certain points. First, if higher education is to realize its potential, the personal response of the student needs to be drawn out.[29] This is no easy matter. Undergraduates of all kinds are often reluctant to express a point of view, to declare themselves and to take a stand. They have to be encouraged, patiently and continually, to do so. Nor is this a requirement solely for students in the humanities or social sciences. If the experience of higher education is to be a genuine rather than a second-hand experience, then all students have to identify with and have a stake in what they themselves are saying and doing. In fact, simply because scientific knowledge changes so rapidly and (in the better courses, at least) students rely heavily on the research literature itself rather than second-hand accounts in textbooks, there are ready opportunities for learning to be authentic, and to have a personal quality at least as much as in other subjects.[30]

Secondly, in many domains of intellectual thought and activity, there is no single truth or even a body of truths to be expounded by the student. The most obvious example lies perhaps in the interpretation of texts, in the humanities and social sciences (not only literature and history, but other areas such as anthropology and theology). Where a text is to be understood, the interpreter has the task of understanding the original author's meaning. But there is no single meaning to be interpreted, for the author's meaning, if the text has any complexity, will not be fully transparent even to the author himself. Indeed, some consider that 'the object is to understand a writer better than he understood himself'.[31] The act of interpretation is inevitably, then, 'a placing of oneself within the mind of the author . . . a recreation of the original act'. It follows that this intellectual process, which came to be known in nineteenth-century idealism as hermeneutics, 'is an art, not a mechanical process'.[32]

Truth does have application here. In helping to promote understanding of the text, 'there is reference to the truth that lies hidden in the text and must be brought to light'.[33] Leavis, in articulating the art of literary criticism, was insistent that the critic's judgements should be seen to be based firmly on the text, and offered with an implied sense of 'this is so, isn't it?', with the critic always able to back up his or her claims by reference to the passages in the text in question.[34] This is, though, an essentially open conception of truth, in which truth claims are invested with personal meaning, commitment and judgement.

Thirdly, as we have seen, what counts as truth in the natural sciences is also, to an extent, open and negotiable. On occasion, we learn, scientific theories not only compete but can be 'incommensurable'.[35] In those instances, the choice between them is not just a matter of the amount or even the interpretation of data, but is dependent on the theoretical framework with which groups of scientists are working. The choice of that framework is, in part, open; it is a matter of a prior decision by researchers. That choice is not entirely open, admittedly; the scientists are *informed* researchers, experienced at working in the field. But in the end, the theory choice is not entirely determined by the data. Lakatos' idea of a 'progressive research programme' (see Chapter 1) was developed to overcome the difficulties of strict falsificationism.[36] The idea, though, begs questions, for one does not know in advance which programme is going to turn out to be 'progressive'. Even as science is advancing, what counts as truth has to contain a non-given element, where the scientific community (or at least an influential part of it) develops and is able to sustain its own *perspective* on interpreting the world.

Finally, in the field of the applied sciences, in the technologies and particularly in professionally oriented areas, effective practitioners have to give something of themselves and commit themselves to what they are trying to do. The teacher in the classroom, the architect engaging with his clients, or the engineer involved in bringing off a new project: in each case there has to be an element of personal commitment if the action in question is to be authentic and meaningful. Another way of putting it is that, far from objectivity being sufficient, many intellectual activities require 'deep subjectivity' for their success.[37]

Conclusions

Where, then, have these reflections led us? In essence, it is that truth is not an end point, or even a set of agreed standards; for both the end points and the agreed standards can change. Rather, truth is the description we give to a particular kind of human transaction. The transaction in question is a conversation, but not just any form of conversation. Following the work of the theorist, Jurgen Habermas, we can see that participants can say what they want, provided that they are trying to get at the truth, they are sincere, and that what they say is intelligible to the other participants in the discussion and is internally coherent.[38] This form of conversation, then, is highly structured, imposing four inbuilt ethical demands (truthfulness, sincerity, intelligibility and coherence). But within this structured discourse comes the opportunity to express a distinctive point of view, of offering a new perspective, and of striking out on one's own. The conversation advances because at least some of the participants are willing to risk failing; they are prepared to risk rejection by the other participants in their particular conversation.

There are several implications of these considerations for higher education. First, it is far from clear that we do ourselves any good by hanging on to the term 'objectivity' within the language of higher education. It can all too easily come to represent arbitrary limits to human thought and experience, rather than the openness that should be characteristic of higher education. At the same time, it is the students' personal responses to the situations they find themselves in that we are after. Their views must contain something of themselves, and be – to that extent – genuinely subjective. A common counter to this line of argument is: Do we want our medical students to be 'subjective'? The answer is yes: every patient with whom the professional surgeon is faced presents particular problems, calling for a definite strategy designed for that situation. The surgeon has to make up his own mind, and convey his interpretation to the rest of the operating team. Talk of objectivity here is inappropriate; and it might even be dangerous.

Secondly, truth is a valuable concept, providing that we see it as a conversation in which anyone can join, including the students. One of the distinguishing aspects of a genuinely higher education is that, in it, students are encouraged to express themselves, to articulate their own point of view. This is entirely in keeping with the perspectival conceptions of objectivity and truth sketched out here.

Thirdly, truth-oriented discourse imposes certain demands on participants. There is a requirement to listen, for every participant deserves to be heard. An intellectual debate is, or ought to be, the epitome of what Habermas has termed an 'ideal speech situation',[39] where no-one experiences any undue constraint on their desire for a hearing. Participants, though, need to listen attentively: one should not join a conversation unless one understands the discussion. There are too, we noticed, other demands, such as sincerity, commitment and coherence. But perhaps most fundamental of all is the willingness to expose one's viewpoint to the critical gaze of others. Habermas has termed this conception of truth a consensus theory of truth.[40] This is not to pretend that consensus is a necessary outcome of an intellectual discussion, but is to make the point that ideas are offered by the participants with a view to securing consensus. Intellectual debate is not cosy, or permissive; it is critical, judgemental and stern. Higher education, on this view of truth, cannot simply be a matter of truths disseminated to the student; it is a much tougher and more demanding process. Through it, the student emerges able to begin to take up an informed position of his or her own, or at least to have some awareness of what that involves.

This chapter has focused on the somewhat abstract concepts of objectivity and truth, but it has ended by pointing to practical implications for academic teachers and students. I have argued that objectivity and truth are not available in any facile sense, for what counts as truth is in part negotiable. The corollary is that students have to be encouraged to offer and to accept responsibility for their truth claims; they have to be prepared to stand by them. Higher education calls for increasing intellectual maturity of individual expression, commitment, resilience, tolerance of other viewpoints, interaction with others and self-critique. If this connection of truth with ethics seems strange, it is because we have lost sight of it in modern society. The Greeks were aware of the connection, and we are now seeing signs of its reclamation in recent social theory.[41] To some extent, the connection has always been present in higher education, although tacitly. The challenge to higher education is to bring those ethical dimensions of knowledge and truth more centrally and more explicitly into the student experience. Ultimately, this means that the student has to be seen not as a recipient of a curriculum, but as an active partner in it.

Part 3

The Sociological Undermining of
Higher Education

5

Ivory Tower?

Introduction

As a term in public use, 'the ivory tower' has had a remarkable innings. It is, of course, both a description and a value judgement. As a description, it points to 'a condition or position of seclusion from the world or withdrawal from the harsh realities of life' (*Shorter Oxford English Dictionary*). As a value judgement, it is nothing short of a term of abuse, so much so that few academics would admit to working in an ivory tower.

The reluctance of academics to accept the purity and separation conveyed by the term reflects their endorsement of its value element: they concur with the general consensus that the implied separation – of higher education from society – is unacceptable. They dissent, however, from the descriptive element of the term: they deny the alleged separation of academe from society. As a result, we have, with increasing frequency, the spectacle of vice-chancellors and polytechnic directors willingly demonstrating the relevance and responsiveness of their institutions to the needs of society.

Certainly, the whole academic community does not respond to the charge (of living in an ivory tower) in this way. There are those of a more old-fashioned liberal persuasion who gladly accept the description of separation, for that is just what they want. Their complaint is that they do not have enough of it, for higher education is not sufficiently separated (as they see it) from society. Their gripe is with the value element of the term: they do not agree that this institutional separation is in any way to be lamented, or is a matter for contrition on their part. On the contrary, they rejoice in the separation. Under their idea of higher education, it is part of the essential character of higher education to stand apart and to offer a contrasting set of values to those of mainstream society.

Both viewpoints are partly right. The apologists for collaboration are right on matters of fact: there is not, nor could there conceivably be, any real institutional separation between higher education and society. The liberals are right, though, when it comes to values. Part of the idea of higher education is that it should offer an open set of conceptual possibilities to the students that pass through. If there are tendencies in modern society for thought, discourse and action to be constrained by a number of dominant forces, higher education has the function of helping to maintain and develop a plurality of styles of thought and action. In this sense, higher education has to be a countervailing force. But how can that demanding role be accomplished, without higher education becoming merely ideological in character?

The myth of the ivory tower

Before we can answer that question, we should have some idea of the situation in which higher education finds itself. We need to sketch out some of the key sociological aspects if we want to identify both the constraints on, and the possibilities open to, higher education. This may seem strange: that, in working out an *educational* theory of higher education, we should take account of the way matters are. For an educational theory is about what ought to be, whereas the sociology and politics of academic life are largely about what is the case. And many believe that no 'ought' can be derived from an 'is'. No claim, though, is being made here to the contrary. All that is being suggested is that if an educational theory is to be taken seriously, and is to be of such a form that it can serve as the basis for action, then it has to be adequate to the institutional dynamics which bear on the matter. This is not the place for a detailed exposition of the sociology of higher education or of academic knowledge; in any case, that work has not been conducted. But we have to understand something of the sociology at work, if our prescriptions are to be feasible.[1]

First, let us reiterate clearly the point already made. Higher education is not, never has been, and never could be, an ivory tower. Ever since its medieval origins, higher education has had the function of supplying cadres for the professions. However, this function has taken on new dimensions since the Second World War, in the wake of the exponential growth of higher education (an international phenomenon across the Western world). With this expansion, more professions have looked to recruiting their members from higher education. In turn, higher education has extended its service role from the élite professions (medicine, law and the church) to provide courses geared to an extensive range of professions. In addition, many graduates enter general occupations in industry and commerce, which do not require a definite professional training.

With this expansion of higher education over the last 30 years has come increased state involvement. In the UK, higher education is costing about £4 billion per year, with the state's direct contribution to the running costs amounting until recently to as much as 85 per cent.[2] And even though, with increased industrial and other 'private' support, that figure has fallen (for some universities to just over 50 per cent), proportionately very little of the financial support for higher education comes from individual students, or even their parents. Where it does not come directly from the state, it comes mostly either from industry or from the banks and other major financial institutions. Higher education, therefore, is big business, and the overwhelming part of the costs is borne either by the state or by the dominant financial interests in the economy.

The upshot of all of this is that, as Galbraith has put it, 'higher education is extensively accommodated to the industrial system'.[3]

Why is this? Why does the modern economy look to higher education for its supply of qualified manpower? There is no simple answer. In surveys, employers are often vague as to what they are looking for in their graduate recruits. They sometimes seem to be less concerned with graduates' specific technical competence than with their general intellectual and social abilities.[4] This ambiguity may mean that employers can take technical skills for granted (or that they will develop them in the work environment), or it may have something to do with changes occurring in the workplace. It may be that, in addition to technical knowledge and skills, the modern economy calls for the ability to communicate in a common language (even if it is one primarily based on the computer).

Nevertheless, the point remains that the modern society is founded increasingly firmly on a knowledge base. Knowledge and modern society are inseparable.[5] And higher education, as an institution for the preservation and dissemination of knowledge, is inescapably a key institution in that kind of society.

Old-style Marxism saw the relationship between the means of production and institutionalized thought as that of base and superstructure. More recent marxian analyses, and social theorists from other perspectives, tend to agree that that image is completely inadequate.[6] Knowledge has become so important to modern society that, if it has not yet become the base itself, it is at least definitely integrated with it. Indeed, with the service society approaching, and manufacturing left to developing countries with their reduced labour costs, brain power becomes as important as machine horsepower. Post-industrial society is essentially a knowledge-based society.[7] As such, knowledge – particularly in its dominant forms of science, engineering and now computing – has become a productive force in its own right.[8] What we see, then, is not just an 'accommodation' between higher education and industry (in Galbraith's terminology), but an incorporation of higher education into the central framework of modern society.

We have to be clear on this. The society–knowledge relationship cannot be disentangled, on any serious reading of our times. That is the way modern society works; a working over which there is a general consensus. Or, at least, the dominant interests are so successful in managing and legitimizing the way things are,[9] that any other ordering of society is literally unimaginable. There may be some softening, or greening, at the edges, as ecological, feminist and ethnic influences come to be felt; but the general shape of post-modern society seems generally given. If this is so, then so too is the general role of higher education given, as a provider of intellectual capital within the wider system.

The sociological perspective

In a sense, both the old-fashioned liberals *and* the traditional Marxists are at fault, in believing that things are not as they are. The liberals hope that if they pretend for long enough that the pressures exerted by the industrial society can be dismissed, they will go away; but they will not. Consequently, the liberals still hanker after a time when undergraduate education was largely built around the humanities, and when higher education was much more clearly a matter of personal development.[10] The traditional Marxists believe that a radically different ordering of society is a real possibility, and that the distinction between mental and manual labour (which higher education sustains) can be overturned. In that event, the distinction between technical and higher education would be abolished and all students would receive, in a genuinely 'polytechnical education', a comprehensive integration of theory and practice.[11]

In both cases, getting the sociology wrong leads to inadequate conceptions of the kind of educational development that higher education can supply. Whether we like it or not, higher education is bound up in, and is a key player in, the formation of modern society. On the other hand, a thoroughgoing polytechnical education, with its implied disappearance of the manual–mental divisions of labour in society, is not a real option either. What we need, therefore, is not less sociology, or even more sociology – we need better sociology.

For example, how far can higher education be said to be part of the 'ideological state apparatus'?[12] Clearly, academics in Western society are not simply apparatchiks, transmitting a limited self-understanding to their students. Party lines certainly exist, however, in the academic community. They may be purely academic party lines,[13] or – and not only in the social sciences – they may be tied to actual political viewpoints (both left and right), and be ideological in character. There are, too, obvious differences between disciplines, notably between technological and professional domains of intellectual life, and those in the humanities and in the performing and creative arts. There are contrasting kinds of ideological function at work here: the training of technical élites for society's production processes is not the same as the education of the producers of society's self-understanding and ideological legitimations.[14]

There is, then, no ivory tower, for higher education is saturated on various levels by society. This is an international phenomenon – as the writings of Nisbet (1971) and Bok (1982) in the USA, and the international symposium edited by Chapman (1983) testify. Far from being an ivory tower outside society, higher education – to move to a more appropriate metaphor of the age – is more like the pit stops in a racecourse (providing some engine power and refuelling). The accusations of higher education being an ivory tower should rather be seen as reflecting the preference of the state for higher education to be even further incorporated into its dominant structures.

Does this matter? Most certainly. In the first place, the liberal conception of the university was founded on two axioms: that objective knowledge was possible, and that the university, as the institution for its uncovery and preservation, should enjoy a significant degree of autonomy. In the last two chapters, we saw how the first axiom has been undermined, although we saw too that not all is lost on that front. Here, though, we are faced with a second undermining, for the sociological basis of the idea of higher education is threatened: in the modern society, there can be no pretence that higher education is autonomous.

The sociological undermining of the idea of higher education matters for a second reason, which we have already noted *en passant*. If we want to develop an educational theory of higher education, which is not lost in fantasy either of a world which never existed (the liberals' perspective) or of a world which is not seriously available (the Marxist viewpoint), then we have to engage in a sociology and a politics of academic life. Producing an educational theory which is not jejune or self-indulgent requires that we be both an epistemologist (the point of the last section) and a sociologist.

The liberal conceptions of knowledge as an end in itself and of the value of individual persons may be fine in themselves, but the world has moved on since the mid-nineteenth century. To continue to talk about the aims of higher education and to teach and fulfil one's professional tasks as if things were unchanged, is liable to render higher education all the more susceptible to undue contamination by the non-educational interests of the wider society. With national planning, with the development of a higher education 'system' (30 years ago, the term would have been almost incomprehensible), and with industry and the professions pressing their claims on higher education, to hold simply to an image of higher education as a transaction between the teacher and the individual student is not just naive; it is, in the end, dangerous. For the ideological currents within higher education will remain largely unrecognized, certainly not confronted, and therefore unchallenged.

The political economy of higher education

Higher education, then, is subject to infiltration by the wider society. Much of this is not at all clandestine, often being overt and transparent. Some of it occurs on the strategic level of the system as a whole when, for example, the government determines that there will be a broad steer towards science and technology in the general balance of undergraduate student places. (The government's difficulty lies in persuading entrants to follow suit, for the majority of them continue, with extraordinary negligence towards the national interest, to prefer places in the humanities and the social sciences.)

Some of the political manoeuvring, though, is felt much nearer the chalkface. In the UK, the Training Agency's Enterprise Initiative is intended precisely to affect the student's educational experience.[15] Higher education, it is felt, is too preoccupied with developing students narrowly in specific disciplines. As a result, the kinds of general competencies and 'personal transferable skills' that employers are seeking are not being given sufficient attention by higher education.[16] As a matter of fact, and as a value judgement, both are true. In the UK, at least, the student experience is extraordinarily narrow, often being confined to one or two disciplines. (Moves have been made over the last 20 years, particularly in the new universities and in the public sector, to develop multidisciplinary and combined programmes of study; and many professional courses, as in the paramedical areas, cover a wide ground. Even so, the general narrowness remains.) In addition, those general intellectual aims of higher education which have widespread appeal to employers and others – such as the improvement of communicative, synthesizing and imaginative abilities – have been given lip-service by academics. The point, however, is that the drive, and the test of success of most of the innovative programmes now under way, is to see that the students are better fitted for the world of work. In other words, the criteria for assessing a major set of processes *within* higher education will be criteria imported from outside, reflecting the dominant interests of work and capital.

In pointing to these developments, my objective is not to disparage them as such. Indeed, some may well turn out to have beneficial outcomes. My intention is to point up the inescapably societal character of higher education. It is called upon to fulfil purposes which are literally not of its making, purposes which are set by interests in the wider society.

Look, for instance, at the introduction of 'contracting', in which new national planning bodies in the UK are paying sums of money to institutions of higher education in the expectation that they will deliver their promised numbers of graduates in stated subject areas (or programmes, as they are being termed).[17] The language of 'contracts', with its implications of 'delivery', of penalties for defaulting, of performance indicators by which institutional provision is to be assessed, and of institutions 'supplying' graduates for the state: all this underlines just how far higher education is perceived not as an educational endeavour but as a financial transaction between parties.

But there is a political economy at work here: it is not just a financial transaction; it is not just a matter of the state securing the maximum number of graduates for the budgets granted by the Treasury. For the state is playing an increasing role in determining the numbers of students in different subject areas, the kinds of education they receive (do they receive sufficient 'enterprise skills'?), the funds available for research across the disciplines, the kinds of institution in which courses are to be offered (universities or polytechnics or colleges of higher education), and the numbers of staff on hand to teach the students in the various subjects. In each case, the resources affect profoundly the character and quality of the student experience. The more unusual options on courses have to be pruned, decisions have to be made about library and non-book resources and, most insidious of all, staff in vulnerable disciplines (in the humanities and creative arts) may sense that they should keep their heads down and not rock the institutional boat.

In all kinds of subtle ways, the agenda of the state comes, then, to influence the internal life of academic institutions. Again, to reiterate the point, whereas some of these influences may be harmful in limiting students' educational opportunities or pointing them in unduly utilitarian directions, others may be beneficial, causing academics to reflect on what they are teaching and to see if the taken-for-granted worth of their curricula is justified. The main point is different. It is that the space available for institutions of higher education to determine their own agenda has narrowed over the past 30 years, and is continuing to narrow further.

It has to be said that, by and large, the academic community has been happy to fulfil the role cast for it. The Enterprise Initiative, for example, was heavily oversubscribed when launched by the UK's Training Agency. And while academics in particular disciplines (such as history, philosophy, and the social sciences together) have acted as pressure groups to protect their own interests when threatened with severe pruning if not extinction, the academic community as a whole has generally acquiesced in the changes and shifts that have taken place. Nor is this very surprising, for the academic community has generally been a significant beneficiary of the 400 per cent growth in higher education over the last 30 years.

At a deeper level, that academics should be willing to undertake certain tasks subscribed by the state might seem strange. For the loss of autonomy strikes at the centre of the academic community's self-understanding as a collective in charge of its own fate. So far, though, the shifting relationship between higher education and state has been rationalized by the academic community in believing that while the autonomy of institutions has been limited, academic freedom has been largely untouched. This sense of freedom is not entirely misplaced; for even though higher education is undoubtedly an institution *of* the modern state (and not just an institution within it), it has retained significant elements of freedom. From one perspective, this is a sociological matter: movement and activity within higher education are not yet under the complete control of the state. (The UK is perhaps better placed than some European countries, in which higher education is much more part of the state apparatus, with lecturers being directly employed by the state.) From another perspective, this is a philosophical matter which reflects the essence of academic life itself. For the intellectual vocation, whether scientist or humanist, is founded on the idea of an open discussion (see Chapter 4). In the end, the mind engaged in debate with others of a like disposition has to have some degree of freedom if that discussion is to be carried forward.

We arrive at a paradoxical situation. The academic community (and higher education) is called upon to sustain the cognitive structure of modern society in all its dominant technical and cultural manifestations; it is implicated, to that extent, in the project of modern society. But it has a genuine autonomy of its own. We can see this tension in its production of ideologies. It produces technicist, managerial and economic ideologies *for* society; and it produces critical ideologies – for example, ecological, feminist, deconstructionist and humanistic ideologies – consciously counterpoised against the former set.[18]

Higher education, it seems, offers a very nice example of the lack of 'correspondence' between the educational system and the economic institutions of society.[19] (Crude Marxism assumed a fairly neat degree of correspondence between the cultural superstructure of society and its economic base.) There is a fit between the requirements of modern society for intellectual capital, of both a technical and a cultural character. But the fit is by no means exact. There is always a lag between the development of a need for intellectual capital, and the ability of the higher education system to fulfil the need. In part, this is due to the sheer inertia in the system: designing a curriculum, developing the necessary expertise among the staff, persuading the academic community of the academic and educational legitimacy of the new offering (for example, in paramedical sciences or in consumer studies), and producing the first cohort of graduates takes time, perhaps as much as 10 years. The time-lag of institutional responsiveness is, though, even more a function of the inbuilt caution, if not downright hostility, to shifting the curriculum in such ways. The utilitarian language of skills, competencies and flexibility does not always find a receptive ear.

Old-fashioned Marxism, or even Marxism brought up to date, can only carry us so far, therefore, in understanding what is going on sociologically. Higher education is managed by the state, and is supported by it, for services rendered. Knowledge has become a productive force, and it is the task of higher education to supply the managers and technicians of that knowledge. It also supplies the managers and technicians of the relations of production, and the patterns of consumption. Witness, for example, the shift that has taken place in the form of fashion design and graphic design in higher education: the task now is to assist in producing graduates who understand the business ethic, and can bring their artistic skills to bear in support of capitalistic enterprises.

Higher education, then, fulfils to a significant degree the tasks demanded of it by the state. Indeed, one of the outcomes of this incorporation of an enlarged higher education system into the apparatus of the state is that the gulf between mental and manual labour in society is growing. The combination of students and workers on the streets of Paris in 1968 may turn out to be a historical quirk: in future, we are likely to see a return to the incomprehension between the two social strata witnessed in the general strike of 1926 in England.[20] In the 1990s and beyond, as access is supposedly made more open, the fundamental break in society will be between those who have had some form of higher education, and those who have not.

Let us try to put some flesh on this argument by following it through in the context of different kinds of courses taken by students.

Science

Modern society would be unimaginable without science (in a way that could not be said of, say, history or literature as fields of academic study). We can see something of the logic of this situation if we look at what might be termed the underlying interest structure of science. We saw in Chapter 3 that Jurgen Habermas has argued that science has an inbuilt interest in prediction and control. His point is that this is not just a contingent fact; it is part of the constitution of science itself. In Habermas' cumbersome terminology, this is a 'knowledge-constitutive interest';[21] on this view, science could not be radically different.

Whether one accepts this view, that the form of science is largely given,[22] it does offer an insight into its centrality for the modern world. For the project of modern man is in part one of power and domination over his environment.[23] This marks modern man off from earlier stages of man's history, when man was either subject to, or sought some kind of rapprochement with, nature. There is a second and arguably even more important factor at work; namely, that through technology, science has made possible ever-expanding opportunities for capital accumulation.[24]

The 'environment', it should not be forgotten, here includes man himself, just as much as the physical world. The exploration of the structure of the atom is paralleled by the ever more detailed examination of the molecular structure of human beings. The massive effort being invested by the state in this research cannot be explained away by a naive faith in the interest of the scientist in knowledge for its own sake. Even the scientific community would agree on that. For example, we find the research director of a major project intended to lay bare the genetic structure of man explaining that 'it's going to lead ultimately to the total understanding of man'.[25] In this claim to 'total understanding', we see signs of scientific reductionism, forms of knowledge other than science being ignored, and the inner interest of science in exerting control over even the human world.

The modern state has, therefore, invested hugely in science, in both scientific research and science education. The proportion of arts to science places has been a key element in higher education planning over the past 25 years. This is not, though, simply a matter of numbers of student places, for a science-based student place can cost up to twice as much as an arts place. Despite this investment by the state, we have seen that, however important and however costly, the nature of higher education is not a crude reflection of the state's 'needs'. The UK undergraduate curriculum is not determined by the Treasury, nor by the Department of Education and Science, certainly not by the Confederation of British Industry, and not (at least not yet) by the Training Agency.

The key determinant of the shape of the science curriculum is the scientific community. Given the extraordinary explosion of scientific knowledge, and the fissiparous tendency of the disciplinary culture to produce more and more scientific sub-cultures, it is not surprising that the science curriculum is often overpacked with material that the student is expected to assimilate. The obverse of this situation is that the science curriculum runs up against the charge that it is educationally narrow. In particular, it is accused of failing to develop in the students a moral sensitivity equal to the power and influence that science plays in the world.

What goes on in higher education is mirrored by larger tendencies in the wider society. Science's understandable belief in itself and the reductionist assumption that human beings are nothing but collections of molecules, are matched by tendencies in social policy to adopt a purely instrumental and scientific approach.[26] Consequently, the realm of the ethical in social affairs is in danger of being expunged.[27]

The science curriculum, then, cannot be understood apart from the uses and effects of science in the modern world. And if, as I have suggested, the general form of science – at least as a research activity – is largely given, a social fact with which we have to reckon, then we cannot sensibly wish it to be other than it is, still less pretend it does not exist (as some humanists seem to want). The real question for those responsible for the education of our future scientists is: Are they prepared to allow the science curriculum to provide a genuine education, or is it to provide simply a training in technical knowledge and in technique itself?[28] The signs, it must be said, are mixed. For example, while science courses which included historical and social elements developed apace in the 1970s, that 'science, technology and society' movement seems to have run into the sands, with the numbers of courses, staff and students involved all diminishing.[29] Personal tutoring, an initiative based at Imperial College in the University of London, which encourages undergraduate science students to teach science to local school pupils, has remained a marginal activity, for which little or no recognition is given in awarding degrees.[30]

It is hardly surprising that the cases of successfully broadening the science curriculum are limited. For if it were to take off, and be firmly established, it would require a significant shift in the way in which scientific research is conducted. Until a significant degree of reflection on the scientific enterprise is built into the mainstream of scientific research, the chances of reflection on the ethical, epistemological and social basis of science becoming a common part of the science curriculum must be limited.[31]

Social sciences

If the natural sciences suffer from a lack of self-reflection, it could be said that the social sciences have a surfeit of it. Particularly sociology but also psychology, and to a lesser extent economics, are remarkable for the time their practitioners spend in debating the nature of their discipline, in discussing the status of their inquiries, and in arguing where the mainstream should lie. These debates reflect something of the epistemological backwash on academic disciplines produced by science. If science receives high marks in this culture, all disciplines that have any scientific pretensions are liable to be influenced.[32] It is hardly surprising if the areas of inquiry that wish to study human behaviour in a rigorous fashion, and which generate science-like methodologies, exhibit tendencies to be seen *as* fully fledged sciences.

The social sciences, therefore, are paradoxical in nature. They can be both excessively theoretical and unduly empirical. The massive computer printouts generated by so many research projects in the social sciences (including, it must be said, some kinds of research in education) and the continuing self-reflection and self-examination are both reflections of an uncertainty in their role. Are they to assist the social planners, by producing huge quantities of data or projections on social groups, and social action? Are they to provide the numerical account of society, so that social policy can be efficiently implemented?[33] Or are they to provide some grounded insight into the nature of human affairs, to assist the general task of self-understanding? Is their role primarily technical or educational?[34]

If the character of the social sciences is affected by their place in society, it is also affected by the way in which they have developed within the academic community. As in other areas of academic life, one of the dominant features is the way in which the various social sciences have become separated from each other, each with its own academic sub-culture and trade union. It is not impossible, but it is exceedingly difficult and time-consuming, for a sociologist to become a psychologist.[35] The boundaries of the academic sub-communities are so tightly drawn that movement of that kind is rare. It is hardly surprising, for that kind of movement represents a threat to the internal cohesion of the discipline; the loss of a member to another grouping is akin to betrayal.[36]

This disciplinary tribalism (Becher 1989) is felt in the curriculum. Certainly, efforts have been made to develop multidisciplinary courses, especially in the public sector of higher education. But we nowhere have a unified sense of what a real education in the social sciences as such would mean. To make the point, should it not be common ground that, as a minimum, social science graduates ought to emerge from their courses with an informed understanding of Freud, Levi-Strauss, Husserl and phenomenology, and the main strands of economics, post-structuralism, and Habermas and critical theory? It is no answer to say that there is insufficient time for a wide-ranging programme of studies of that kind, and that attempting to cover such ground would lead to dilettantism. Those are merely the defensive postures of the academic professions. There is plenty of time, if the aims and content of such a programme were seriously thought through.

Again, the academic dimensions of this state of affairs are not to be seen simply as a contingent fact about academic life. The limits on understanding, thinking, self-comprehension and, indeed, social criticism, which this segregated approach to curriculum design fosters, are entirely understandable. For such an education will not rock any boats, and will leave society largely as it is. This disciplinary apartheid supports not just an academic division of labour, but a wider social division of labour.[37] The social sciences would claim to offer a critical education, but their anxiety over their own role and their lack of vision of a genuine social science education has a conservative outcome falling far short of the rhetoric.

Professional education

I use the term 'professional education' to embrace all applied and practical domains of study, from engineering to nursing, from rubber technology to social work, from remedial gymnastics to librarianship, from accountancy to teacher education, and from pharmacy to graphic design. There are some 90+ professional bodies directly associated with courses of higher education in the UK. In addition, many courses which are overtly practical in orientation (such as business studies) are not endorsed by any one professional body. The professionalization of the higher education curriculum probably represents the biggest – and largely unrecognized – shift in UK higher education over the past 30 years. Precise figures are not available, but in the UK polytechnic and colleges sector, nearly one-third of the students are taking some form of industrial or professional placement (supervised work experience, as it is called) as part of their degree course.[38] There could be no better demonstration of the inapposite nature of the term 'ivory tower' than in this proliferation of courses in professional education.

Few generalizations will have application across such a diverse range of fields of study; however, perhaps some are possible. We can recall Stuart Hampshire's observation, quoted in Chapter 3, that 'the opposition between thought and action has been wholly confused'. This can be seen in the curriculum in professional education. By and large, we have not sorted out how professional education can both be educative and provide a professional training. Debates over the relationship between theory and practice are either endless (as in teacher education or in the creative and performing arts), or they are non-existent because there is an unquestioned division of labour between higher education (which looks after the theoretical components) and the profession (which subsequently provides the training elements, e.g. pharmacy, law and engineering).

It is certainly true and with justification that professional bodies have been criticized for an excessively conservative approach to higher education, manifest not only in the curriculum and examinations but even in the admissions criteria. On the other hand, many professions are now scrutinizing their relationship with higher education, and are helping to review radically in some cases (engineering, law, social work) the character of the educational programme. Admittedly, much of the impetus of these reviews comes from a desire to improve professional competence, rather than the educational development of students. Nevertheless, it remains the case that worthwhile initiatives in the higher education curriculum have been seen in professional education. Open learning, project work, group work, experience integrated with the educational components, and students encouraged critically to appraise their own professional practice: these are just some of the developments in train. (Medicine, paramedical subjects, teacher education, civil engineering and law are some of the professions beginning to promote such developments; though sporadically even within those professions.)

In the best of these developments, what we are witnessing is a genuine partnership between the academic and the professional communities, with consequent mutual benefit.[39] For example, we see academics and the profession accepting 'practice' as a valuable developmental opportunity, with students expected to keep a log-book of their experiences, and to be able to evaluate their actions in conversation with their supervisor or mentor. In other words, it is becoming increasingly recognized that a profession will be the stronger if its practitioners are used to plan, to execute, to accept responsibility for, and to evaluate critically their own actions. 'The reflective practitioner' is not, or should not be, a woolly piece of rhetoric.[40] It signifies an idea of real value both to the world of thought and to the world of action.

Humanities

Surely, if nowhere else, we can see evidence of the ivory tower in the humanities? Well, perhaps. But we can also see signs of its disintegration. The humanities have been 'in crisis' for at least a generation;[41] since, that is, the dawn of the post-war expansion of higher education. With justification, whatever the blandishments of successive Secretaries of State for Education, the humanities feel under threat. They sense that, in some quarters, they are not considered to offer real knowledge at all,[42] and that, if they are to survive, they need to demonstrate their relevance to the world of work. This kind of self-presentation works at two curriculum levels – the syllabus and the teaching and learning methods used.

On the first level, we can just begin to see signs of movement; as we saw earlier, transferable skills have begun to appear in the language of educators, if not yet seriously in the curriculum itself. On the second level, we see an increasing willingness to introduce the computer into the learning process, though that too is by no means universal.[43] The commitment to developments of this kind must be suspect because the momentum is largely generated outside the academic community; they do not spring from an internal agenda.

At the same time, while cosmetic curricular changes are happening, the role of a humanities education in the modern world goes unexamined, in any serious sense. Leavis (1943, 1969) was perhaps the last to set out a manifesto, and that solely for English literature. We might today have reservations about its élitism, and its complete repudiation of industrial culture. But his vision of university education did recover a sense of the critical function of higher education.[44] On this view, higher education is not simply a vehicle to reflect society's consciousness, but has the crucial task of perceiving alternative visions, or extending the sense of the possible. The humanities of the 1990s urgently need redirection, and a new sense of their contesting mission in society.

Unfortunately, we see again a set of disciplines failing to live up to its own rhetoric: if they have not actually been eroded, the concepts of person, imagination, judgement, value, and even of the 'humane', as represented by the humanities curriculum, are failing to match the post-industrial world we live in.[45] The humanities are needed more than ever, but not as a super finishing school for the civil service or to provide the managers of advertising agencies. While they have not been incorporated into the mainstream of society to the extent of the other disciplines, neither have they provided any serious alternative vision to that society. The hermeneutic project, as providing a realm of meaning consciously set off against the instrumentality of the age, remains only an evocative prospect. Sensing their own vulnerability, the humanities have instead allowed themselves to be reduced to a neutral blandness, lacking any real educational purchase.[46]

Summary and conclusion

Higher education is not an ivory tower; even if it wished, it could not be one. Given this situation, the instrumentalists (who believe in the existence of the ivory tower, but think it should be destroyed) and the liberals (who also believe in the ivory tower, and think it should be defended) are both mistaken. Higher education is, as a social fact, incorporated into the modern state. The question, then, which an educational theory of higher education has to answer is: What ought we to do to see that a higher education fulfils its emancipatory promise, so that it does more than providing qualified manpower for the state, and acting as a cultural finishing school?[47]

There are two options, by no means mutually exclusive. The first possibility is to accept willingly into the curriculum the vocational elements that are being pressed on to higher education, *provided* that these elements can be used as educational vehicles. Those who advocate the development of vocational skills or wider transferable skills can have their way, just so long as they are prepared for the practices in question to become the object of critical appraisal on the part of the student. A practice can only be tolerated in higher education provided that it is susceptible to examination, evaluation and, if necesary, repudiation. It cannot be allowed to become a routine, a technique, a mere habit.

The other option is complementary. It is to take a theoretical approach and to build in, systematically, levels of reflection within bodies of knowledge. Making that insertion into the curriculum will be easier in some subject areas than in others. In some subjects, as we have seen, self-reflection already exists as a dominant strand in the discipline's own self-development; in other areas, forms of knowledge have largely failed to develop a level of self-reflection. The effort has to be made, however. For if, as indeed it does, a corpus of knowledge in part represents social interests, then the emancipatory promise of higher education can only be redeemed if the corpus itself comes under critical evaluation.

In the end, the two strands of strategy come together. Higher education has been sucked into society, at least into the fringes of the state apparatus; and with that incorporation, knowledge has been institutionalized and colonized. In that situation, it is imperative – if higher education is to recover anything approaching the liberal qualities that it promises – that students are encouraged to stand back, to reflect deeply, to consider the ethical dimensions of both thought and action, to understand something of the place of their knowledge in society, to glimpse something of what it might be, and to gain their own independence from all that they learn, think and do.

6

Living with Ideology

Introduction

Ideology is a slippery term, and its scope is hotly debated by social theorists. It may not be true to say that it has as many different meanings as it has users, but it sometimes seems like it. However, just as with 'objectivity', 'truth' and many other concepts, if we want to develop a well-founded educational theory of higher education, we cannot leave the debate over ideology to the specialists; for ideology impinges on higher education in several dimensions.

The connections between ideology and higher education are at least three-fold. First, ideology is to be found in theories and beliefs about higher education. This was touched on in Chapter 2, where we explored historically the idea of higher education. Secondly, ideology enters the processes of human action and interaction within institutions of higher education. This will be taken up later, in a chapter on higher learning. Thirdly, ideology forms an element of the knowledge made available to the student in a programme of studies. It is this level of ideology in higher education which will be the focus of this chapter.

Why, though, should ideology warrant special attention? The general point of ideology is that, either alongside a message or, more often, somewhat under the surface, there is a further message. The idea, for example, of a hidden curriculum is not unfamiliar (Snyder 1971), although it is largely given lip-service. Those responsible for the higher education curriculum talk much of the encouragement given to students to be independent in their learning styles, and to take up a critical stance in what they have to say; whereas, all too often the student experience, driven by an overheavy and formal examination regime, is one of sticking to a syllabus, and of learning and marshalling prescribed facts. This is a hidden curriculum in a very real sense, because it is hidden even from the academics themselves. Or rather, it is not so much hidden from them, as that they fail to notice the real character of the student experience, even though it is so close at hand. This is an ideology in the fullest sense, not only because there is a gap between the rhetoric and the reality, but also because those who produce the rhetoric (about open learning and critical perspectives) delude themselves that that is the reality.

There is no deliberate conspiracy here. It is in the nature of ideology that those who produce it do not always know that they produce it. The reason for this blankness is that the rhetoric matches their picture of the world. And the lack of self-reflection that goes with it indicates that it is in the interests of the rhetoric-espousers to hold such a view. With ideology goes either a defence of power or a claim to power: ideology is the story of those who wish to maintain a position of power or who aspire to it. Typically, the social relations between those who teach and those who are taught are unequal, and the stories spun about the student experience by the academic community are a means of legitimizing that situation.

Although these introductory comments have focused on the student experience, they bring into the open a number of features of ideology in higher education. The target of this chapter, though, is the knowledge and thought that students are expected to get on the inside of. Knowledge, after all, is central to the higher education enterprise; and if ideology can be found there, the legitimacy of the whole enterprise itself seems to be in doubt. Just that is being claimed here.

The social basis of academic knowledge

One of the inner beliefs of this book is that the formulation of an educational theory of higher education cannot be accomplished in a purely abstract way. By this, I mean that a well-grounded educational theory cannot be achieved purely philosophically. Even if we were to draw on epistemology, ethics, the philosophy of action and the philosophical studies of the various forms of thought (philosophy of science, of history, of the social sciences and so on), and even if we were to include the philosophy of education, our background studies would still be incomplete. Those speculative studies, while necessary, cannot provide a sufficient grounding in themselves. This is simply because higher education has an inescapable social basis, as we saw in Chapter 5.

The second section of this book (Chapters 3 and 4) outlined what I termed the epistemological undermining of higher education. The central idea developed there was that, in the light of modern epistemology and indeed social theory, it is impossible to provide an absolute legitimation of our cognitive claims. A neutral framework, within which we can gain an assured epistemological security, is simply unavailable. There is always an epistemological gap between our knowledge claims and the world to which they are addressed. At best, there is a partiality about our claims; at worst, there are embedded in them social interests. Pure objectivity is a chimera.

We now take up that story again, as we focus on the social basis of knowledge. Pointing out that knowledge has a social basis can mean a number of things. We could simply be implying that if our social institutions, our wider culture and our knowledge-producing arrangements were different, our knowledge claims would be different. By and large, the knowledge that is important to the Borneo headhunter is clearly not that sought by a Western academic. Closer to home, we can see signs that there is a tendency for the kinds of knowledge on offer in higher education courses to differ across the sectors. In the UK, in comparison with their university counterparts, public sector degree courses more usually include societal components, or seek to develop social or community links in the core of a programme of studies. This is apparent not only in public sector courses oriented towards a specific profession, but even in much 'purer' subjects, from philosophy, through modern languages to the sciences.

Such contrasts in the priorities given to different forms of knowledge are not in themselves a matter of concern, from the point of view of an educational theory. For what are being revealed here are simply associations between the classification and distribution of knowledge on the one hand and social groups on the other. This is the province of the sociology of knowledge: linkages between knowledge as it is perceived, pursued and disseminated on the one side and social formations on the other.[1]

This view of knowledge can have a powerful impact, for in the variant known as 'the strong programme' of the sociology of knowledge, *all* knowledge claims can come under the sociological microscope.[2] The causes of the beliefs of the Borneo headhunter and the nuclear physicist can be understood in precisely the same terms. In other words, a thoroughgoing relativist account of knowledge is possible. But despite the anguish this view of knowledge generates, both among professional theorists and the academic community more generally, it is rather benign in its implications. Nothing follows for the truth of a belief from the fact that its social causes can be identified.

Where things become more serious, however, is where social causes can be shown to be accompanied by social interests. In that case, the story changes from 'this is the way things are here', to 'things are this way here because there is a set of social interests at stake'. Where that kind of story can be told, we have moved from the sociology of knowledge to the uncovering of ideology.

In the process, something else has happened. We have moved from a relativistic description of the world (this is how it is here; and that is how it is there) to a critical account of the world. The implication behind the ascription of 'ideology' is that the representation in question not only is explicable in terms of underlying social interest but that, in being explicable in this way, it contains a hidden dimension of closure. If there is an interest at work in forming the knowledge corpus, that interest structure will be working to maintain that formation, and will act to prevent a different kind of formation (possibly serving a different set of interests) taking shape.[3]

This has to be of concern to us in working out an educational theory of higher education. If the knowledge clusterings on offer to the student could plausibly be associated with a structured configuration of social interests, the implication would be that, instead of being available for open examination, those orderings of knowledge would contain elements of resistance. Students, in other words, would not be working their way around and within a body of knowledge as an open learning experience. Rather, their learning would have become a cage, albeit with rubber bars that could be bent a little.[4]

These are, admittedly, highly abstract remarks, and deserve some examples if they are to have any substance. Before offering one or two, it is worth admitting also that the notion of interest has so far been left as an undefined term.[5] Both defects can be redressed at once by identifying examples of the scope of the different interests at work in academic knowledge, within the curriculum.

I regard it as a form of ideology, for example, where we find that a subject is dominated by a profession (for instance, the influence of the medical profession on medical science, with the relatively limited attention given to preventive medicine, to epidemiology, and to complementary medicine; or the influence of the business community in shaping uncritically the agenda for undergraduate courses in business studies). I also regard as ideological those cases where boundaries are erected by disciplinary sub-cultures (for example, where problems in the social sciences are defined as purely sociological or purely psychological, so that a teacher in one discipline will exclude accounts given by a student wishing to draw on findings from the other discipline). And as a final example (for now) of ideology in the curriculum, I would want to point to the wider links between knowledge and the state, particularly in science and technology, and the way in which science and technology can assume the character of an ideology, with their adherents believing uncritically in their worth.

What this last example points up is that there has developed in the modern state a general *Weltanschauung*, or societal outlook, supportive of science and technology, and that – as Habermas argues – consciousness is ideological by virtue of its implicit interest structure.[6] We see the associated resistances emerging where its internal assumptions are questioned (as with nuclear power). Higher education is not separated from society, and so any ideology of this kind will almost certainly find its way into the curriculum, unless firm countervailing measures are taken to open up those forms of thought from purely technical considerations to embrace value positions.[7]

Now let me qualify all those examples. Although each is made as an authentic example, their purpose here is not to make polemical points. Rather, they are offered as exemplars, as markers of the range of ways ideology can intrude into curricular knowledge. To summarize the three examples: ideology can be present when academic interests alone are at work; it can be present when the interests of particular external reference groups are involved (such as professions); and it can be present when the interests of society-wide institutions or groupings are affected. Picking up the query about interests made earlier, we can see that interests may be narrow or wide-ranging in their scope; they may be internal to the academic community or lie largely outside it.

Vacuous concept or critical edge?

Those familiar with the historical origins of the concept of ideology may feel a little cheated by what has been said so far. For, once it got going after its eighteenth-century origin, the idea of ideology played a key part in the birth of social theory. In its classic Marxist form, ideology both had a basis in social class and was contrasted with science. The dominant ideas of the age were those of the ruling class, the owners of production. Through analysis, however, they could be shown not simply not to represent reality, but actually to provide a complete inversion of the 'true' state of affairs (Mepham and Ruben 1978). One of the images used by Marx was that of a camera in which the picture is turned upside down on the lens. Centrally, Marx was here attacking general conceptions of human beings, and their economic and social relationships with each other. Against ideology of this kind, Marx was determined to develop a science of man. In other words, he believed that it was possible to attain a non-ideological form of cognition, even in human affairs.

However, key elements of the classic Marxist use of ideology have not been retained in its application here. Its class basis, its contrast with science and its focus on ideas are nowadays commonly eschewed, as indeed I have here. Today, the idea of ideology has broadened into a much more catholic concept, and we need not feel constrained to remain within the Marxist framework.[8] There is, though, a danger that in allowing more flexibility in the use of the term, the concept itself will become vacuous, for the range of its applications seems endless. And if everything – from ideas to practices – is a potential candidate for the appellation 'ideology', does the term not lose its critical edge and, ultimately, its meaning?

That is a possibility against which we must guard. Ideology is not, nor should it become, a vapid concept; and it is possible to widen its use beyond its original Marxist meaning while retaining its critical edge. And the critical edge has real point here. The idea of ideology does its most work when it reveals a partiality in a truth claim, or belief or practice, a partiality which is not accidental but is shown to serve a limited set of social interests. Its application is both explanatory of, and pejorative towards, its object. It implicates its object as suffering from a blankness, a refusal to be open and self-critical. It is not necessarily saying (after Marx) that what is on offer is untrue, but that it is partial in a self-serving way. This state of affairs is particularly awkward when the corpus of knowledge in question pretends to be fully open, self-critical and transparent. In such a case, there is an epistemological gap between the self-understanding of the corpus and its real status. Instead of openness, we have closure, exclusion and boundary maintenance. This is not how it seems, however, to the initiated, to those on the inside of a form of thought, to the converted.

I believe that we can see signs of all these ideological features in knowledge packages presented to students in the higher education curriculum. They do not, though, have to be widespread to warrant our attention: they only have to be present as possibilities. If we seriously want to minimize the element of ideology in knowledge within the curriculum, then we have to be permanently vigilant in combating it. Ideology is always threatening to take over. In some senses, it is permanently present. The influential interest structures of the wider society, of professional groupings and of the academic disciplines are ever with us. Ideology cannot be entirely shaken off. We must therefore do what we can to reduce its effects.

The production of knowledge and the educational class

Before easing the burden, the problem has to be further compounded. Following the work of Althusser (1969), we should remind ourselves that knowledge as systematized thought does not exist in some pure domain of its own (in some kind of Popperian third world). Rather, it is the result of interactions and negotiations between claimants in a discussion. It is not even necessary to say that knowledge is the result of human interaction, the outcome of human practice; rather, we can say that knowledge is itself a practice. It takes on form not as some end point of human activity, but as the concomitant of it. It follows that just as we can raise questions about the mode and relations of production in the mainstream economy, so we can ask questions about the mode and relations of production of the practices constituted through the search for and the maintenance of knowledge.

To bring to the surface this way of looking at knowledge is, at one level, only to give a theoretical backing to the idea that academic disciplines have a tendency to generate their own ideologies. Within disciplines in the context of the discovery of new knowledge, we can see definite relations of production. There is a relatively limited number of those who control, if they do not actually own, the means of production, through their publications and journal editorships. There is a larger number, who have only their intellectual labour to sell, perhaps as a research worker (note the use of the term 'worker'), with very limited rights over the direction of research inquiries and emerging intellectual property. The professor's name may well appear as a joint author, even though his or her contribution may have been quite limited.

This way of looking at knowledge suggests that ideology may well arise out of the knowledge enterprise itself. The owners of the intellectual property emerging will have invested much in its production, and will tend to defend it, rationalize it and cloak it with spurious legitimations against those who seek to overthrow the dominant intellectual order. But if ideology can be said to be lurking in this way, is the idea of a non-ideological form of thought a practical possibility?

It may seem that behind an ideological framework there lies a non-ideological perspective not far out of our grasp. But to entertain such a prospect implies the possibility of a genuine (even scientific) form of thought arising in parallel to the form of thought it replaces. This is simply not feasible; and it raises endless questions about the relationship between the ideological form of thought and the 'real' form of thought. Having advanced to a materialist perspective, having taken on board the intellectual world as it really is, we would be back in the unsatisfactory idealist position of imagining that thought forms exist in themselves and that a rational choice can be made between them.

But that option is unavailable. We have to accept the general messiness of the situation. As Gellner has aptly remarked, we cannot jump out of our sociological skins.[9] We have to accept that there are no pure states of cognition. What we can do in this position is to go on struggling, as Feyerabend argues, to open our forms of thought ever wider, and to allow all kinds of theory to proliferate.

These reflections on the ideology of knowledge have implications for our understanding of the academic community's independence. Higher education is a pivotal institution in society, producing the qualified personnel for its central professions and institutions. With its research functions, the academic community also produces, refines, preserves and legitimates society's cognitive structure. As a result, the academic community has taken on the characteristics of a social class. This educational class is in a position of some influence, seeking with some success to have its intellectual currency adopted as the cognitive currency of society.[10]

Admittedly, this is a class with its own internal strata and divisions, and so no simple model of a class acting in and for itself will adequately describe the activities of this social group. It is the general picture which concerns us here, though. Once we recognize that members of the academic community are not just bearers of social relationships within the academic community, but stand in a social relationship with the wider society by virtue of their academic role, the opportunities for ideological contamination are multiplied. This is not to allege any simple model of social determinism; but it is to suggest the possibility of 'overdeterminism' at work (Althusser 1969). It is plausible to suggest that the cognitive structures developed by the academic community reflect the interests of both the academic community itself and the wider society.

These two dimensions of interest are, of course, interrelated. The educational class will try to press its cognitive structures on to society and, in seeking to find a purchase on society's wider value systems, will inevitably end in acknowledging those societal interests. The two sets of interest take in each other's washing.

Ideology in academic knowledge

Certainly, we have to acknowledge that somewhat different processes are at work in different forms of knowledge. Ideology – both of society and of the academic community – enters indirectly into the natural sciences, and directly into the hermeneutic forms of study of the humanities and social sciences (where personal meaning and interpretation are at stake).

The indirect entry of ideology into the positivistic sciences is no less significant than the potentially direct assault on the humanities and the arts. Science, for instance, is happy to present itself as being concerned with facts rather than values; as identifying means to fulfilling ends rather than determining the ends themselves; and as being objective rather than reflecting the personal and group motivations of scientists. To these components of scientific thought have to be added the tendency of science to impose itself as the supreme form of human cognition in modern society.

All this amounts to ideological surreptitiousness,[11] and is arguably more serious than the more direct entry of ideology into the humanities. First, undergraduates are prevented from asking questions about the ends to which science is put, and the values represented by science itself. Secondly, it pretends to a purity over value-freedom in its truth claims that cannot seriously be maintained. I have in mind not simply the value ascribed to such components of a theory as elegance, or simplicity, or comprehensiveness; but the way in which, through history, science has reflected wider social values even in its internal truth claims and evaluations. The mechanistic world-view of the eighteenth century had its parallel in the science of the day; now, we are seeing signs in modern physics and cosmology of the fragmentation of thought and belief that is a part of the post-modern world.[12]

It is worth seeing where this discussion has taken us. One natural reaction to the charge of being ideological or even being just susceptible to ideology is to try to clean up one's act by removing the ideological component in question. The supposition is that if some of our beliefs, theories or thought patterns are contaminated by ideology, the offending elements can easily be detected and removed. But the picture presented here is that the situation is much more problematic. Ideology is endemic to all thought, including the knowledges carved out by the academic community. It is not just an element, a stratum within each corpus, that can be sliced off. Rather, the picture given by certain strands in modern social theory and taken on board here is that ideology is eradicable; it is a necessary element in systematized forms of thought.

The temptation is to think that even if ideology is present in the softer disciplines of the arts, the humanities and the social sciences, at least we can find some havens in the more muscular disciplines in the natural sciences, in mathematics and in logic. If we picture the position in the form of Fig. 1, and ask ourselves how far to the right the arrow might move, we might feel that sooner or later we can find a boundary to offer it some definite resistance. But, if the argument here has any substance at all, we have to say that there is no secure redoubt available. Potentially, at least, ideology can be found in all disciplines. The arrow moves across the whole range.

The self-refuting argument

To some, the claim that all thought is susceptible to ideological contamination will appear to be contradictory and incoherent. That point of view runs something like this. The claim that all thought is ideological – even if only potentially so – must apply to itself. But that means that the claim itself is ideologically tainted and, therefore, is itself devalued. So the claim that all thought is potentially ideological cannot be taken seriously. The claim undermines itself simply in being made. It must, therefore, be false. It refutes itself; it can therefore be dismissed.[13]

Before tackling the argument, I accept that some will wonder what, in any case, is the significance of it. The argument that has just been raised will seem to some to consist of scholastic debating points, which should not be allowed to hold us up when we are interested in developing aims in higher education. This

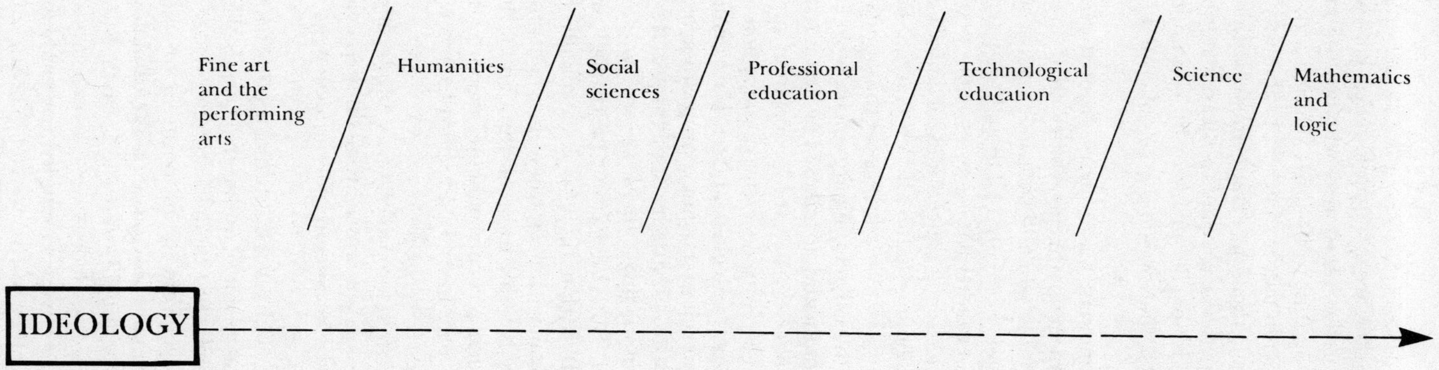

Figure 1 The range of ideology.

is simply not the case, however; the argument just outlined, and the general issues raised in this chapter, are of the profoundest kind within the enterprise we have set ourselves. For the question is whether the knowledge purveyed in higher education can be said to be pure, offering a disinterested grip on the world, or whether it is tainted in some eradicable way. If the latter situation is even possibly the case, then our arrangements within higher education, the kind of educational experience we want to offer our students, can hardly remain unaffected. We would not be justified in continuing to offer the same educational experience that would be on offer if knowledge was entirely objective.

The self-refuting argument has to be confronted, therefore. For one of the things it does is to open up the possibility that there must be some non-ideological space which thought and knowledge can occupy. The implication is that the claim being made here – that all thought is potentially ideological – can only attain some kind of validity if it occupies a non-ideological space of its own. If this is so, then traditional conceptions of knowledge pursuits in higher education can perhaps be saved after all. A way might be found of showing that they too inhabit a space free from ideological contamination.

Both that hope and the self-refuting argument, however, can be shown to rest on two simple but fundamental mistakes. The first is to assume that the charge of being ideological implies that the proposition or theory in question is necessarily false. That is an unnecessary assumption. While they have some relationship, the concepts of ideology and truth are distinct. It is not necessarily the case, in claiming or even in showing a proposition or a body of thought to be ideological, that it is false. Admittedly, something of the kind was present in the classic Marxist view of ideology: there, as we saw, ideology amounted to an inversion of the truth. But the account of ideology which I have offered is somewhat different. It is that thought is essentially perspectival, giving an account of the world from within a framework which represents social interests. In this sense, ideology is liable to break through all thought, even if it is not actually present. As such, a corpus of knowledge provides us with a view of the world which is necessarily partial and shot-through with interests of various kinds.

Ideology does not, therefore, necessarily imply falsity; but it does imply partiality, reflecting social interest. From the judgement that all thought is potentially ideological, we should not immediately suspect that falsity is ubiquitous.

The second problem with the self-refuting argument is this. The claim that all thought is potentially ideological, or that that corpus of knowledge or this theory is ideological, are claims *about* thought and knowledge. They are propositions made on a different level from the propositions to which they refer. This is a singular fact about human consciousness. We can know about the world, and so, arguably, do other sentient beings on the earth. But, uniquely, we can form judgements about our knowledge, we can evaluate it and take up stances towards it. In turn, if we were so minded, we could form observations about those evaluations. In other words, we can generate a hierarchy of knowledge claims; we might call them first-order, second-order, and so on.[14] The central idea of this book is that a true *higher* education will be located essentially at these higher levels of thought and knowledge.

Drawing on this hierarchical conception of knowledge, we can see that even if truth and falsity were to come into play at the basic level of propositions as a result of the ascription of ideology, nothing follows about the truth or falsity of the higher-order claim employing the concept of ideology. To go back to the self-refuting argument: even if it were the case that there is an implication of reduced truth value, when it is said that all systematic thought is potentially ideological, nothing follows about the truth value of that claim itself, for it is being made on a different (indeed, higher) epistemic level than the knowledge claims to which it refers.

For both these reasons (the conceptual distinction between ideology and falsity, and the hierarchy of knowledge), therefore, the self-refuting argument fails.

Reducing the ideological component of knowledge

So where do we go from here? If we cannot altogether shake off the presence of ideology in our structures of knowledge, in which we invite students to participate, is there any move we can make which might at least mitigate the worst effects? For a framework which offers just that, I want to turn again to the work of Jurgen Habermas. There, we find two possibilities presented to us, one a theoretical solution and the other a practical solution. Habermas does not pretend that either is a complete 'solution', but they do at least offer us a way forward.

The theoretical solution has been hinted at already, both in this and in previous chapters. It is to take seriously the idea of criticism. Throughout his work, Habermas has insisted on the inescapability of human interest embedded in our structures of knowledge. For him, there are two fundamental interests at work: the will to control, which underlies the natural sciences and purposive-rational thought in general; and the will to communicate, which underlies humanistic forms of understanding. Habermas (1978) goes on to argue that alongside these two fundamental interest structures, we can see a third fundamental human interest in emancipation. And this emancipatory interest finds expression in critical modes of thought, whose purpose very often is to offer a critique of conventional knowledge expressing the other kinds of interest. On this view, ideology can be counteracted to some extent through the formation of a critical discourse. The argument of this book is that it is in this critical discourse that a genuine *higher* education will be attained, if at all.

The other 'solution' Habermas offers is more practical. For Habermas, the fundamental source of ideology lies in our social relationships: unequal social relationships are likely to produce distorted communication, in which the powerful seek to impose their own view of the world on the powerless.[15]

Consequently, the way to reduce this kind of distorted communication lies in so arranging our social relationships that all those involved have an equal opportunity to be heard, and to have an appropriately proportionate effect on any outcome. This requires nothing less than the formation of what he calls, as we saw earlier, an ideal speech situation.[16] I return here to this central idea of Habermas because it offers a way of countering the presence of ideology. If ideology is symptomatic of a communication process which has gone wrong, then we should attempt so far as possible to iron out the components of our social interactions which are responsible for that distortion.

What might this mean in practice? So far as higher education is concerned, the idea of a discourse freed of unnecessary constraint works on two levels. First, there is the discourse in which the student is a participant, with opportunities available to the student to form and communicate ideas either with other students or with teachers. Secondly, there is the discourse of academics, a discourse which sustains and advances their own disciplinary communities. If the ideological component of a corpus of knowledge is to be kept at a minimum, then the epistemic community has to find ways of keeping the communication flows fully open and equal. The interests of powerful groups, both inside the academic community and beyond (particularly for professionally related forms of knowledge), have to be kept in check so that they do not exert a disproportionate weight.

The point of countering ideology

If we cannot reach a situation where we can say ideology has been banished from a form of thought forever, if no such pure vantage place is available, why bother? Is there not a hint here of trying to guarantee just that which cannot be guaranteed? If so, who guarantees the guarantors?

The questions are worth asking, but they too betray signs of a yearning for perfection which neither is available nor is being claimed. There is no complete solution; permanent vigilance is the watchword. Just because we cannot reach perfection does not mean that the effort is not worth making. I have indicated that the concept of ideology is an epistemological concept, as much as it is a sociological one. Being aware of its possible presence encourages us to stand back, and to adopt a sceptical stance towards a corpus of knowledge as a whole. The suspicion of ideology does not in itself supply a different corpus of knowledge, or a new theory. But simply in raising critical questions (why this set of representations or theories or concepts?), the mind is released from passive acceptance of the knowledge on offer as such. This attitude is wholly to the good, in trying to develop a genuine higher education in which the student's mind is freed to ask and to answer questions of its own.

Ideology is not the demonic, irrational form of discourse it is often made out to be. On the contrary, it is often highly rational, offering an account of the world, and demanding to be taken seriously (Gouldner 1976). It can give reasons, can be couched in elaborate garb employing complex concepts and theories, and can even be aware of itself. Indeed, as we know, Marxism has itself often been said to constitute an ideology *par excellence*. Ideology can catch us unawares, therefore. It can appear surreptitiously, in a guise which hides its true character. Academic knowledge, accordingly, provides a most suitable home for ideology.

But if we are seriously interested in developing a higher education in which the minds of students are really free, and do not succumb unwittingly to ideology, we have to develop, within the curriculum and within our institutions of higher education, reflexive strategies that encourage students to stand back from their core course of studies, see it in various perspectives, and take up critical stances towards it.[17] We cannot produce an absolutely non-ideological curriculum; we cannot begin *de novo* and invent a disinterested corpus of knowledge. We have to start from where we are, both sociologically and epistemologically, both in terms of the prevailing interests inherent in knowledge, and in terms of the 'leakiness' of knowledge. Interest-freedom is not possible, nor is a watertight epistemological experience. Let us therefore admit as much not just to ourselves but also to our students. Let us also put the onus on them as much as on the teaching staff for developing their own independence from what is put before them. Ideology will not be overcome in higher education, but it may be neutralized to some extent.

Conclusion: Whose interests?

One of the conclusions of this chapter is that interests cannot be expunged from knowledge, and they cannot, therefore, be eradicated from knowledge as presented within the higher education curriculum. We are obliged, consequently, to ask ourselves: Which interests do we want our knowledge to serve? What view of knowledge do we want to pass on to students? To pretend that it is interest-free is just to revert to an ideological stance, of the academic community no less. Higher education, in its knowledge offerings, will be bound to reflect the disciplinary interests of the educational class, and the interests of industry, commerce and the professions where they bear on the curriculum (increasingly so, irrespective of the subjects that students study). But higher education has an interest of its own, an emancipatory interest in developing students with liberated minds of their own. Only through sustaining that emancipatory interest actively and continually throughout the curriculum can ideology be confronted with any seriousness.

Part 4

Key Concepts

7

Culture

Introduction

> Finally, there is a function . . . that is none the less fundamental: the transmission of a common culture and common standards of citizenship . . . It is a proper function of higher education . . . to provide in partnership with the family that background of culture and social habit upon which a healthy society depends.[1]

For the Committee chaired by Lord Robbins, there was an essential link between higher education and culture. So much so, that the cultural function of higher education was one of the four functions identified as the core of Robbins' idea of higher education. Looking back a quarter of a century to that statement, perhaps the most obvious awkwardness today lies in its easy assumption that there was, in the 1960s, a common culture to be transmitted. As writers like Leavis and Raymond Williams saw it, although educational institutions had a duty to do what they could to sustain it, the common culture was almost irredeemably lost.[2]

Let us put that difficulty aside, at least for now, for there is something much more significant in the silences within that passage. The Robbins report looked to the culture of the wider society and the relationship of higher education to that. In looking for its cultural bearings, the report correspondingly failed to give any serious attention to the internal culture of higher education. This is a striking omission, because the inner life of higher education institutions was, for Robbins, an essential ingredient in the development of the system. The failure to engage in that kind of self-reflection was part of a self-assurance over the wider common culture. It never occurred to Robbins that there was any need to describe the internal culture of higher education; it was taken for granted that everyone knew what it was, or at least what it should be. As we approach the year 2000, with an increasingly complex system of higher education, with more students, more kinds of institutions and more kinds of courses, we cannot make such assumptions.

In addressing the inner culture of higher education, we must not forget that inescapably it will and should have some relationship with the culture of its host society. It would be a contradictory state of affairs to believe that higher education could maintain one kind of culture within itself and could underpin a quite different kind of culture within society at large: there could not be any fundamental incongruity between these two cultural functions of higher education. It follows that, in offering a view of the cultural characteristics of higher education, we must also keep an eye on the wider culture and say something about their interconnections.

Two levels of internal culture

The inner culture of higher education works on two distinct levels. First, the idea of culture has application in relation to the academic community. So, we can ask questions like: What, if anything, is characteristic about the culture of academics? Is there one, in fact, or are there now only the multitude of disciplinary sub-cultures? Can we, at a deeper level perhaps, identify elements of a form of life, with its own values, which is distinctive of the academic community in general?

That set of questions has to be distinguished from those we can pose on the second level of culture. This is the level of the process of higher education itself, the level which comes close to that of the student experience. The questions this analytical level raises include: What kind of cultural enlargement, if any, can higher education hope to offer the individual student? Is it a matter of exposing students to some kind of culturally rich material (like the American 'great works' approach) or is it more a matter of a particular educational experience? In other words, is it a matter of content or process?

If it is a matter of process, what are the limitations on the process of learning considered as a human transaction, if the sought-for cultural enlargement is to take place? For example, a traditional assumption was that a genuine higher education experience could only be offered in a collegiate setting, with its communal and residential qualities. Red-brick universities, inner-city polytechnics and the Open University have dented that assumption; but perhaps there are still features of the student experience which we should hold on to if higher education is to offer a cultural enlargement? On the other hand, if it is a matter of content, does the idea of culture only have meaning for students in the humanities and the social sciences? Or do those taking science, technological and professional courses also deserve some kind of cultural experience?

Before moving on, two brief observations. First, at the level of the student's developmental process, culture as process seems prima facie to offer the prospect of an integrative element working across disciplinary cultures. Culture as content seems to point, on the other hand, to different answers for different kinds of educational programme, and even begs the question as to whether it makes sense in some subject domains.

The other point is that, while I have distinguished between the culture of the academic community and the cultural dimension in the student's educational experience (and this book is mainly about the second of those), there has to be a strong connection between them. Logically, and as a matter of fact, the quality of the student's experience is affected by the character of the life of the academic community. Individual members of the academic community will also often readily admit that their own continuing development is heavily influenced by their interactions with their students (a symbol of which is the dedication 'to my students' to be found in many of their books).

With these two levels of culture within higher education having been distinguished, let us look in more detail at them.

The academic culture: One culture or many?

The idea of culture suggests a shared set of meanings, beliefs, understandings and ideas; in short, a taken-for-granted way of life, in which there is a reasonably clear difference between those on the inside and those on the outside of the community.[3] Part of the sharing, and sense of community, resides in the taken-for-granted aspects of the culture. The unquestioned stock (of dominant ideas, concepts, theories, research practices) bestows personal identity and sustains the community as a community. Consequently, those on the inside recognize each other as one of themselves. The recognition takes several forms, including modes of communication. All these features of a culture are apparent in the academic community. However, they are less obviously to be seen in the academic community as a whole than in the discrete disciplinary sub-cultures, where they take different forms (Becher 1989).

The point can be made in the form of a question. What, if anything, do the following members of an academic institution have in common: the business studies lecturer, the philosopher, the pharmacist, the nuclear physicist, the archaeologist, the civil engineer, the social work lecturer and the law lecturer? Other than their having the same employer, what does it mean to say that they are each members of the same community? For, if pressed, many are likely to say that they feel more in common with others in the same discipline in other institutions – even on the other side of the world – than with academics in the same institution but in different subjects. Indeed, there is a greater likelihood that they could give the names of more researchers in the same field in another country than they could give the names of staff in other disciplines in the same building. The invisible college is a more influential community than the visible college (or so it might seem).

One of the enduring terms which speaks directly to the academic culture is that of the 'community of scholars'. Although heavy with its medieval resonances, it can still be encountered, especially – and perhaps surprisingly – in American books on higher education. 'Surprisingly' because it is the large American universities that typify most obviously the apparent disintegration of the academic community into a multitude of discrete disciplinary cultures. Clark Kerr put it aptly enough in his famous observation that the 'multiversity', as he called it, had become 'a series of individual faculty entrepreneurs held together by a common grievance over parking'.[4]

The unity of purpose across the academic community comes through, too, in the term 'university', with its suggestion of a single universe of knowledge.[5] It reminds us of the idea that, while we have carved up knowledge and put it into the hands of separate academic professions, ultimately all knowledge is bound up together. There may be, as Paul Hirst claims, different tests for truth in the various forms of knowledge,[6] but at least those different corpuses of knowledge all make a contribution to the total sum of knowledge. And that entire pool of knowledge then becomes a single resource on which we can draw in solving our problems. Many of the divisions between disciplines are not arbitrary, for they have a logical basis. That, though, should not stop us losing sight of the partiality of single disciplines. Their development is strengthened, not weakened, by being placed in the proximity of other disciplines under the epistemic umbrella offered by the university (and its sister institutions).

It has to be admitted that signs of an internal common culture, of a shared unity of purpose, and of a common means of communication are not immediately apparent. Perhaps the most significant aspect of any culture is its language, and there, above all, we encounter the most obvious signs of difference across the disciplines. For while it is the case that the academic community is distinguished by its 'elaborated' discourse (Gouldner 1976), it is more to the point that each disciplinary community has developed its own elaborated discourse. This is not just a matter of words: one does not become a member of a disciplinary community simply by having access to the latest dictionary or even the fullest encyclopaedia on the subject. The discourse reaches beneath concepts, theories and ideas, and beyond the practices intrinsic to the discipline, to background assumptions, beliefs and even ideologies.

There are ways of going on (in Wittgensteinian vocabulary) that mark out one discipline from another, with their tacit rules that can only be learned by being active in that community. For example, it is almost a requirement for publication in some academic journals that diagrams (and high-quality diagrams at that) be included; in other disciplines, diagrams are simply unacceptable. These editorial policies are not the result of idiosyncratic requirements on the part of journal editors; they are simply part of the disciplinary culture, which every aspiring academic has to pick up.

The question, though, remains: given these differences, is there any sense in which we can still refer today to a single academic community? If there is, it has to be at a deeper level of thought and interaction than we have so far identified.

Disciplinary cultures: Conservative or revolutionary?

We can begin here by reflecting that the account so far given of the internal culture of the academic community is somewhat misleading. Any culture, because it has to retain traditional customs and beliefs, has to be in a sense a conservative institution. In this respect, academic disciplinary cultures are no different; they impose their own boundaries on what is acceptable from their adherents. But disciplinary cultures are not just conservative in character, fixed for all time. Change takes place continually. Arguably, more change takes place in disciplines than in any other kind of culture. This is hardly surprising, for part of the rationale of the academic enterprise is a refusal to take aspects of its culture as given. Theories, concepts, models, practices and interior assumptions are all, supposedly, on the table for debate, for approval or rejection. Certainly, this picture deserves to be qualified. Following Kuhn, we cannot but be aware of the internal resistance to change that disciplines exhibit, even in the supposedly open-ended inquiry of science. The point, though, remains. The disciplines are always on the move, generating new meanings and insights. In theory, every aspect of their constitution is a candidate for reassessment by the disciplinary grouping charged with its custodianship.

Each sub-culture of the academic community, then, declines to be a culture in the normal sense, for each sub-culture is potentially critical of just those elements which constitute its culture. The taken-for-grantedness of those practices around which a conventional culture is formed represents closure; a genuine academic community, even one built round a well-defined discipline, on the other hand, abhors closure.

Towards a common culture

We seem to have reached a contradictory position. The groupings that form around academic disciplines are both cultures and anti-cultures. Both views are true. From the outside, the immediate impression is one of a traditional culture, with its own way of going on, more or less impenetrable to an outsider. Just under the surface, though, we can see signs of a willingness to take nothing on trust, to maintain a permanent self-vigilance, and if necessary to overturn the cultural idols. But does this observation not give us an insight into a deeper foundation on which the individual disciplinary culture is based, a foundation which is common to all disciplinary formations permitted entry into the academic community?[7]

Recalling the analysis contained in Chapters 3 and 4, the tests of truth, the relationship between theory and practice, the degree of objectivity and the human element, all vary across the disciplines. But they all share a common interest in self-reflection. They each exist as an organic entity, with an internal dynamic. The movement of thought happens not directly through any outside intervention, but through the sub-culture's inner compulsion to reflect on itself, if only at the level of current findings, theories and views. Occasionally, the form of thought itself comes up for reassessment, and usually then as the result of some external influence (as we see in the case of modern technology-driven medicine beginning reluctantly to embrace complementary medicine). Nevertheless, whatever the scope of this self-examination, it remains a constituent part of every disciplinary sub-culture.

Each disciplinary sub-culture is, then, a critical enterprise; but with the critique turned in on itself. It follows that, underlying the variety and very real differences across disciplines, there is a common interest in self-criticism as such. It is this propensity to engage in self-critique that is perhaps the key distinguishing feature of the academic community. It is on this level that members of different disciplinary cultures can recognize each other as engaging in a common activity, if at all.

Picking up Jurgen Habermas' analysis of truth-oriented discourse (Chapter 4), we can go further along this path. That kind of discourse, which after all is the kernel of academic discourse, contains within its own deep structure implicit claims as to veracity, sincerity, coherence and comprehensibility. Any speaker, claiming to offer some definite view on the world, can be questioned in any of these domains, for all truth-directed speech acts have this inner structure. If this is so, then academic discourse contains this hidden structure as a kind of metadiscourse. Even if none of the domains is invoked against the speaker, it is still there, within the discourse. Even where a definite assertion is made, there is an implicit invitation to the reader or listener to assent or dissent. But to say this is to reinforce the point already made: that academic discourse has a common foundation in being self-critical in its inner structure and underlying interest. Gouldner was just three-quarters right in describing it as a culture of critical discourse;[8] for it is essentially a culture of self-critical discourse.

It may be felt that this analysis has only theoretical value at most. Precisely because academics have their identity, language and conversation within their own sub-culture, there is little if any sign of a shared discourse. The idea of each institution forming a coherent academic community seems to have little purchase in reality. In medieval times, Latin provided a lingua franca, a common means of communication for scholars from different countries. Where, though, do we see evidence today of any analogous common grounding, and of a felt shared set of interests running across the academic community and its various disciplines? Admittedly, we see the academic community being collectively self-critical *within* the disciplines, e.g. through the peer review system which operates in research activities. We also see, occasionally, the academic community rising up *en masse* to defend itself against some perceived *external* threat – usually further diminutions in its autonomy. But these are not instances of the academic community acting concertedly as a single corporate body, being self-critical about its own internal affairs and activities.

Restoring an academic community

Still, the idea of an academic community, with its connotations of sharing and common commitment, dies hard. Even the state believes in it, quite apart from the academics themselves. Recently, we have seen in the UK, in the Lindop Inquiry, not only a group of academics subscribing to the notion of a 'coherent academic community', but also the government in its response accepting that the best safeguard of 'standards' lies in the maintenance of a 'coherent, self-critical academic community'.[9] Is this just the state having been convinced by the academics' own rhetoric about themselves, or hoping that the academics will actually be prepared to keep their own house in order (for instance, by closing down a course of their own volition)?

It is worth pursuing this example. The Lindop Inquiry was set up to examine the maintenance of standards in the polytechnics and colleges sector of UK higher education. Its principal focus was the work of the Council for National Academic Awards (CNAA), the body established in 1964 with the task of 'quality control' in the public sector of higher education. Essentially, the Inquiry found that the major institutions in the public sector (many of which were larger than some universities) should be exercising much more responsibility for the standard of their work, and be accountable for that task. It was wrong, so the Inquiry judged, to expect a central body to possess the primary responsibility for maintaining standards, particularly if the institutions had now reached 'maturity'. The institutions themselves, being closer to the work in question, were much better placed to fulfil that responsibility.

The argument was, as we have seen, founded on the notion of an academic community. The assumption was that each institution would behave like a mini polis, in which all full members of the community would be actively involved in its *corporate* life. How could this be, given the fissiparous nature of academic life, with its discrete disciplinary sub-communities? Where lay the basis for the belief that there was a corporate life, a level of interchange over academic matters in which all could feel themselves to be involved? When Lindop was talking about 'academic community', it was against the background of a CNAA-directed national peer review system. This system was based on an examination of individual courses by external academics and others drawn from the subject or professional area in question.

There were two ideas at work, then, in the proposal that public sector institutions should be self-validating, ideas which did not obviously hold together. On the one hand, the public sector institutions were thought of as being capable of maintaining the *subject-specific* national peer review system for themselves. On the other hand, there was the reflection that all universities, through their senates – composed of academics drawn from *all subjects* taught in the university – were responsible for keeping a self-critical eye on their own work, and it was time in this sense that the public sector caught up with established university practice. Now, irrespective of the soundness of believing that universities did actually work vigorously to review and develop the quality of their courses and did in practice operate as self-critical academic communities,[10] these ideas are not immediately compatible. Were the public sector institutions being urged to develop a modified national subject-specific review system, or a new kind of system drawing on their own internal intellectual resources as academic communities spanning a wide range of subjects?

Surprisingly, out of this mish-mash has come a positive development, in which the public sector institutions are giving the idea of 'an academic community' a completely new reality. It has three ingredients: the retention of a face-to-face critical dialogue between the course team and a review panel; the inclusion in the panel of some members external to the institution; and the incorporation of panel members internal to the institution, usually from disciplines other than that of the course up for review. The review is normally chaired by an internal member of staff, often a head of department unassociated with the course; and it may take the form of two or three meetings with the course team, enabling the course team to go on developing the course in the light of advice from the panel.

These changes are shifting the character of the dialogue between the course team and the validation panel. It takes on more of the form of a consultation, aimed at course development, rather than simply being a judgemental exercise. In addition, the inclusion of academics from a broad range of subjects or chosen for particular expertise (in student learning, for example) means that a wider range of critical questions are more likely to be explored. With growing confidence, members from outside the immediate disciplinary fraternity can raise issues not just over resources (important though these are), but over assumptions taken for granted within the discipline. So matters such as the teaching process (Is the student given sufficient autonomy?); the fundamental aims of the course (Is the course designed to promote the student's general education? Has the professional body exerted too dominant, and too narrow an influence?); the learning process (Is there an undue balance towards the student having to assimilate and memorize material, rather than engaging in active reflection and exploration?); and the examining process (Will it allow the student to demonstrate his or her higher-order abilities?) are often more likely to come to the fore, when staff from outside the immediate discipline are sharing in the course review process.

We are seeing, in this development, none other than a new embodiment of the idea of an academic community, and one that is at the heart of the higher education enterprise. The message is that all staff of an institution have more than an 'academic' interest in the activities of staff in other departments. There is, here, the view that the student experience on every degree course is a collective responsibility, across the whole institution. Staff, in offering a course, are becoming directly accountable to colleagues in other subjects, not in an abstract sense, but face to face. This development is quite new in British higher education (and there are signs that it is being incorporated in some universities). It offers nothing less than the prospect of giving substance to the idea of 'an academic community', unknown since the medieval foundation of the university. It does justice to the belief that the teaching activities of an institution of higher education are proper matters for collective responsibility. And it legitimately widens the scope of who can count as an academic peer: no longer can peer review amount to a cosy chat among academics sharing but not exposing taken-for-granted assumptions. The individual course, and the student experience on that course, cannot constitute a 'secret garden',[11] but must be open for critical examination by the staff acting together as a corporate body.

This development is, though, a delicate innovation. It will need to be watched, encouraged and supported. There are no guarantees that it will survive. If the new higher education funding bodies established by the Education Reform Act (1988) were to rely over-heavily on numerical 'performance indicators' in assessing the extent to which institutions have fulfilled the contracts for which they are funded, institutions are likely to develop course appraisal systems which record performance in just those terms. Internal review will then be just a matter of mechanically scrutinizing numbers on a balance sheet, rather than engaging in a critical dialogue over the educational effectiveness of courses.[12] There are also signs that in the new era of competitiveness between them, institutions are becoming reluctant to open their course offerings to the critical gaze of panel members drawn from institutions competing for contracts with the funding bodies.

More familiar than detailed critical self-reflection on the level of individual courses are the corporate processes of decision making at the institutional level. The senate or academic board, with its central committees, is the outward sign of a willingness on the part of academic staff to engage in cross-disciplinary dialogue for the general benefit of the institution. There are, however, some caveats.

First, academic institutions have made only moderate progress in developing internal processes which encourage self-reflection and self-criticism at the institutional level. For example, every institution would claim to accord high priority to the quality of teaching. As evidence, one might point to the staff appraisal procedures being introduced across the system; or to the units for staff development, which many institutions (especially in the public sector) have organized; or to the 'teaching week' run successfully by some polytechnics, where staff are encouraged to experiment with teaching styles as a means of enhancing the student experience. But these developments, while welcome, do not usually amount to a cross-disciplinary vehicle for systematically reflecting on the quality of the student learning.

There are certainly other signs of institutional self-reflection worth recording. For example, we see individual universities establishing their own central committee for overseeing academic standards across all disciplines. We see (again, particularly in the public sector) institutions collectively framing their own mission statements, as they seek to define the particular role they see themselves fulfilling in the national system of higher education. We can also see some colleges and institutes of higher education, in trying to develop distinctive degree courses for the first time, taking pride in acting as 'coherent, self-critical academic communities' when difficult choices are made in determining where effort and scarce resources are best applied in the short term. Very occasionally, too, we see the formation within an institution of an overarching committee to monitor and evaluate degree results and the examining process.

These are welcome indications of the academic community enhancing its capacity to engage collectively in self-criticism. They show that institutions of higher education have the capacity to go on developing as self-critical corporations. Drawing on Habermas' analytical framework, we can say that in developing in this way, institutions of higher education are expanding the scope of their self-reflection and, in the process, are increasing their own self-understanding. They are learning about themselves, with the internal academic community growing as a community. In theory, there is no limit to this evolutionary process of self-development.

If the first caveat is that these processes are at a relatively embryonic state, the second caveat is that such movements towards greater institutional self-reflection are liable to be arbitrarily arrested by external pressures. The drive towards numerical and managerial performance indicators has already been mentioned. In addition, in the wake of the current managerial approach to institutional governance, we see signs that the role of the committee structure is being reduced, whereas that of the executive (the vice-chancellor or director) is being increased.[13] At the same time, the powers of the Court or Board of Governors, with its lay representation, are being reasserted, while, in universities at least, new small planning committees under the chairmanship of the vice-chancellor are being established.[14] Whatever their merits, these developments must have the effect of diminishing the extent to which policies and strategic decision making are the expression of the will of an institution's academic community.

This is, then, a critical moment in the history of higher education institutions in the UK. There are real signs that institutions are ready to advance to new levels of self-understanding and self-criticism. There are also ominous indications that these positive movements are coming under the severest threat. The medieval idea of a community of scholars, of an internal culture of sharing, of a common set of interests, of a common discourse, has a unique opportunity of being realized in a completely new and exciting form. It is doubtful, though, that that hope will be allowed to be fulfilled. Instead, the governance of academic institutions is liable to be reduced to mere technique, under the control of managers with an eye on the bottom line.

The student experience

I have been arguing for institutions of higher education to do justice to the idea of a culture of critical discourse (as Gouldner puts it). I now turn to the other dimension of culture within higher education; namely, higher education as a cultural experience for students.

In depicting higher education as a cultural experience, it might be helpful to take a historical approach. It is often pointed out that higher education was centrally seen in this way in the nineteenth century, but that very different models were on offer. Whereas England (i.e. Oxford and Cambridge) evolved, through its tutorial system, an educational process in which the student's character was developed, Germany (following von Humboldt) sought to raise the quality of the student experience through immersing the student in an atmosphere of the pursuit of knowledge.[15] The contrast was stark: the English system was founded on a social interaction, with knowledge as the vehicle of communication; the German system was founded on a personal interaction with knowledge, and any human interaction rode on the back of that experience. The balance in the two models between human interaction and knowledge interaction was inverted.

These models were derived from quite different perceptions of the cultural function of higher education. The English model looked primarily to the eventual social role of the graduate as a 'gentleman', and the face-to-face interaction between student and tutor was crucial.[16] The German model looked to the elevation of mind being attained by the student in personal pursuit of knowledge. It was a more austere and intellectually demanding conception of the role of the student, though one which removed the student even more from the culture of the wider society.[17]

Any proper examination of those models would need to set them in their philosophical and social contexts. Connections would need to be drawn, for example, between empiricism and the English model and between idealist thought and the German model; and between each form of higher education and the social class system and roles for which their graduates were intended. Here, though, rather than distinguishing between them, I want to assert that the two conceptions had important common aspects. The key common element is that both systems took seriously the possibility that, whatever students were study-ing (for specialization had begun in the nineteenth century), higher education offered a general enlargement of the mind. Newman himself used the term 'enlargement' (as we saw in Chapter 2), but it is equally applicable to the German conception. Ultimately, there might have been differences between them in what enlargement meant, but the point is that higher education stood for an overriding and widening development of the mind.

On this conception, higher education was a cultural experience in several senses. First, there was an assumption of an integrating culture informing the student's experience and studies, which ran across subjects and institutions; it was a common inheritance in which students were being invited to share. Secondly, in so far as it spoke to a general enlargement of the mind, the student experience was not confined to the acquisition of mere technique. It was a developmental enrichment. Thirdly, both conceptions of the higher education enterprise were developed and indeed articulated within the framework of a set of wider philosophical values and meanings. (Again, 'philosophical' was a term employed by Newman.) Finally, in both forms, the student was conceived as being actively and personally involved in a process larger than himself, whether in interaction with others or directly with knowledge itself. In all these senses, the nineteenth-century formulations of the idea of higher education had to be accounted a cultural experience in their own right.

These ideas and the systems associated with them carried over well into the twentieth century, but we also see steadily developing the view that higher education has more limited functions. This was by no means simply a matter of higher education becoming more utilitarian. Previously, I emphasized how the academic community had taken knowledge unto itself and, in proliferating disciplinary sub-cultures, had 'professionalized' knowledge. The result has been that 'in the modern university, the product [has become] knowledge as much as students' (Scott 1984: 63). In this, there was both a narrowing of vision of what higher education had to offer and a compartmentalism of that offering. The major shifts have been quite recent. Although the sciences had begun to develop in English universities in the nineteenth century (following Scottish innovations), it is probably fair to say that the dominant culture of the universities was founded on the humanities up to and even a little beyond the Second World War. We have only to look at the disciplinary background of vice-chancellors over the past 30 years to see evidence of the modern superior position of science and technology.[18]

From the point of view of the educational process considered as a cultural experience, this shift would not, in itself, necessarily have been an issue. After all, Snow forcefully reminded us that science had at least an equal claim to that of the humanities in the full development of the mind of the student: they were two cultures, formally equal in status.[19] The problem was that the cultural experience offered by an education in science and technology was in practice a completely different kind of experience. It was a move from a concern with the intrinsic character of the student's experience to an interest in what the student knew and could do at the end of the course. In other words, in the contrast between a humanities and a science and technological education, there was an underlying gulf in the conceptions of what a higher education stood for; and it was Snow's failure to recognize *that* that lay at the heart of Leavis' attack on Snow's association of the two cultures.[20]

This is not to say that a science and technological education had to take on this character, for clearly there were and always have been those who are committed to inspiring in students a love of, and a care for, their subjects in those disciplines. It is to observe the way in which things have in practice turned out, an outcome not unconnected with the logic of those disciplines in supplying means to fulfil ends, rather than inquiring into ends themselves.

Another way of making the point is that higher education traditionally formed a culture of the written word,[21] albeit a kind of literacy which embodied a restricted code, understood by the few.[22] With increasing rapidity, though, as technological and professional education develops, and as bodies such as the National Council for Vocational Qualifications attempt to point higher education towards the acquisition of 'competencies',[23] higher education becomes a culture of technique. Again, though, it is the acquisition of stratified techniques in which, at the highest level, only the few are competent. Knowledge élites *and* technical élites are now emerging from our higher education institutions. In this way, higher education is sustaining a societal stratification characterized by different levels of understanding and of performance.

It was against the background of these tendencies that the 'counter-culture' and 'counter-course' movements of the late 1960s and 1970s took off.[24] While these movements may still have residual effects in the attitudes of some staff in academic institutions, they are largely defunct. One suggestion for their short-lived character comes out of Gellner's view that they were parasitic on the very society to which they pretended to offer a counter.[25] Far from providing a new kind of experience and 'meaning', at bottom (on Gellner's view) these counter-cultures depended on the existence of mainstream society and culture for their critiques to have any purchase. I believe that Gellner's criticism is misplaced. The main reason that these alternative approaches failed to gain any substantial long-lasting purchase is that they were naive. They seriously underestimated the dominant interests (of the state, industry, the professions and the knowledge industry itself) against which they were contending. They did not deserve to be taken seriously because they did not take seriously the main currents of the culture they were attacking.

The extra-mural cultural function of higher education

I began this chapter by pointing out that much of the talk about the cultural function of higher education concentrates on the interconnections between higher education and society. As a result, the way in which higher education can support and even develop the general cultural base of society is given attention before the internal culture of higher education. This is putting the cart before the horse. Having made some observations about the internal culture of higher education – both that of the academic community and that of the student experience – we are now in a position to say how, if at all, the internal culture bears on the wider cultural relationship.

Like it or not, there is at work a sociological aspect of this particular cultural dimension that is insidious and is probably unshakeable. I refer to the way in which higher education, as an institution within society, acts not just as a vehicle for economic reproduction within the social classes, but also as a means of 'cultural reproduction'. This is, of course, the territory mapped out in detail over many years by the French sociologist, Pierre Bourdieu.[26] It brings home the manifold and almost surreptitious ways in which the internal life of academic institutions serves to sustain, reinforce and reward class-related forms of style, language and behaviour. There is an unspoken recognition of a certain disposition or *habitus* among the social classes.[27]

It will be said that all this is long past, that academic institutions today are much more egalitarian in their evaluations and actions. We only have to look at the interest being shown, especially in public sector institutions, in recruiting their students from a wide social background. But the objection makes precisely the opposite point. For it is the non-élite institutions that are in the vanguard of recruiting non-standard students. There is a hierarchy of academic institutions that is founded much more on their social status than on their academic reputation. A first-class honours degree from a college of higher education still counts for less in the world than a third-class degree from Oxbridge, and even less than a sporting 'blue' from the ancient universities.[28]

It might be countered that that is because the Oxbridge graduate has more to offer in social 'maturity', in interpersonal skills, in self-confidence, and in being articulate. But again, the objection only serves to make the point. Our academic institutions help to maintain a flow of the kind of cultural capital on which our wider social institutions are based. The difficulties that public sector graduates have in getting into the senior positions in the professions have little to do with their academic accomplishments and much to do with the cultural stratification in society of which academic institutions are a part.

A more substantial criticism of this line of thinking is that, being sociological and stating what is the case, it does not offer us any positive conception of what *could* be the case. The picture it offers is, too, a negative one. So can we conceive of a more positive relationship between the culture of higher education and that of society? I have said that this is a theme that has attracted the attention of past thinkers. We started the chapter with a quotation from Robbins; it might equally have been drawn from other writers, such as Ortega y Gasset, F. R. Leavis or G. H. Bantock. Each has argued for higher education to preserve the cultural fabric of society. But whether it is Ortega's 'vital system of ideas of a period', or Leavis' sense of an 'organic life' which it is the university's function to foster, or Bantock's concern that the organic relationship between education and (what he admits to being) a minority culture was being attenuated, or Robbins' view with which we started, we are in each case being asked to accept an unduly conservative function.[29] Although we can see elements of a critical function (especially in Leavis), the dominant approach of these writers is founded on a base of a certain set of social ideas which it is the duty of higher education to guard and transmit. The function is essentially largely passive and uncritical, and addresses a minority culture.

Couple this with the earlier sociological observations about the students' experience being describable in terms of intellectual, technical and general cultural hegemony. Couple it, too, with the reflections about the abortive and incoherent nature of the counter-culture and counter-course movement in higher education, and we seem to be emerging with a depressing set of conclusions about the wider cultural function of higher education.

All is not lost, however. Recall the first section of this chapter, where we outlined ways in which the academic community has the chance of revitalizing its self-critical capacities. The original (i.e. medieval) idea of the university looked to a self-governing community of scholars, in which there was no distinction in kind between those who mainly taught and those who mainly learned – all were embarked on a process of intellectual discovery. The Socratic dialogue was another example of this openness and collaboration, as was the Humboldtian conception. We can generalize from this: there need be no fundamental distinction between the culture of the academic community and that of the student experience. The culture of the student experience is one of a self-questioning voyage, not in any self-indulgent form, but rooted in a rigorous self-critical examination of what is being taught, learned and achieved. But this also describes, if only in ideal form, the character of the academic community.

What, then, to pick up our last theme, is the carry-over of this conception into the culture of society? The answer follows through: it is, as a minimum, to provide the graduates of higher education with the capacity not merely to go on learning, but also to go on being critical of all they encounter in thought and action. The transferability and the value of the culture of higher education to society lie not in the acquisition of specific competencies, but in the propensity of graduates to take up a sceptical stance to what they come across (in truth claims, in concept, in value, in ways of going on). The steady injection into the wider culture of such a questioning and critical element will be uncomfortable to society. The value of higher education, on this view, is in direct proportion to the critical capacities of its graduates. In an age where there is no common culture, but where there are threats to open debate, the strengthening of the culture of critical discourse is all we have.

8

Rationality

Introduction

Higher education and the life of reason are inseparable. At the very least, the idea of higher education implies an educational process in which students are not simply initiated into forms of thought, but are encouraged actively to engage with them. Students should come not merely to know that such and such is the case, or that this procedure works, but should be able to offer their own account of why it is the case or why it works. They should be able to offer reasons for their beliefs and actions. In short, rationality is a condition of the full realization of the meaning of higher education.

The general argument of this book is that the idea of higher education has been undermined both philosophically and sociologically. Philosophically, we cannot provide any absolute epistemological underpinning for our knowledge endeavours; and, sociologically, higher education and its manifold forms of thought have lost any pretensions to occupying an independent position in relation to the modern state. Both these underminings have their impact on the life of reason, and how we view it. Seen against that double undermining, reason seems no longer to offer its traditional security. What counts as reason stands in the dock accused, on the one hand, of being mere appearance (the emperor never had any clothes syndrome) and, on the other, of representing vested interests of the academic community and the wider society. How, then, can we reconceptualize the idea of rationality within higher education so as to convey something of its traditional promise, while confronting the dual problematic it faces?

The attack on reason

What are the forms of threat to rationality? I will cite just a few examples, without any claim to being comprehensive. First, all societies develop their own ideas as to what is to count as rationality. This holds for modern society as well. Our ideas about rationality, within a pluralistic society, are bound to be complex and fuzzy, but even so we can readily see that certain kinds of rationality are dominant. At one level, this exhibits itself in the place that mathematics and science have come to occupy, mainly in virtue of their underpinning of technology in all its forms, including information technology and computerization.[1] One consequence is that the thought patterns of primitive society, being felt to lack a scientific approach, are generally felt to be beyond the bounds of reason.[2] As we saw in Chapter 3, witchcraft and astrology are generally not available in the higher education curriculum, except as objects of study by anthropologists and sociologists.

But, and secondly, what counts as rationality takes on much more subtle hues. Even within the legitimate forms of reason in society, some are ranked as being more 'reasonable' than others. With mathematics and the natural sciences occupying such a dominant position in the culture of modern society, other forms of thought are obliged to jockey for position somewhere behind. It is hardly surprising that we emerge with 'a crisis in the humanities'. The general point is this: what counts as rationality in modern society is a selection from the total available forms of rationality and that, even within the legitimate forms of rationality, some acquire a higher authority than others.

Thirdly, forms of rationality are actually multiplying within modern society. The French theorist Lyotard has recently pointed to the fragmentation of intellectual culture. New sub-disciplines are taking off at an extraordinary rate, associated in particular with the integration of computer systems into society's systems of communication, management and finance. One reading of this situation is that society's thought patterns are developing in an anarchic fashion, with their adherents less able to communicate meaningfully with each other.[3] This multiplication of forms of life is without obvious integrating features. Seen in this way, the post-modern society is increasingly anarchic and irrational.[4]

Fourthly, one of the hopes behind reason considered as a historical project is that rationality offers the prospect of establishing a realm of thought and, therefore, ultimately of life, pure of ideology. There is the belief that even if criteria of rationality differ across forms of thought, at least individual forms of thought could be said to contain discrete pools of rationality. But one of the striking lessons of much of social theory over the last 30 years (picked out in Chapter 4) is that science – the apparently supreme epitome of rationality – turns out to exhibit various kinds of non-rationality. From Polanyi's account of the tacit knowledge with which scientists operate (they 'know more than they can tell'), through Kuhn's picture of incommensurable paradigms (their proponents 'practise their trades in a different world') to Feyerabend's idea of scientific growth through unbridled Machiavellianism ('anything goes'), it has emerged that even science cannot live up to its self-congratulatory belief in its own reasonableness.

The general lesson to be grasped from these observations is clear. Rationality, both in its definition and in its realization, is not 'given' in any absolute sense. But if this is a feature of modern society and its thought patterns, then inescapably the point holds for higher education as well. In short, we cannot assume that higher education is a site of pure reason.

Critique of rationality

The points just made have their imprint on higher education in fairly obvious ways. However, it is worth making a further point about the link between modern society's sense of rationality and higher education, which emerges from the analysis of rationality offered by Jurgen Habermas.[5]

Habermas has argued that there are essentially two different forms of rationality, and that these are intimately linked with different forms of action. 'Cognitive-instrumental rationality' is linked to 'action oriented to success'; and within this form of rationality can be distinguished two sub-forms. Habermas calls action oriented to success 'instrumental' when it can be understood as following technical rules, and can be evaluated in terms of efficiency (typically when operations are being performed on the physical world). He calls action oriented to success 'strategic' when it can be understood and evaluated in terms of its effectiveness in influencing the decisions of other social actors (typically in the worlds of politics or business). Alongside these forms of 'cognitive-instrumental rationality', Habermas argues for a realm of 'communicative rationality'. The associated form of action here is one in which actors work jointly to understand each other, and to influence each other purely by the force of argument.

Habermas, in developing his analysis of rationality, is not interested in disparaging 'cognitive-instrumental rationality' as such. Rather, his purpose is to do two things. First, to show that the means–end rationality which has come to dominate the thought of modern man as *the* form of rationality is simply one kind of rationality. Secondly, to open up the possibility for modern society of a rational discourse, freed from artificial domination, in which participants share equally in the conversation. His analysis also allows him to argue that the rationality which typifies our social institutions, and our transactions within them, is tending to take the form of strategic (i.e. cognitive-instrumental) rationality, rather than a genuinely interactive communicative rationality.

The consequence is that reason in modern society has been reduced in scope to a means–end form: debate is too often a technical discussion among experts about the means. The ends are seldom on the agenda for serious debate, for society is unable to handle that kind of discussion. We see precisely this happening in higher education. Discourse about higher education focuses on structure, finance, numbers and performance indicators: it is about means, method and systems for planning and resource allocation. The values or ends for which higher education stands are seldom raised as a serious matter for discussion. What appears on the surface as a reasoned form of life is in reality a mask for a partial approach to reason, if not sheer irrationality.

The question facing us, then, is simple enough. How can we justify our practices, our structures of knowledge, and our interactions in higher education as manifestations of reason? At best, our claims to reason in all these spheres seem to be limited or partial, and at worst ideological. If we are to confront these matters, they need to be worked out at the levels of the individual student experience, the curriculum and the institution as a whole.

The limits of rationality

One way of summarizing the general points of the previous section is to say that there is a dynamic interplay between reason and non-reason. We can see this dynamic at work at different levels within forms of thought.

First, bodies of thought take on a solidity through being structured around dominant paradigms.[6] This is not to say that all members of an epistemic sub-culture – say economics or anthropology or even nebulous professionally oriented clusterings of knowledge such as pharmacy or business studies – subscribe to the dominant concepts, theories and approaches of the corpus. But even where there is debate and conflict, there is usually a consensus over the central questions. By and large, there is general agreement as to what counts as doing economics or pharmacy. To attempt to change the dominant perceptions of what the corpus is all about will literally be irrational, because such a move would run counter to the form of life represented by the discipline. Being part of a disciplinary community is partly a matter of following a set of rules; stepping outside the conventions of the discourse invites opprobrium, if not downright excommunication. If knowing how to go on in a discipline is largely a matter of rule-following, it remains the case that the rules are as much socially imposed by the disciplinary tribe as they are by epistemic considerations (Becher 1989).[7] It is hardly surprising, therefore, if disciplines are largely characterized by inertia, for substantial change very often counts as heresy.

Secondly, the very act of generating new ways of seeing and doing things is itself non-rational. The traditionalists have a point. To break totally new ground is to abandon the conventional rules. The creative act is indeed anarchic. There are no rules for that kind of process. However, it is not purely random. Where significant innovations have happened, it is astonishing how often through history other individuals or groups have been working along parallel lines of thought. The desire to establish that one was the first to arrive with the finding, and the priority disputes which are part of the scientific game, are testimony to the point. The old ways of going on within a discipline may, from time to time, become inadequate; but finding new ways forward is not totally without direction.[8]

Thirdly, at a higher level still, we can see the dynamic between thought which is rule-governed and thought which is far less bounded where different forms of reason collide. The complexities of modern society not only cause new forms of thinking to emerge; in due course, they also compel them to interact with others. Professionals, we are frequently reminded, have to be sufficiently 'flexible' to work alongside other professionals and possibly even with them in 'multidisciplinary teams'. The presence of different styles of thinking, being brought together and being compelled to intermesh, provides the basis for even further innovations in thought and action. Such new admixtures of cognition provide unforeseen resources for conceptual, theoretical and practical innovations. In effect, this is to widen the sense among practitioners of what is reasonable within a mode of thought.

Finally at the highest level, the limits of reason are exposed when a critique is mounted of a form of thought as such. Forms of thought are bounded; they occupy but a portion of intellectual space. A critique of a form of thought will attempt to mark out its location, describe its boundaries, indicate its limitations and bring out its implicit assumptions and any ideological undercurrents.[9] To those on the inside, the critique will probably seem unreasonable. To the critics, however, it is the corpus itself which is irrational. Ultimately, what counts as rationality is partly a matter of where one stands, and what intellectual position one is taking up.

So, whether we look purely to the way in which a corpus sustains itself internally, or to the production of new perspectives for the corpus, or to the intermingling of different corpuses, or finally to standing outside a corpus altogether and developing a critique of it, we can see that reason is exhibited within and given sense by a framework with its own tacit rules. Those rules are not immutable; at each level, the rules can be bent and perhaps have to be if progress is to be made.[10] Equally, innovation and critique require, if not irrationality, then the adoption of different kinds of rules. It transpires, therefore, that the boundary between reason and non-reason is far from absolute.

The ethics of reason

Minimally, reason implies method.[11] It means using evidence, making deductions, seeing conceptual connections and drawing conclusions. It also means, as we have seen, following the conventions of the discipline, whether it be conducting experiments and assessing the results, or engaging in a case study in management studies, or constructing a model in studio-based work. But this is all technique. Following reason in this way shows that one knows how to go on (to use again Wittgenstein's phrase) within the discipline. The term 'discipline' implies, after all, following a particular set of rules and being prepared to stick to them. This reason is the reason of the bureaucrat or the accountant. It is devoid of values and judgement. That cannot be said to be a full description of reason within the disciplines, for they cannot be sustained without values and judgement.

Indeed, if we are going to give a full account of what practitioners do within a discipline, we are bound to use such terms as deciding, assessing, evaluating, judging and criticizing. These are all value terms and point to valuing activities. They are not activities which can be accomplished with a slide rule or computer or calculator. In other words, the routine operation of reason is not just a matter of routine. It is not simply that comparisons and choices have to be made; for computers can sometimes do that. It is, to put it another way, the difference between quality and standards.[12] We can reach for the tape measure or stopwatch to see if a standard has been reached; but we turn to our inner judgement to assess the quality.

Even within a discipline, values are not all of a piece. We saw in the previous section that there are limits to rationality, and that thought can and does break through those limits on different levels. The rules break down, or can be circumvented, both within disciplines and between them. These movements of thought have their parallels in the sphere of values.

First, the truth criteria within a discipline will often be value-laden. From mathematics to sociology (as we saw in Chapter 4), offerings are judged partly in virtue of such features as comprehensiveness, elegance, simplicity, neutrality, social impact or wit, the criteria varying not only across disciplines but also within a discipline over time. This means that our assessments of what is on offer are not governed solely by what is before us. Those assessments partly reflect values. In turn, those values are partly constitutive of the form of life held to be valuable by the adherents of the discipline. Ethical choices, then, enter into a discipline at all sorts of levels, from its overarching framework of values, through the specific truth criteria in current use, to their application on specific occasions. It follows that our practices and assessments in the disciplines carry ethical layers within themselves: were our choice of values at any of the levels to be different, our practices and our evaluations of truth claims would also be different.

Secondly, the ethical dimension of reason is apparent in the communicative process of a discipline. This is so whether we have in mind disciplines which are largely cognitive in character, or those – such as in the performing arts – which are built around action. For the term 'reason' implies the giving of reason, and a recipient who understands both the reason that is offered, and that it is a reason (inviting a response). 'Reason' points to a particular kind of discourse. We saw in Chapter 4 that the academic community is built around a structured conversation, with its members adhering to certain norms: they are truth seeking; they are sincere in their utterances; they offer understandable propositions; and they adopt appropriate forms of communication. But this analysis (from the work of Habermas) shows how ethics enter inescapably into the processes of rational communication. Although truth criteria and the rules of discourse vary across disciplines, members are obliged to speak the truth as they see it, to put it in a form that other members of the discipline will comprehend, and to mean what they say. What follows from this is that reason cannot survive unless general values of this kind are maintained. To enter the life of reason is to accept its values.

The hierarchy of rationality

I have been talking about the different levels at which reason operates in relation to individual disciplines: we can take up stances within disciplines, across disciplines, and in being critical of disciplines as a whole. But there is an even more profound way of differentiating reason, and that is in terms of its meaning for, and impact on, those who pursue it. It was part of the Greek conception of reason, after all, that reason was not just a purely intellectual affair but carried over into the life-world, with considerable practical implications.[13] Three levels on which rationality has practical significance may be distinguished, which I shall call groundedness, enlightenment and emancipation.

Groundedness

In its most basic form, rationality is a matter simply of giving reasons for one's beliefs or actions. Minimally, therefore, it conveys the idea of giving grounds for what one is saying or doing.[14]

What is going on when we give reasons for our beliefs or actions? It is, surely, a way of giving legitimacy to what we say or do, of providing some kind of backing or security. It deflects the charge that 'that is simply your view' or 'that is simply the way you prefer to do it'. Giving reasons, therefore, raises our thoughts and actions from the here and now and from their singularity by placing them in the context of a wider perspective or tradition. It is a way of making connections within a public discourse. To employ Popper's terminology, it is to move from the world of subjective knowledge to the world of objective knowledge.

What counts as giving a reason? As I have just implied, reasons have their home and meaning within a tradition of thought. Disciplinary sub-cultures are real cultures in this sense (see Chapter 7). They contain their own perspectives, meanings and values. A reason makes its point by having resonances in such a wider set of meanings. But my argument seems to be running in opposite directions. I have just said that giving reasons is a move in the direction of objectivity. Now, though, I am saying that being reasonable is partly a matter of falling in with the conventions – in time and place – of an intellectual form of life or culture; and this surely raises the spectre of relativism. This is, in fact, precisely the situation. Objectivity has its limits (Chapter 3). There is a strong element of conventionalism in rationality.[15]

There are two obvious moves which could be made to counter this argument. First, at least in the kinds of knowledge on offer in higher education, it could be said that knowledge 'progresses'. In other words, the knowledge which is the stock-in-trade of the academic community has a degree of reliability to it and is not pure whim. The rejoinder to this is to accept that the counter is pointing to a real feature of academic thought, which is that the consensus of the relevant disciplinary community does indeed offer some measure of reliability and raises knowledge claims above mere whim; but that does not in itself amount to a demonstration of the 'progress' of knowledge. The work of Feyerabend and Kuhn suggests that unqualified talk of progress even in the natural sciences is going too far. Neither in Feyerabend's image of theory proliferation nor in Kuhn's paradigm shifts is there any simple model of progress.

The second move which might be made to counter the relativistic flavour of my earlier argument would be to argue that, despite the changing discipline-bound truth criteria, the intellectual enterprise as a whole is founded on certain context-independent truth criteria.[16] Unfortunately, while superficially attractive, those context-independent truth criteria which have been suggested turn out to be vacuous or tautological.[17] In fact, the search for universal criteria of rationality has so far proved fruitless.

So, giving reasons for our thoughts and actions does not perhaps have the solidity and universality that we might believe. None the less, a person who gives reasons is engaging in a valuable activity. The person is implicitly saying that he or she subscribes to the network of rules of the discipline in question. There is a tacit affirmation in a form of rule-following. The academic who describes himself at cocktail parties with the words 'I am a physicist' or 'I am a historian' is saying something about his self-perception (essentially a researcher, not a teacher); but is also saying that he subscribes to the disciplinary code imposed on its practitioners. Even granting the limitations of the rules in question, the giving of reasons implies the willingness to engage in a structured conversation. This adherence to a discipline-specific set of rules, which we can term substantive rationality, places demands on the individual of a worthwhile kind.

In parallel to this substantive rationality (giving particular kinds of reason according to the discipline), the rational life also requires, as we have seen, the participation in a certain kind of dialogue. In order for the dialogue to function effectively, there are rules of procedure which all participants have to accept. To recall and build on the earlier analysis, these rules have to do with truth-telling, sincerity, intelligibility, empathy and active listening. Significantly, while the particular rules of what counts as a reason (substantive rationality) vary across disciplines, the rules of procedural rationality (as I will call it) are more or less universal across disciplines. They are binding on all academics engaged in their profession, whatever their discipline. This is hardly surprising, for the disciplines of the academic community have an underlying unity in open communication, which is what procedural rationality is all about.

On this analysis, it follows that *ir*rationality could mean either a reluctance to adopt the particular norms within a mode of thought (i.e. a disinclination to fall in with the substantive rationality of the discipline in question) or a determination, perverse or otherwise, to impose a constraint of some kind on the open discourse of the discipline (in other words, to distort the procedural rationality of the academic community).

Enlightenment

Beyond groundedness, there is a level of rationality which reflects an idea almost lost to modern thinking. The central belief is that by being immersed in, and contributing to, the life of reason, one can attain a truer level of understanding and perspective on the world than is ordinarily available through personal experience. There is the sense here that reason is more than the sum of its parts, and that the serious pursuit of truth can, over time, generate a way of looking at the world and an approach to forming judgements on it that stands over and above any particular truths that may be assimilated on the way. We encountered this view at the beginning of this book, in the dialogues of Plato, where we found talk of 'the ascent to see the things in the upper world [which] you may take as standing for the upward journey into the region of the intelligible'.

More modern views of this kind have dispensed with the metaphysical baggage of a pure Platonic universe of knowledge way above the senses of the uneducated, but the idea that reason can bring a new level of understanding still persists. We saw, for example, signs of it in Popper's differentiated model of the three worlds of knowledge, with objective knowledge residing in a quite different world from those of human consciousness and of physical objects. More recently, Habermas has distinguished a domain of critical thinking separate from the two domains of purposive means–end thought and thought founded on human interaction. Admittedly, Popper and Habermas may seem to be strange bedfellows; for they have entered the lists against each other precisely over their views on knowledge and reason, both of them seeing the other as an unwitting ideologue. None the less, the striking point here is that they have this central feature in common: not just that they both see the life of reason as important, but also that there is a distinctiveness about the quality, character and significance of reason when it is taken up seriously, which marks it out from conventional human experience.

Put simply, it is (to recover the Platonic imagery for a moment) a matter not just of seeing the light, but also of living in the light. The underlying idea here is that reason can be more than going through the techniques and operations that reason demands; and more than paying attention to particular truth claims. It is that reason can come to play a central part in one's life, so that we can properly talk of 'a life of reason'. That form of life, with reason as a constitutive part, brings with it a larger transformation in the way individuals approach, view and take up stances towards all their experiences. It is in this sense of 'cognitive perspective' (as Peters puts it[18]) that we can talk of the transcendence which comes through the life of reason, without resort to the metaphysical world-picture of heavenly spheres of intellectual existence. In a word, the life of reason offers the prospect of enlightenment.[19]

This idea of enlightenment, of living in the light, takes on particular importance alongside the notion of ideology (Chapter 6). One of the strands of that concept is that even rational thought may not be just what it seems on the surface. It may harbour undisclosed interests or values. Enlightenment, considered as a continuing enterprise, warns us to be perpetually on our guard; and not to be seduced, even by apparently rational thinking. It suggests the need to keep our distance, especially from those bodies of thought to which we are most drawn. Whether we get interested in mainly cognitive pursuits (such as philosophy or chemistry) or more practical endeavours (like physiotherapy or graphic design), we should try to avoid becoming dominated by them, and being identified with them (as a chemist or graphic designer). Enlightenment demands that we should not simply engage in the practices that are part of these rational pursuits (submitting to their different forms of 'groundedness'), but that we should maintain our own integrity. Every so often, rational pursuits need to be 'seen through'; and their practices and concepts, which all too easily take on the form of rituals, need to be demystified. But it is the practitioners themselves who can do this most successfully, for only they carry authority with their peers. So a degree of scepticism is required from practitioners towards their own forms of thought, with their associated practices and values.

Enlightenment, then, points to a level of reason above the routines, conceptual manipulation and judgemental procedures of a corpus of knowledge and its associated practices. Beyond competence, there is insight. Can we see the wood for the trees?

Emancipation

The third and highest form of rationality is emancipation. The term 'emancipation' reminds us of the liberal aspiration – and indeed the Marxist claim – that self-knowledge and self-understanding can offer new possibilities for thought and action. The essence of that hope is that through self-knowledge, existing constraints on thought and action can be better appreciated and thereby overcome. When fully carried through, self-knowledge can bring new freedoms. But how do we get to the ideas of self-knowledge and self-liberation from the two previous levels of rationality – groundedness and enlightenment?

The link is quite simple. If the giving of grounds is seriously taken on board by the individual as an integral part of this valued form of life, then the individual will be led to pose to himself or herself some of the likely questions from an external observer. In other words, groundedness, taken seriously, leads to an internal dialogue. In that process of internal dialogue, discoveries are made by the person about himself or herself. Rationality at the level of enlightenment should lead on, then, to self-awareness, self-reflection and self-criticism. In turn, this continuing dialogue with oneself provides the basis for self-transcendence, for the development of the self, such that entirely new possibilities of thought and action are opened up.

In short, the life of reason is a process of self-development. The internalized dialogue that it brings acts on the mind so as to generate a continuing cycle of reflection and intellectual advance. Pursued further, as a form of enlightenment and emancipation, it opens up the possibilities of critical self-reflection, of seeing one's central pursuits in a new perspective. Even more ambitiously, it can prompt new kinds of practices. A lawyer might be encouraged to work for, say, professional arrangements which opened up the profession's services to the general public; or a chemist might seek to reduce the impact of the chemical industry on the environment; or a doctor might act to bring about a new balance between preventive and restorative medicine, as practised by the profession.

Ultimately, then, reason can have emancipatory effects on thought and action, through the power of self-reflection and self-understanding.[20]

In this section, I have offered an analysis of rationality, by showing three levels on which rationality can have practical effects. At each level, the examples have picked out individual academics and professionals. But these levels of rationality also have applications in terms of the development of thought, of social institutions and of society. Rationality is not just a matter for individuals as individuals becoming reasonable people. We can enquire into the extent to which a form of thought is rational (How open is it? To what extent does it have rules of debate and procedure?); we can ask about the degree to which our social institutions are rational; and we can assess how far society itself is rational.

Conclusions: Rationality and higher education

This analysis has implications for higher education on several levels. We can look to our institutions of higher education becoming more rational in their inner processes, with their members working together in articulating a shared view of an institution's aims and fulfilling them in a corporate way. We can justifiably expect that academics will adhere to the demands of rationality in their professional work, developing the open character of their discipline. And we can expect to see the curricula they offer encouraging students to enter the highest levels of the rational life.

To take these points in reverse order, the initiation of the student into the rational life should occur in two directions. First, the student should go beyond simply acquiring the particular forms of reasoning within a mode of thought (i.e. go beyond what I have termed 'groundedness'), and should even go beyond embracing the life of reason as such ('enlightenment'). Ultimately, the student should reach the stage of continuing self-reflection and self-transcendence in thought and action ('emancipation'). This process cannot be achieved solely by the student working away diligently at the programme of studies before him or her. On the analysis offered here, rationality is partly a matter of engaging in a dialogue with others in an appropriate way.[21] So we come to the second implication, which is that the student has to understand the practical aspects of the life of reason. In short, the student comes to an insight into both the cognitive and the practical dimensions of the life of reason.

What does this mean in reality? Cognitively, it means that students will go on examining their own beliefs, thoughts, values and practices, and will make connections between those intellectual activities and their wider life and their general values. Out of that self-examination, other actions in their lives may follow. Practically, it means that students have to become used to expressing a point of view and exposing it to the critical evaluation of their peers, and in this way take on the ethical demands of rationality. Not just truth-telling, but sincerity; not just intelligibility, but empathy; these are values which ought to be taken on board.

There is a double-bind at work here. The corpus of knowledge in which the student is most interested will be neither interest-free nor value-free. So the emancipatory promise of higher education cannot be realized through students stepping onto a plane of value-freedom and interest-freedom. It is simply not available. But even if it were, the attempt would misrepresent the character of higher education. For the cognitive and practical forms of emancipation sketched out here are also neither interest-free nor value-free.

Turn now to one of the other levels of rationality in academia – rationality within the disciplines. Each discipline can be assessed for its rationality. We can, for example, assess the degree to which a form of thought incorporates an element of self-reflection. Is it considered legitimate for members of a discipline to reflect critically on the discipline which provides them with their intellectual identity and status? We can also enquire into the extent to which a discipline promotes an open debate. Is there a range of journals, with contrasting editorial policies? Is the discipline controlled by the big guns, or can individuals – even those without tenured posts in institutions – really expect to get a hearing? To what extent is dissent tolerated?

Finally, institutions of higher education can be seen as being more or less rational in their organization, their internal arrangements and their managerial processes. As we have seen, it is all too easy for institutions to be governed by means–end purposive models of rationality, rather than by those of communicative discourse. Ideas of efficiency, numerical performance indicators and managerial top-down decision making can seem to be justified in terms of their 'rationality'. But this is artificially to restrict the sense of what it is to be a rational institution. And this restriction is ultimately anathema to an institution of higher education, which must be founded on a continuing conversation about its ends and its values, and their fulfilment through its internal human transactions.[22] (Chapter 7 contains an attempt to follow through the implications for the internal life of institutions of their practising such a Habermas-type communicative rationality.)

These reflections carry over into institutional appraisal. Assessing the performance of this kind of institution cannot be solely a matter of adding up figures on a balance sheet, whether they are the finance officer's financial data or the registrar's data on student performance. Ultimately, we can only know our institutions of higher education by coming to understand the quality of their internal life.

In drawing this chapter to a close, there are two riders, both significant. The first is that whether we have in mind the student taking on the demands of the rational life, or the individual discipline considered as a rational endeavour, or an institution of higher education: for each of them rationality is neither static nor a definite end-point. In each domain, what counts as being rational can go on being developed. Students can pass through the stage of giving reasons for their beliefs and actions to enlightenment and emancipation; disciplines can become more open and more self-critical; and institutions can go on becoming more and more rational.[23]

The second rider is that just because, in all these senses, higher education is the supreme site of rationality in society, higher education can become the model of rationality *for* society. There are tendencies towards closure, partiality and sheer irrationality in society, and these admittedly affect higher education. It is not an island and not immune. Still, higher education contains within itself, if only it would realize, an essential rationality: academics, students and disciplines have to be rational. But institutions of higher education do not. They can either follow the path of instrumental reason or they can recover their true character as a modern polis, a site of developing communicative reason. As communities sharing a common but critical discourse over ends, values and achievements, institutions of higher education can become a microcosm of the rational society, a reminder to society of what society itself might be.

9

Research

Introduction

What is the relationship between research and higher education? Is there one? By speaking of a relationship, I want to raise the question as to whether or not there is a conceptual connection between the two. Clearly, much research goes on in institutions of higher education. Indeed, we can probably find some kind of research in progress in each of the 200 or more institutions which offer some kind of higher education in the UK. The question, though, is whether or not, *qua* institutions of higher education, they have an obligation to sponsor research. Is it part of the meaning of 'institution of higher education', such that we would not be prepared to grant the name to an institution in which there was no research taking place?

This issue has formed a key element in the historical debate over the idea of higher education.[1] Or, rather, over the idea of the university. Views are to be found on both sides. Among those who have argued that the university need not or, indeed, should not engage in research, we find Newman, Ortega y Gasset and Sir Walter Moberly. On the other side, in arguing that research is indeed part of the meaning of 'university', we see Jaspers, Phillips Griffiths and Wegener.[2] So there is no unanimity of view on this issue.

Today, this is not just a philosophical issue: it has political importance. The UK government has suggested that universities should be separated and funded on the basis of their research capability, so that we might have 'research' universities and 'teaching' universities.[3] However, our concern in this book is higher education. It might make sense to argue that no bona fide university could exist which did not also conduct research. But even if that were the case, we could still maintain that research is not part of what we understand higher education to be. That is the argument I shall make here.

Before we get into the argument, however, there will be two objections to what I have just said. First, that making a conceptual distinction in this way between 'university' and 'higher education' is to engage in philosophical pedantry. Secondly, that it is politically naive, because such an argument could be said to justify the kind of political move I have just mentioned, in which some institutions of higher education might be denied research funding. Research might then be seen to be a mere luxury add-on, not an essential part of what it is to be an institution of higher education.

Against the first objection, I hope to show in this chapter that the conceptual distinction is far from mere pedantry. It forces us to consider what we mean by higher education and, indeed, I shall argue that research is not an essential part of the process of higher education as such.

So far as the second objection is concerned, any such political argument would be missing the point. Precisely because my focus is the relationship between higher education and research, I am not concerned with research *per se*. Consequently, in distinguishing higher education and research, nothing said here will imply that research is not worth conducting or supporting. Indeed, I shall argue that while research is not part of the idea of higher education, it is presupposed by higher education. Any attempt to withdraw research funding on the basis of the argument I am offering would, therefore, be quite illegitimate.

The ideology of research

Over the last 30 years, research has become big business, and has been a key element in the formation of new academic disciplines. The aspiration to conduct research on the part of the academic community has been a vital ingredient in the process of 'academic drift', of new institutions of higher education measuring their performance against the more established and élite institutions.[4] Being a costly enterprise and having many uses to the modern state, research has at the same time come under increased scrutiny from the paymaster. The debate over research has become the battleground for the competing ideologies of the academic community and of the state.

Quite apart from the rhetoric, what is the character of research in reality? Clearly, there are differences across subject areas, and so general observations are fraught with difficulty. None the less, certain aspects stand out. First, a significant element of research is not only funded by the government, or quasi-governmental agencies, but also organized on a customer-contract basis.[5] The initiative for a project very often comes from the funding agency, which adopts a 'proactive' stance (in the jargon), setting the agenda, administering a steering committee and ensuring that the project is running towards the desired end. Under this set of structural conditions, research has taken on an instrumental character, extrinsically oriented to external goals. Accordingly, in many fields, the conventional idea of a disinterested researcher having his or her own idiosyncratic interest and pursuing it wherever it might lead is a matter of history.

Secondly, this form of research endeavour can all too easily produce a state of alienation in those conducting the research. I use the term 'alienation' in its marxian sense of the workers being separated from their work; for literally their work is not their own.[6] This is especially the case where large budgets generate research 'teams' with different grades of research workers, the individual members having little control over their work.

Thirdly, research is largely uncontrolled by democratic means even though it is directed by state agencies.[7] The fiction is that those state agencies are able to and do exert democratic influences; or at least, they impose a measure of accountability to the public. But the argument should be recognized for the fiction it is.

Finally, research is increasingly conducted outside institutions of higher education. It is pursued not just in specially funded research institutes, but on a large scale in industry, and by private foundations and policy institutes.

How do these broad-brush sociological observations help us to understand the conceptual connections between higher education and research? On the picture just conveyed, research appears to have something of the character of a commodity, largely unconnected with 'improvement', whether improvement of society or of the individual. The metaphor of commodity suggests itself (with its marxian overtones) precisely because research has become part of academic currency, bestowing credibility on those who possess a curriculum vitae listing their research publications. That kind of curriculum vitae brings a reward in terms of career advancement, with the inevitable monetary gains. And those rewards bear more of a relationship to the length of the list of publications than its quality. There should be nothing surprising about this: in a competitive market, where the number of would-be senior academics considerably exceeds the posts available, an 'objective' means is required to allocate the scarce goods. The list of publications meets the bill: it is a form of intellectual capital, bartered in exchange for the sought-for advancement.[8]

The general point of all this is very simple: knowledge in the context of discovery and knowledge in the context of transmission are entirely different enterprises. Sometimes they are to be found in close proximity; and there are certainly empirical connections between them. Curricula which are project-based can be linked to staffs' research programmes. Alternatively, curricula which are weak in certain areas may prompt the need for particular kinds of research. The key point remains, however: research is seldom driven by curricular considerations, but is normally given direction by an interest structure based on academic careers and the public use of knowledge.

The significance of career advancement in driving research is evident enough, but the use of knowledge in determining the shape of research should not be overlooked. In an age of the commercial exploitation of discoveries, and the marketing of research work, the division between pure and applied research has almost vanished.[9] Certainly, there remain some domains of research which are disinterested, but the incentive to have an eye to the main chance grows. Not only in biotechnology and in computer science; even in archaeology and fine art, we see that academics (advising new museums and making television films) are finding with no little alacrity that their intellectual capital is highly marketable.

Research, then, is born by a coincidence of social interests: of the academic community, of industry and of the state. Whether it is the academics' interests in the livings that come in the wake of a research career; or industry's wish to produce new drugs or insecticides; or the state's desire to develop new military armaments or better traffic flows or even to reduce truancy in schools; these are motivations quite unconnected with the education of students in higher education.

All this leads to a distortion in academic life. Academic excellence comes to be defined in terms of research excellence, irrespective of an academic's qualities as a teacher. Correspondingly, high-level achievements in research all too easily serve as a sufficient criterion for academic excellence. We have to see through this framework of thought for what it is: nothing short of academic ideology.

The logic of research and higher education

By the logic of research and higher education, I mean the general conceptual relationships that exist between these two sets of activity, and I should like to explore those relationships in the following six theses.

First thesis: Research is public whereas higher education is private

Research and higher education share much in common. Both activities are built around structured inquiries, which are persistent, deliberative, more or less organized, and set within a context of present knowledge, and which contain elements of interaction, dialogue, problem solving, creativity and criticism. This is such a formidable list that we might be tempted to assume that research and higher education must at least be species of the same genus of activity, even if not actually identical. But such a conception is to overlook a fundamental distinction about the two activities.

Research is an attempt to produce objective knowledge, independent of personal viewpoint. It is the knowledge which inhabits world III of Popper's schema. (I argued in Chapters 3 and 4 that knowledge cannot attain the state of disinterestedness implied by the schema, but here I am concerned with intentions.) The point of research is that it is a systematic human endeavour intended to produce a level of impersonal knowledge, standing outside individuals. And, as Popper reminds us, this is so in a literal sense: we can find the outcomes of research on the library shelves, or on the computer disc. Its public character has a solidity and a substance to it.

Higher education, on the other hand, is oriented differently. It is directly concerned with individuals, with their minds and with their own way of looking at things. In that sense, it is deliberately idiosyncratic. This is a genuine kind of knowledge, but it is shot through with subjectivity. To return to Popper, his schema allows for this form of knowledge, but as forming the inhabitants of world II, the personal knowledge contained in the human consciousness. *Qua* researcher, the academic may inhabit world III; but *qua* teacher, he or she works in the realm of world II. Admittedly, from time to time, the development of the student's mind is assessed, and the student is required to give a semi-public demonstration of the extent to which his or her consciousness has advanced. But in the end, higher education is a matter of what goes on in the mind of the individual; it is essentially a personal affair.

Second thesis: Research is a matter of outcome whereas higher education is a matter of process

Research is a painstaking business. Much time is spent getting anywhere. Progress is often slow, and can be counted in years. Sometimes, the model or theory being examined leads into a blind alley or the methodology turns out to be faulty, and the researcher feels as if the effort involved was worthless. Outcome is everything. And not just any outcome. The outcome, whether a journal article or a book or a commercial patent, has to be significant and recognized as such. First, it has to get past the gatekeepers, the publishers and the journal editors, the referees and reviewers. Secondly, it has to beat the clock. Particularly in the sciences, time presses heavily as research teams around the world struggle to be first to the finish, and then engage in priority disputes to determine just who was successful. But other areas are not without their temporal aspects: even philosophy has its intellectual fashions.[10] Then, if a new thought does see the light of day, it still requires the approval of the researcher's peer group within the academic or professional world. The outcome can be conventional or revolutionary; to develop another of Popper's metaphors, it can amount to mere filling in of the mortar, an additional brick or two, or even a completely new building.[11] Either way, in research, the outcome is all. Except for the historians and the sociologists of knowledge, the process of getting there is signally uninteresting.[12]

In higher education, it is entirely the other way around. There, there is no outcome as such. This may seem odd. After all, the government, employers and other agencies are talking precisely about student outcomes.[13] That is understandable, given the desire of those agencies to ascertain that the 3 years or more spent in higher education lead to some definite outcome. Higher education, though, is a matter of getting students launched on a process of self-development, in which they take responsibility for enlarging and deepening their own consciousness. Admittedly, after graduation, many students go no further in their reading and thinking. But at least they have sufficient grounding to do so, if they wish.

Seen in this way, the moment of graduation is just an arbitrary point in the formation of the individual's consciousness. Graduation day symbolizes no end-point; merely perhaps a getting-off point, or an interlude, or a marker in the continuing process. The degree cannot be an outcome; for the development of the human consciousness has no outcome. It is a process which can be continuous, or halted, or intermittent. In one sense, though, there is an outcome. And that is – perhaps when receiving the undergraduate degree – that the student has reached the point when he or she intellectually can take off on his or her own, if so desired. The BA or BSc is a symbol to the world that the student has attained a level of intellectual independence. But the key point remains: higher education is a continuing developmental process.

Third thesis: In higher education, learning is intended whereas in research, it is a by-product

In higher education, the focus is the mind of the student, and its development. For the moment, let us call this developmental process 'learning' (although, in Chapter 11, I shall show that there are problems in using the term). It is the private world of the student's mind that is at issue, a world that should expand and take on a rich array of colours, within the course of studies.

In research, however, with its emphasis on demonstrable outcomes and the public world of knowledge, we are completely uninterested in the mind of the researcher. Still less do we want to know if the production of the book or research paper represented a learning experience for the academic concerned. Even if we were, there would be no necessary relationship between research as public outcome and research as personal learning. A modest journal article might have produced for the author a significant learning experience. In reverse, we can imagine a researcher producing a paper which had a profound impact on the research community and even the wider society, but for some strange reason had little personal impact. In reality, of course, such events are rare; researchers do undergo a process of intellectual development in the course of their work. But this is incidental, for it is not a condition of research taking place.

Research and learning, then, are conceptually unrelated, whereas higher education and learning are conceptually interwoven.

Fourth thesis: Higher education is open whereas research is closed

Research is highly specific. The researcher has to have some idea of what he or she is looking for, even though the outcome may be unpredictable. Sometimes, the sought-for object may be entirely predicted in advance, as with the 'discovery' of the planet Neptune in 1846 (which in reality was just the astronomers' confirmation of the mathematicians' predictions). On other occasions, a model or theory may emerge in an act of discovery; but that is the result of deliberate endeavour, perhaps over several years, devoted to some particular inquiry.

Higher education, as the opening of a person's consciousness, is in contrast unpredictable. Certainly, that movement of mind normally takes place in a bounded framework of study, i.e. the student's 'course'. The very term 'course' implies a definite path of study; the student is not going to go wandering all over the intellectual map. But higher education produces a dynamic interaction between the mind of the student, the teachers, the other students on the course and even on other courses in other subjects, and the array of resources the institution has to offer. And students are expected to make their own responses to what is put in their way. There is, accordingly, an element of uncertainty about the educational processes in higher education. Indeed, the better the course, the more the students will feel welcome to offer their own insights, reactions and ideas to which the staff will want to respond in turn. Higher education, as we have seen, has the character of a conversation: the participants may have their own roles, but improvisation breaks out continually as they interact with each other.

One way of putting this difference between the bounded nature of research and the comparatively unbounded nature of higher education is to say that, in research, the researcher starts off with a fairly hazy idea of what might emerge and ends with a precise formulation or conclusion, whereas in higher education, this is reversed. The student starts off with a fairly definite hold on the world, built on reasonably stable concepts and ideas, but at the end of the course has grasped that very little of the intellectual world has enduring substance and that there are always more cognitive spectacles to put on. In theory, students should always be welcome to go beyond the immediate limits of their studies, and 'read round their subject'. The pity is that we do not sufficiently encourage them to conduct those explorations.

Fifth thesis: Research is a necessary but not a sufficient ingredient for higher education

Precisely because others have conducted research in the past, and knowledge has 'exploded', the opportunities for the development of the student's mind have grown and widened. Not all research is important in this way: it is not the accumulation of detailed findings, but the occasional additions to our conceptual frameworks which make possible the expansion of the student's understanding. The position that Newman held, in seeing higher education as unconnected with the search for new knowledge, is no longer tenable. Over the last 150 years, the world of knowledge and understanding created through research has opened up infinite possibilities for higher education, and so research has become undeniably linked to our modern understanding of higher education. For a genuine higher education to take place, research has to have been undertaken somewhere, upon which programmes of study will in part be based. It does not follow, though, that an institution offering a course of study should be conducting research in that topic. It does not even follow that the research base should have been developed in *any* institution of higher education. (It could be established in research institutes and, in some branches of science, it largely is.)

While, then, higher education and research are separate and separable activities, higher education inescapably draws on research. But if institutionalized research is a necessary condition of higher education taking place, it cannot be a sufficient condition. Introducing research into the curriculum is justifiable provided that it is used to expand the student's intellectual horizons, and not because it propels students towards becoming embryonic researchers. The relationship between research and higher education is such that someone, somewhere, should have engaged in research; but that does not mean that research is part of the meaning of higher education.

Sixth thesis: *The academic community is directly related to research, but indirectly related to higher education*

Earlier in this book, we saw that there is no single group which forms the academic community. Academics are intertwined in networks which operate at different administrative levels, from the department to the institution itself. More importantly, they are locked into their own epistemic community, composed of others who are working in the same subject areas. That community not only traverses frontiers, to form an invisible college; it also extends, for some subjects, beyond institutions of higher education to include research institutes, industrial laboratories, professionals working in the field, and the individual scholar who (no longer based in an institution) still goes on contributing to the literature.

Kogan and Becher have argued that, beyond the individual academic, the department is the basic unit of academic life.[14] Certainly, academics will tend to identify with their department more than their institution; but there is a sense in which the worldwide subject-based invisible college could be said to be basic. For academics *qua* researchers can operate without a department in an institution of higher education; many academics are located in quite different settings, as I have just mentioned. As researchers, though, they cannot operate without reference to that wider community of others who are active in research, wherever those others are based. It follows that the academic community and research are directly interrelated.

The academic community figures much less prominently in higher education. Clearly, students are not (or only exceptionally) full members of the academic community. Occasionally, a student – perhaps in mathematics or logic – can be seen actually to make a contribution to the research literature, but that is so rare as to appear precocious. Many of their teachers will certainly be making a contribution to research, but in their role as researchers, not as teachers. And the process of higher education is not, or should not be, intended to produce new cohorts of researchers. We have seen, however, that it is entirely proper that the results of research will be drawn on, within that educational process.

It follows that we can describe the human transactions between students and staff that constitute the processes of higher education without mentioning 'the academic community'. The academic community is not directly part of that process. It is on the fringes of higher education, through its contribution to research, which provides an educational resource for students. Accordingly, we can say that the academic community stands in a direct relationship to research but in an indirect relationship to higher education.

Teaching staff and students

What are the implications of these rather abstract remarks for the key people in higher education?

Teaching staff

We have seen that for effective teaching in higher education to take place, someone, somewhere should have engaged in research. This does not imply that all teachers should engage in research. It does suggest that teachers corporately have a responsibility to assist in keeping alive the research tradition, but that there is also only a minimal obligation on individuals to participate in the research enterprise. On the other hand, every teacher has a professional obligation to understand the key conversations going on in the research community. This is sometimes called 'scholarship', but that term carries unfortunate overtones of separateness and aloneness. A better term might be 'informed eavesdropping'.

Some might be willing to grant the general thrust of what has been said, that teaching and research are different kinds of activity, but still be reluctant to accept that teachers in higher education do not have a major responsibility to conduct research. Is that not one of the distinguishing characteristics of an institution of higher education, that its staff do, by and large, conduct research and feel themselves under an obligation to do so? As an empirical observation, that is normally the case; that set of shared norms *is* part of the culture of institutions of higher education. But my argument is that that culture should not be accepted uncritically. Indeed, the balance between teaching and re-search obligations as they are felt is weighted too much towards research, for, in some respects, the research culture can have deleterious effects on the teaching process.

I have in mind, for example, that research can often consist of narrow problem-solving routines, with little theoretical content and even with little empirical content.[15] Researchers, too, can sometimes be carried away in delving deeply into some issue in the minutest detail. This may be entirely proper for the evolution of knowledge in a particular field; or it may be simply that the researcher has developed a tunnel vision, and is unable to see beyond a very narrow focus. Whatever the reason, that kind of perspective is anathema to higher education, where we are trying to widen students' horizons.

Another counter to this argument might be to point out that one of the defining characteristics of higher education is that students are brought to the 'frontiers of knowledge' in a particular field. Students, the argument continues, can hardly be brought to this level of understanding unless their teachers are active in research. But the argument does not work. The notion of bringing students to 'frontiers of knowledge' is tendentious. A corpus of knowledge does not have a single well-defined boundary; it has many fuzzy debates going on. Secondly, as a matter of fact, it is accepted in many areas of the higher education curriculum that the basic conceptual understanding cannot be fully accomplished at the undergraduate stage, in which case the 'frontiers of knowledge' can be shown only to students who follow on to a postgraduate programme.

But apart from these largely empirical objections, the argument is flawed theoretically. One can reach a frontier without crossing it. Teachers in higher education are bound to have a close understanding of much of the current thinking and work in their intellectual field. They have professional obligations to engage in that kind of scholarly work; and, in that sense, be right up against the 'frontiers'. It does not follow that the teacher has to be engaged in actually moving the frontier.

The relationship of the teacher to research is analogous to the relationship of the musical soloist to the score. There is no demand on the soloist that he or she be a composer, and therefore be able to produce new scores. But it is paramount that the soloist be so directly acquainted with the score that he or she is able to offer us a personal interpretation of it; in a sense, a critical commentary on it. Indeed, being a composer may even be a drawback, for it might lessen the critical distance that the soloist needs to maintain in order to bring a fresh interpretation to bear.

Put this analogy into the teaching situation, where the argument often runs that the teacher in higher education should not just be doing research, but that that research should be brought into the curriculum. The musical analogy suggests that there is no general obligation of that kind; the responsibility of the teacher lies much more in having an intimate understanding of other academics' research and in being able to give an interpretation of it. But the musical analogy also suggests that the picture of the teacher giving an interpretation of his or her own research is likely to reduce the chances of an independent viewpoint being brought to bear. This is vital, for ultimately we want students to branch out on their own, to develop their own viewpoints, and not simply to imitate the views of the teacher bound to a particular research methodology or paradigm. Higher education is notorious for producing disciples, as students take on the mantle of a teacher who has created a great impression. The teacher in higher education should be trying to promote genuine independence of mind, rather than act in the guise of a pied piper.[16]

The point I have just made, about the dangers of the teacher being so bound up in her or his research that a genuinely critical perspective is made more unlikely, links to another argument that is often heard. This is that the research effort in a department should underpin the courses it offers. There are two assumptions at work here. First, that there should be a direct transfer of that knowledge base into the curriculum and, secondly, that there is a more general 'spin-off' in terms of the intellectual energy and commitment which staff will put into their teaching responsibilities.

I have partly dealt with the first argument. It is simply undesirable for there to be a direct transfer of research findings into the curriculum, particularly the undergraduate curriculum. Course design should be led by educational objectives, and not by research perspectives.

The second argument is more diffuse and therefore more difficult to counter.

If it were true that research effort in the area of the curriculum promoted teaching commitment, few would quarrel with the proposed obligation on the department. But is there any evidence for it?[17] It admittedly makes intuitive sense, and fits in with the general observation about staffs' professional identities being a function of their research identities. If that is the prime source of their professional motivation, then the more their research is oriented towards their students' courses, the more likely is their commitment to those students. So, yes, if staff are conducting research, the more they can be persuaded to work in areas which directly 'underpin' the curriculum, the less is the intellectual distance between their teaching and research activities. But this is an argument about departmental and institutional management, as much as it is a matter of professional ethics. It does not amount to an argument that staff should be conducting research as such; merely that if they are engaged in it, there is an advantage to it being undertaken with an eye to their teaching commitments.

Some may think that these are just nice debating points, and that they bear little relationship to what actually happens. For, in reality, the research and teaching activities are so closely interwoven that they are inseparable. There is good reason for this; at its best, the teaching situation takes on much of the character of the research process, with an open dialogue between the students and teacher, the teacher being the first among equals. The teacher may lead the discussion or the activity, but he or she is also learning from the students. That is a very common situation.[18] Indeed, not infrequently, a teacher in higher education will use a set of lecture notes – polished over the years through interactions with students – as the basis of a book. This kind of close integration between research and higher education is obviously highly desirable: discussion with students so advancing the teacher's understanding and insight that a stronger publication emerges. That being so, suppose we have another member of staff who is equally as effective as a teacher but who does not work up the lecture notes in the same way: could we not say that his or her teaching is integrated with research to the same degree? Critical reflection is there; so too is the dynamic dialogue with the students and with it the continuing development in the teacher's own thinking. The only difference is that the work simply does not get published.

That difference, while immaterial from the point of view of teaching, is vital from the research point of view. It is the difference between worlds II and III, between the private and the public worlds of knowledge (thesis one). Getting one's work published and counted by one's peers as a contribution to the intellectual debate is a significant step in its own right. The individual teacher may well have made a significant development in his or her own understanding, but that is not a sufficient condition of securing publication (thesis three). That is why the academic community has erected its appraisal systems, with anonymous referees and appraisers.

But to go down this path of analysis is to put things in an unreasonably negative light. It suggests that the difference between the successful teacher and the successful researcher is that the teacher is a failed researcher. It misses the point that being an effective teacher, leading students to a measure of intellectual and professional independence such that they are able to articulate with others their own viewpoint, is a major achievement. There are many gifted teachers who are extraordinarily successful in this way, who are not just animated interpreters of complex concepts and theories, but who are able to galvanize their students into grappling with the issues for themselves. From the student point of view, and from the point of view of their higher education, whether the teacher is also involved in research is quite irrelevant.

From all this, we can say quite simply that the roles of teacher and researcher are distinct. Individuals may perform either role by itself; or they might be active in both roles, and successfully at that; or they may be strong in one but not in the other. There is nothing odd in that, for the two activities call for separate sets of accomplishments.

If we sense that academics could improve the quality of their teaching – if, for example, we find that there is a high rate of students failing to complete their courses – the attention of the academics concerned should be directed to their teaching rather than their research activity. It is a truism, but worth stating for all that: as teachers, academics' first responsibility is to their teaching (i.e. to their students); it is not to their research.

The student

I have tried to indicate that the role of the student should not be construed as that of embryonic researcher. The intellectual, emotional and practical development that goes on – or should go on – is much wider than that. For that reason, it is a second-order matter whether the student is actually brought to the 'frontiers of knowledge', even putting aside the tendentiousness of that notion. It is much more important that the student is given an understanding of a conceptual structure, and is able to take up stances within it, to understand something of the fundamental debates taking place within it, to see the difference between sense and nonsense, and to stand back and form critical evaluations of the wider social role of the form of thought.

Certainly, in writing essays, conducting experiments, citing sources, marshalling one's findings, reading part of the relevant literature, and finding one's way around information sources, students are undertaking tasks which are found in the research enterprise. But these tasks are not expected of students *because* they are quasi-research activities. Rather, being quasi-research activities, they are a means of promoting in students the higher-order thinking and reflection that are characteristic of a higher education. Those higher-order levels include being critical, forming independent judgements, authenticity of thought and action, and problem setting and problem solving by the student. It is in these higher-order achievements that we can talk of a logical correspondence, although not identity, between the roles of student and of researcher.

So the idea of the student as an embryonic researcher turns out to be a metaphor referring, at its best, to just some of the activities employed by the student. At its worst, the metaphor is misleading and dangerous. It can reflect an academic ideology, seeing the student programme of study as a narrow training which initiates the student into the world of research. On the contrary, the higher education experience should be a challenging and unsettling experience, opening the student's mind to a sense of ever-widening possibilities, in concept, supposition and approach to the world.

The research student

Even if all this is granted, even if it is accepted that higher education and with it the roles of teacher and student are in principle separate from the world of research, the sceptic still has one final card to play. It could be suggested that my argument has merit in relation to undergraduate education, but that it makes no sense at all at the level of postgraduate education. There, research and education are surely intimately connected. We would have to say, for example, that staff responsible for research students have a definite obligation to engage in research. The point appears to come through even more strongly in the role of the postgraduate student, particularly the research student. For that looks like a situation in which research and higher education are one and the same process. There we have a student who is in receipt of a higher education (almost by definition) and, at the same time, an individual who is engaged in research.

This counter has point to it, but it is a one-sided reading of the situation. In preparing a thesis at the master's or the doctorate level, the student is clearly engaged in research. Indeed, particularly in the humanities, and perhaps in the social sciences and in professionally related fields, it will be a substantial work of research when considered against any criterion. But it is still wrong to think that here research and higher education are one and the same thing. To see research students in that way is educationally shortsighted.

Given the way that research is structured, where for instance research students in the sciences and social sciences are often engaged to assist staff in large-scale research projects, research students as a matter of fact are part of the total research enterprise of the academic community. That much has to be admitted. But precisely on that account, it is all too easy for the work of the research student to be governed by the interests of the director(s) of the research project. As a result, the student is directed into exceedingly narrow channels, and the work is a matter of going through some methodological routines and writing up the results. Pressures of this kind have led the PhD work to become a narrow research training, rather than a proper educational process of making ever-wider connections and expanding one's intellectual compass.

In other words, the pretence that research and higher education are inseparable results in driving out higher education. Is it possible now, given the huge weight of academic ideology and the interests of the research councils bearing down on it, to inject an educational dimension into the work of the research student? Or is the situation beyond retrieval? This is not to press for a reversal of the present position, but to understand that if the work of research students is to be understood in educational terms, then the first step is to accept that the role is a hybrid of research and of higher education. The point also holds for those postgraduate courses which are hardly more than programmes of professional training. If they are to be more than mere training, then a process of informed reflection has to go on at the same time. Research theses and postgraduate courses can fulfil ends other than purely educational ones; but they cannot become, as part of higher education, simply instrumental, whether in the direction of academic careers or professional careers. They also have to fulfil the higher-order objectives implied by the title 'higher education'.

Conclusion

Institutions of higher education do not need to conduct research in order to justify the title 'institution of *higher* education'. We have so distorted our conception of higher education that it is difficult to realize the point. Research and higher education seem so inseparable that they are almost synonymous. Admittedly, there is some substance in this way of thinking. A genuine higher education today cannot be offered entirely separately from some kind of research base. But that does not mean that either institutions of higher education or their staff are obliged to conduct research. Staff, though, do need to have the time and resources to so keep up with their field of study that they are immersed in its conversations. The argument here is not just theoretical, therefore; it has policy implications.[19]

There are, however, major forces at work sustaining the present occlusion of research and higher education. Research is the fulcrum of the academic community. It is the point on which the academic community turns, and it is by their research performance that academics take on their professional identity and are judged by their peers. Teaching accomplishments take a back seat. One justification for this has been given: research is public, whereas higher education is private. Exposing teaching performance is tantamount, in Lawton's phrase, to invading 'the secret garden' of the curriculum.[20] But if we are seriously interested in promoting the quality of higher education, of improving the effectiveness by which teachers teach and students learn, it is to the teaching process that we must look. In short, if we are concerned about higher education, it is to higher education that we must turn, rather than research.

10

Academic Freedom

Introduction

It may be no surprise to see a chapter given to 'academic freedom', in looking at key concepts in higher education. But pause for a moment. Does academic freedom necessarily have anything to do with higher education? Or at any rate, with higher education as sketched out in this book? For on the argument here, higher education is essentially a developmental process experienced by students; staff and institutions are largely incidental. That being so, what connections exist between academic freedom and higher education?

The question makes particular sense given the way the debate over academic freedom has been cast both in the UK and in the USA. For academic freedom is usually seen on both sides of the Atlantic as a matter of rights which owe to fully paid-up members of the academic community. Issues of academic freedom attract heated public discussion when academic staff see themselves as being prevented from pursuing the *research* in which they are personally interested. In discussing the topic, the academic community also talks of its right to *teach* as it wishes, although it is remarkable how seldom, in reality, the right to teach arises as an issue over which the academic community feels especially aggrieved. The naive observer might be forgiven for believing that this contrast has something to do with the different weight given by members of the academic community to their research interests compared with their 'teaching interests' (the very awkwardness of the term makes the point).

None the less, it remains the case that academics' public debate over academic freedom is grounded in their wish to defend their rights – as they see it – to conduct their own activities in the way they see fit. This is entirely in keeping with the theoretical debate over academic freedom which we find in the literature. Not surprisingly, different viewpoints have emerged over the range of activities which can be justified under the name of academic freedom, over the kinds of threat which are most felt to be present, over the circumstances in which appeal can be made to academic freedom, and over the justifications which academics employ to claim a right to 'academic freedom'. Irrespective of these differences, though, we can – I think – encapsulate the whole debate in a simple principle: That academic pursuits, carried out in academic settings, by academic persons, should be ultimately directed by those persons.[1]

   Admittedly, this formulation is relatively empty, for questions can be asked about each of its main terms. Does the killing of an animal in a laboratory for research purposes count as an academic pursuit (over which the academic concerned should enjoy some measure of academic freedom)? Does the television studio, in which a group of academics are gathered together for a discussion on an 'academic' issue, count as an academic setting? Do research assistants count as academic persons (and should they be entitled to publish as freely as the research directors who carry contractual responsibilities for their research activities)? These questions are worth asking, but they must not be allowed to detain us here.

   I believe that the formulation just offered does amount to a shorthand summary of much of the somewhat tortuous justifications that are available in the literature on academic freedom. From the fact that it leads on to all sorts of other questions, we can reasonably infer that many of the justifications given in the literature are indeed question-begging. The traditional discussions of academic freedom, whatever their superficial differences, are also depressingly uniform. They frequently exhibit the following characteristics: a lack of specificity; a concern for the academic freedom of staff and not students; a defensive proclamation of the rights of academics; and a disinclination to say anything about the *duties* that should accompany academics' rights.[2]

   Where the rights in question are spelt out, they are often lumped together, as if they were all of the same kind. In particular, freedom to teach and to conduct research are often mentioned in the same phrase, as if the authority by which an academic engages in the one activity is exactly the same as the authority under which the other activity is undertaken. But the expertise by which an academic may justify embarking on research is not the same as that by which teaching is undertaken. Correspondingly, the authority by which research expertise is acknowledged is that of the academic peer group, the relevant epistemic community; in contrast, teaching authority comes at least in part from the students.

   To return to the main point, the debate over academic freedom, whether in the columns of the quality press, or in academic conferences, or in the academic literature on academic freedom itself, is conducted by reference to the felt interests of the full members of the academic community. It is characterized by concerns over the threats they perceive to their right to conduct their own activities (as they see all three – threats, rights and interests). Excluded almost universally from this debate is any consideration of the students' rights. Because debate is framed in terms of those who are fully competent to exercise academic freedom, and because students almost by definition are not felt to be properly 'competent', the exclusion from the debate of students' rights is hardly surprising. It is precisely that exclusion that I want to address in this chapter.

Whatever happened to *Lernfreiheit?*

It was not always thus. Most notable of all, the German universities from the early nineteenth century onwards were founded on a conception of inquiry, and of educational development, in which the student took centre stage. Admittedly, the definition of the student role that emerged in that conception of higher education had much to do with the idealist epistemology in which von Humboldt and the other founders of the modern German university were themselves scholars and contributors. It was an epistemology in which knowledge was ultimately not grasped, or uncovered, but was attained through debate. Today, the idealist baggage – of entering a world of spirit, for example – seems at least obscure, if not downright obscurantist. However, rather than serving to dissuade us from finding some base for the notion of students' academic freedom, the epistemological grounding of the German universities holds some definite clues that are worth pursuing.

Indeed, those who recall the account of knowledge developed in the second section of this book may feel that there are definite similarities between the epistemology underlying the formation of the German universities and the epistemological position we find ourselves in today. In both, there is an absence of absolute authority, and of definitely grounding our claims to knowledge independently of the knower. There is also a sense that what counts as knowledge is negotiated through a discourse allowing a critique and a counter-critique by participants subscribing to the conventions of a shared form of life. That being so, it is worthwhile recalling the view of the student that went with that earlier epistemology and which generated the idea of students' academic freedom (or *Lernfreiheit*, as it was known[3]).

On the idealist view, knowledge was not to be simply read off the world but was to be gained through entering a critical dialogue with others. Consequently, there was no difference in kind in the formal position of teachers and taught. Both were engaged in the same kind of activity, in exploring accounts of the world through participation in a conversation. Given this epistemology and this view of the role of the student, it was entirely apposite for the notion of student academic freedom to arise. For, if students were to fulfil the role cast for them, they had to be free – institutionally and intellectually – to pursue their own inquiries and cognitive interests.

It would be wrong not to acknowledge the allegation that that educational philosophy had, in practice, many damaging results in modern European higher education, for example the separation of students from professorial staff, so that the students were often left too much alone by professors who were much more interested in their own inquiries; the free movement of students across universities and its impact on the coherence of the students' programme of studies; and the slow completion and very often non-completion by students of their courses. Whatever the validity of these observations, they are salutary warnings in moving over-boldly in the direction of student self-learning; and they may point to the value of ensuring the existence of an adequately supportive learning environment.

Even so, these cautionary comments should not dislodge us from the main point. If the formation and acquisition of knowledge has the character of a conversation, then students must be accorded an appropriate measure of freedom to engage in that conversation in their own way. No doubt, most will require considerable assistance to be able to participate effectively; but no-one can be forced to engage in a conversation with sincerity. The students have to pick up the threads of the conversation, to make sense of it, and to make a contribution – if they wish – in their own way. The shorthand way of putting this is that students must have the freedom – the academic freedom – to exercise due responsibility for their own learning.

These reflections amount to no less than this. The conventional concept of academic freedom as adumbrated in the UK and the USA is completely inadequate. It needs to be recast, so that it extends beyond academic staff to embrace the student body. Or, to put it slightly differently, in characterizing academic freedom in terms of the rights of the academic community, we need to draw the bounds of the academic community widely enough to include students. Students need to be rehabilitated in our idea of academic freedom, *and* in the practices associated with the idea.

Precisely what, in the modern age, does this amount to? Exactly what academic (as opposed to, say, more general civil) rights might students legitimately claim?[4] They are simply those rights which underpin the conditions under which it is meaningful to talk of the student's right to learn. And, just as with academic freedom for academic staff, we can distinguish negative and positive rights for students.

Among negative rights, we should include the rights: not to be indoctrinated; not to be subject to unnecessary ideology; not to experience racialist, sexist or religious bias; and not to be subject to unprofessional practices by teaching staff in admissions, in teaching and in examining. *Among positive rights*, we should include the rights: to have all one's experience and knowledge assessed in the admissions process; to determine the subjects studied; to have a legitimate measure of control over the pace and the methods of study; to be able to follow a particular academic interest, or develop a point of view of one's own; to be examined in ways which do justice to the student's achievements; and to be credited with those parts of a course which have been passed successfully (should the student wish or need to move to another institution, or to take a break in the programme of study).

Certainly, there could be argument over some of these suggested rights, if only in their extent and their implementation. Additionally, other rights might be invoked. That kind of detailed examination could and should go on. That further exploration, though, is second order to recognizing that students need freedoms of an academic character if their learning is to be fully effective.

There are two parallel considerations at work here. The first is that students are adults, and enrol and attend their courses voluntarily. However it may feel at times to them as individuals, and whatever compulsions they sense from relatives and friends to 'get through' their course, the fact is that they could withdraw without any legal penalty at least. Attending their institution of higher education betokens a degree of 'wittingness and voluntariness' on their part.[5] That being so, their continuing participation in their programme of studies represents a contract between them and the providing institution. By 'contract', I mean an educational contract, in which the institution is in effect undertaking to provide the student with the kind of programme that he or she wants, in return for the student's active participation.

The second consideration is that students require a degree of intellectual space if they are properly to develop their own intellectual maturity. The abilities not just to comprehend, to take things into one's own understanding, and to make something of them, but also to be able to evaluate critically the available theories and traditions, and to be willing and have the mental toughness to take up a stance of one's own: all these abilities point to an intellectual independence, requiring real academic freedom for their realization.

We have, then, student wittingness and intellectual maturity both pointing in the same direction. If students are really to be involved in their own learning, then they must feel they do, in part, own it. They not only must enjoy negative freedoms (freedoms not to be unduly constrained), but also must experience positive freedoms (of the kind sketched out above). The freedom to learn cannot be an empty slogan but must be made real for every student on every course of study of higher education. In practice, most students do experience many of the positive freedoms I have cited. The question is whether something approaching a Bill of Rights for students would not be worthwhile, spelling out the academic freedoms which all students have the right to expect. This would act as an agreed convention against which programmes of study could be evaluated.

An educational Bill of Rights would not stand in place of students' legal entitlements; students would, as now, still have the right to pursue a legal claim if they felt themselves to be the victim of an injustice. A Bill of Rights would fulfil a different and a prior purpose. It could, indeed, help to establish the kind of ethos which might make recourse to legal remedies unnecessary. Legal and quasi-legal moves are made when things have gone wrong, where expectations have not been fulfilled on both sides, and often where students have not played the compliant role expected of them. Those manoeuvres arise in a situation of unequal power. It is surely time that students, as adults in part responsible for their own higher education, were formally accorded the rights and academic respect they deserve, and the social relations between teacher and taught were made more equal.[6]

A student ethic

The enjoyment of special privileges, such as the freedom to learn, carries with it corresponding responsibilities. If the kinds of academic freedom for students just outlined are to be vigorously sustained by the academic community (as they should), then students have to play their part in the exercise of those freedoms. There is nothing odd in this; the academic freedoms that the academic community enjoys generate their own academic ethic which members of the academic community should fulfil if they are to warrant those privileges (Shils 1984). Academic freedom, whether for teachers or students, cannot mean academic licence; the role of the academic, in whatever capacity, is a demanding one, with its own obligations.

Among the responsibilities that accompany academic freedom for students are the following. First, there are the *substantive responsibilities* which go hand in hand with the moral virtues that are inseparably part of the intellectual life. These include sincerity, honesty (not to indulge in plagiarism or cheating), truthfulness, the avoidance of self-contradiction, a determination to be comprehensible, the intellectual courage to develop and hold a position of one's own, a willingness to be subject to the demands of reason and evidence, an openness to other viewpoints or ways of going on, and according due (but not undue) respect to teaching and other staff.[7] Secondly, there are the *procedural responsibilities* associated with the conventions of the student role. Among these are the completion of assignments on time, attendance for appointments (including tutorials and examinations), undertaking the necessary groundwork for the course – whether in the laboratory, studio or library – and accepting the customary house rules, such as not interrupting (or barracking) the lecturers.

Significant measures of freedom are necessary if the student is to acquire the virtues of intellectual independence, toughness, empathy with others' views, and willingness to engage in meaningful conversation. But the acquisition of those very virtues requires the student to submit to the demands of intellectual life, as experienced within an institution with all its vicissitudes. With the best will in the world, the library is not always going to have the book on its shelves that the student is after; and nor are members of staff always going to be available to answer students' enquiries.

All this is tantamount to saying that, even in the role of student, the academic life exerts particular and considerable demands on the individual. The image of the irresponsible student may have a basis in various periods of higher education (in medieval times, in eighteenth-century Oxbridge, and in the late 1960s across the Western world). None the less, the moral imperatives that are intrinsic to the student role will always reassert themselves.

If students' academic freedom imposes responsibilities as well as rights, how might we understand student radicalism? Here, as with academic freedom for teaching staff, we should distinguish between freedoms which derive from civil rights and those which derive from the character of academic life. Student action on the streets – as in China or South Korea – does not as such raise issues of academic freedom.[8] That kind of action is defensible or not in terms of the students' civil rights, and in terms of the constraints such activities present to the civil rights of the general public. (Even if the activities do present curbs on the rights of the general public to go about their business, street action might still be justified where, for example, it brings to public consciousness some injustice that would not otherwise receive a public hearing.)

Student action on the campus, on the other hand, does raise issues of academic freedom, and in a double sense. First, it raises issues of the academics' academic freedom (*Lerfreiheit*): are the academics' rights to teach and research constrained? Just this, indeed, happened in the student radicalism of the 1960s. Secondly, the other students' own right to learn (*Lernfreiheit*) can be called into question. Whatever mitigating justifications could be cited in favour of overt action on the campus, in much of the 1960s' action, students were often reducing other students' right to learn, were therefore abusing their freedoms and were, as such, forfeiting their own rights as students.

To say that the student role must be confined within the boundaries of the academic ethic does not mean that the student role is a docile one. On the contrary, if the student body were to take its right to learn (*Lernfreiheit*) seriously, and were to be vigilant in seeing that it enjoyed the kinds of academic freedom I spelt out earlier, it would necessarily take on an assertive role. The trouble today is that the student body has moved so far away from asserting its academic rights that it has become largely passive, simply accepting the fare put before it. Although individual students may seek to press the system to its limits, whether in securing credit for prior learning in the admissions process, or in pursuing a formal appeal against a felt injustice over assessment, or in taking advantage of such open learning arrangements as are available, the student body as a whole seems depressingly unconcerned about its academic rights. It would rather mount a protest over student grants (probably in the UK the most generous in the world per student) than attempt to frame a Charter of the academic rights which should fall to every student.

Even if students were to conceive of their role in this way, the academic freedoms and the associated student ethic could not be maintained solely by the students. Implications follow for their lecturers and other teachers. If students' freedom to learn is to be made a reality, academic staff must provide the intellectual conditions for students to be intellectually free. Again, there has to be a balance. It is right that students be initiated into the conceptual apparatus, skills and ways of going on within the teacher's own discipline; and it is right that students therefore acquire the discipline required for the necessary under-standing and competencies. But it is not right for a member of the teaching staff to so present that disciplinary framework that the student is unable to view it from the outside or is discouraged from offering an alternative perspective from another discipline. Student academic freedom and its associated academic ethic imply a high degree of intellectual maturity not only from the students but also from the academic staff. The teacher needs to be open to, and supportive of, the student who has an alternative view to present, even if it does not fall squarely within the teacher's own disciplinary expertise. In the learning enterprise, everyone has a share in it, the teachers as well as the taught.

Finally, there is another student freedom to which the teacher in higher education needs to be especially alert. It is the freedom for the student to make his or her mistakes. This is not simply a matter of learning through one's own mistakes. I argued a moment ago that if the student is to enter into his or her own work, and is to be committed to it, he or she simply has to be given the intellectual space – to a degree – to follow his or her own inclinations. But this means that, from time to time, the student will pursue hunches which lead nowhere, or adopt a method of analysis which turns out to be unfruitful. This may sometimes prove inefficient, seen from the perspective of crude perform-ance indicators. But it is a necessary price to pay, if we want students to emerge with minds of their own, who do not merely know but understand in some depth what they know, and who are able to form and develop their own ideas.

Institutional autonomy

We have seen that, if students' freedom to learn is to be a reality, it has to be acknowledged by the academic community in all the academic processes that affect students, from the time of applying for admission through the course arrangements and the curriculum experience to the final assessment. Another way of putting this is that students' academic freedoms should be reflected in the internal culture of institutions of higher education. But we saw in Chapter 5 that, as key institutions in the modern state, institutions of higher education cannot attain a position of pure autonomy. That being so, are these institutions in a position, even if they so desire, to guarantee the student freedoms argued for here?

In the context of the conventional debate over academic freedom, a standard move in response to this point is to claim that academic freedom is a concept applicable to individual persons, and that academic autonomy is a concept applicable to institutions.[9] It is certainly possible to argue both on empirical and on conceptual grounds that there are institutions – for example, German or Swedish universities – which are not autonomous, but offer academic freedom to their academics. And it makes obvious sense to say that autonomous institutions are not necessarily homes of academic freedom. In other words, you can have one without the other: academic freedom and academic autonomy are distinctive concepts. This is neat, but it does not work entirely.

The lack of academic autonomy will show itself in some form or other. Perhaps in the selection of students for admission; or the promotion of the faculty; or the apportionment of priorities for institutional expenditure; or the direction of research projects; or the range of teaching and research subjects pursued in an institution; or the character of the curriculum. Now, the latter three are clearly matters of academic freedom, given the way in which academic freedom is commonly understood. Whether or not we describe the three preceding ones as activities that fall under academic autonomy or academic freedom is a matter of judgement. It looks, therefore, as if there is at least an empirical connection between academic autonomy and academic freedom. Take the first away, and effects will be felt on the second.[10] We can still retain the conceptual distinction; we can say that academic autonomy is descriptive of the relationship between the institution and the state, while academic freedom characterizes the institutionalized accountability of the individual academic. But, in practice, it appears that a degree of academic autonomy is a necessary condition of academic freedom.

Secondly, the same point can be turned round. Academics have their livings in institutions established to conduct academic activities. As they are practised in the modern world, high-level teaching and research only make sense in institutions. Higher education has been thoroughly institutionalized; an Illich-style 'deschooling' is simply not on.[11] This means that, for most academics at least, research and teaching require an institutional framework. The logic is that academic freedom requires academic autonomy if it is to mean anything more than rhetoric. Again, then, we see a close interweaving of the two features of academic life.

Thirdly, autonomy at any rate can be applied to an individual academic. In one sense, admittedly, it has a disparaging overtone, implying something of a freewheeling character, adrift from his or her institutional or collegial obligations. But it might also be used to convey the idea of an academic willing to take up a bold independent stance, outside the disciplinary currents of the age. Indeed, autonomy has been seen as a general virtue in philosophical thought of the Western world. Much ink has been spilt within the philosophy of education in proclaiming the virtues of promoting autonomy among those on the receiving end in the education system, from the youngest of school pupils.[12] There is, though, something of a paradox here. Educators want to develop autonomy in those who pass through. But there seems something faintly quirky about trying to describe someone who is well-educated as 'autonomous'.

Where does all this get us? In many respects, over the past 40 years, UK academic institutions have experienced a significant loss in their autonomy.[13] As the new funding councils for the universities and for the polytechnics and colleges develop systems of contracting, the institutions' room for manoeuvre in the subjects they offer may diminish further as their programme performance and their accounting arrangements are subjected to ever closer scrutiny. Both sectors have long experienced the eye of professional bodies, which accredit the degree courses designed to produce recruits for their profession. It is not impossible, too, that an overarching agency with responsibility for quality assurance will eventually be established to perform for the whole system something of the role performed by the Council for National Academic Awards for the public sector. And the part played by Her Majesty's Inspectorate in monitoring and advising on the quality of work in higher education has recently begun to increase in a remarkable way.

All these interventions have an impact on the internal life of institutions; and, arguably, not all are of a deleterious character. But academics are not yet told who to admit, precisely which books or theories to teach or to avoid, how to teach and which methods of assessment to adopt.[14] The question 'Can academic freedom survive?' is a matter of determining whether academic institutions can reach a *modus vivendi* with the state.[15] For the moment, most essential academic freedoms remain, and the question can be answered in the affirmative, with the tongue only slightly in the cheek.

The present position, then, is that institutional autonomy is still such that there are no serious external constraints in the way of students' right to learn. Academics have no excuse not to provide students with the academic freedoms outlined earlier. The onus lies with them in the first place, because the design of the programmes of study is their responsibility. Given a willingness on the part of the academic community, all the student freedoms I have cited – from the right of applicants to have their experiential learning taken into account in the admissions process, through allowing students a significant measure of control over their curriculum, to submitting to an assessment regime which is explicitly designed to allow students to do justice to the higher-order abilities they have acquired – could be assured to students. There are no state controls forbidding such developments, although we should acknowledge that some professional bodies do act in just this constraining manner.

Admittedly, providing these essential conditions for the students' growth will not by itself ensure that the sought-for maturation takes place. Students' personal autonomy cannot be guaranteed even by the best curriculum in the world. In the end, students in higher education have to give something of themselves.

An achievement concept

The debate over academic freedom has been structured as if attaining academic freedom is part of a zero-sum game. All too often, academic freedom is thought to be of such a form that its possession by one group implies its denial to another group. If the members of the academic community do not possess the rights in question, then they must belong to some other grouping, whether agencies of the state, local councillors, professional bodies or even students. It is as if academic freedom were a largely fixed commodity that was passed around among the groups contending for the right to make the key academic decisions.

In this chapter, I have shown that we do not have to think of academic freedom in this way. Although my major concern has been to rehabilitate the idea of students' academic freedom, I have also said sufficient to show that academic freedom cannot just be granted by one group or agency towards another. Ultimately, it has to be worked at so that its possibilities are realized fully by those who possess it. We saw earlier that academic freedom means not just rights, but responsibilities. To put it in more formal philosophical language, we can say that academic freedom is an achievement concept. If it is not to be mere rhetoric, then its scope has continually to be exercised and its limits stretched. Otherwise, the freedoms that it implies are likely to atrophy through lack of use.[16]

But we can say more than this. Far from being a zero-sum game, far from being fixed in the amount that is technically available, those in possession of academic freedom can go on continually expanding its scope. Just as the notion of civil rights has not been fixed in its eighteenth-century formulation but has undergone continuing expansion, so too with the rights that go with academic freedom. Our notions of who constitutes the academic community, the freedoms at stake, and the ways in which they might be protected, all develop over time. There is a further point to be made. The academic community depends upon, as the term implies, communication among its members. The forms of communication and the subjects thought proper for comment by members of the academic community also widen through time. For some years in the public sector and just beginning in the university sector, we see academics willing to have their teaching activities subjected to the face-to-face evaluation and commentaries of their peers. On top of this, it is always possible for the form of discourse to be made more open, so that all academics have a hearing, irrespective of their rank or reputation.

All this translates to the situation of the students and their right to learn. Indeed, we have already noted that allowing students the rights spelt out earlier is not sufficient for students' academic freedom to be taken up. That requires students to explore and exploit the freedoms given to them. Indeed, as in social history generally, the rights are likely to be given to them partly through the students pressing for them themselves. And the retention and widening of those rights – as we approach a new wave of expansion of higher education – will require a continual vigilance on the part of students. In the end, whether applicants have their experiential learning counted in the admissions process, or whether students go on expanding the degree of influence they exercise over the curriculum, will be up to them. In short, in the domain of *Lernfreiheit*, as well as *Lerfreiheit*, academic freedom is an achievement concept.

Personal autonomy

Finally, I return to my earlier comments about autonomy, in so far as they apply to students. The reader may have found those remarks somewhat quizzical, for I pointed out that while philosophers of education have advocated 'autonomy' as an outcome for the educator to aim at, there seemed something quirky about describing, say, a graduate who had just successfully completed a course as autonomous. I believe this discussion about academic freedom has helped to resolve the puzzle.

In effect, I have been saying that students' academic freedoms are necessary conditions in the realization of the emancipatory promise of higher education. What that points to, minimally, is a developmental process in which students are enabled to be critical and to be self-critical in an informed way. That kind of independence is not to be achieved by the student acting purely independently. Becoming educated in the way being argued for in this book requires a willingness and an ability to participate in a discussion oriented towards truth. It implies a sharing and an interchange of viewpoints. Certainly, to a degree, it is possible to educate oneself; and teachers in higher education often overestimate their own importance. But the independence being sought for in higher education, and for which the rights to learn are necessary conditions, is an independence of thought which is exercised within a dialogue with others. Ultimately, if it is to count, the independent thought or action has to be offered or at least to be open to others for their evaluation. In the world of work, this is one of the distinctions between the professional and the technician. Students' academic freedoms are reminders, then, of our hope that students will develop their own autonomy, but it is an autonomy exercised within a shared form of life.

Part 5

Restoring Higher Education

11

Beyond Teaching and Learning

Introduction

No book which offers an overarching educational theory of higher education can afford to neglect teaching and learning; or so it must seem. For surely they lie at the heart of higher education. Certainly, these matters – and particularly the student's learning – are unjustly neglected in the debate on higher education. We look at research, at structures, at planning, at evaluation, at the curriculum and, to a lesser extent, at teaching. Learning, though, seems hardly to figure, unless it is in technical discussions about its psychological character, and how it might be improved.[1] The place of learning and how we construe it is barely on the public agenda. We are not asking critical questions about learning.

This chapter might have been called 'higher learning'. Two reasons suggested otherwise. First, the phrase will appear odd to many, particularly in the UK. And some would think it pretentious. That reaction is a little parochial. It is certainly not so unusual in the USA, where we find books bearing the phrase in their titles.[2] One reason for its presence in the USA might be that the American higher education system is so heterogeneous, fulfilling such different functions and admitting such a diversity of students, that questions about the character of the learning experience arise naturally. Analogously, as the comparatively uniform character of British higher education begins to dissolve, so questions are arising in the UK about the aims and character of student learning. In this context, the phrase 'higher learning' is particularly helpful, because it prompts us to ask whether in higher education there is anything especially 'higher' about the learning we expect students to achieve.

I shall argue that there is. But my argument will be double-edged; and this brings me to the second reason for discounting 'higher learning' as a chapter title. Strictly speaking, learning as such is not part of the idea of higher education. Obviously, learning has to go on in our institutions of higher education, but the idea of higher education points to a separate aspect of personal development. The learning that goes on in higher education justifies the label 'higher' precisely because it refers to a state of mind over and above conventional recipe or factual learning. Learning is necessary; but it is not part of what is meant by higher education. What counts for the sake of higher education is the student's ability to understand what is learned or what is done, to conceptualize it, to grasp it under different aspects, and to take up critical stances in relation to it.

Learning, then, is a misnomer, or at least an inadequate way of construing higher education. That much the reader may have gathered from the argument so far. But there are issues here worth exploring further.

The concept of learning

There is a weak sense of 'learning' in which the student is taught or the student reads that x is so and so. Tests would show that the student can recall that x is so and so, can write it down and can repeat it orally. Perhaps much learning in the natural sciences, in the medical sciences and in technology is like this. The student is faced with an overwhelming amount of material to get through, in an exceedingly short time. (Medical students are given just 8 weeks for a unit on obstetrics and gynaecology, for example.)

There is also a strong sense of 'learning', in which the student identifies with the truth claim he or she is faced with, and can offer it (for example, back to the consultant physician) as something with which he or she had personal experience (having had an opportunity to examine some patients). This stronger sense of learning also carries with it the idea that ultimately the student is able to evaluate it for him or herself, and form a personal view about its validity (by reading the relevant articles, by listening to the different views of the authorities on the topic, and perhaps by assisting in a clinical trial).

Some will say that that is all very well as a conceptual distinction. But, the critic may sense, in some subject areas it is simply not appropriate to expect students to form a view of their own. In medical education, or in the teaching of some scientific or technological subjects, it could actually be dangerous. When it comes to saving lives or building bridges, the last thing we want is for un-informed and inexperienced students to form their own ideas. Well, yes and no.

It is obvious that students should not believe that their own ideas by themselves are valid. In our earlier discussion of truth (see Chapter 4), we saw that it is not available in any absolute sense; but this does not mean that 'anything goes'. Students' views are not necessarily as good as those of recognized authorities, but it is still essential that the ideas to which students hold should be their own. They should enter into those ideas, and see them from various angles. This is, after all, what we mean by 'understanding'. The ideas might even have come from elsewhere – their tutors, or books, or perhaps a tape/slide presentation – but the student has to embrace them as his or her own if he or she is claiming them to be true. It is in this sense that we can speak of students forming their own ideas. And that is a general point, which holds across all disciplines, whether English or engineering, whether mathematics or medicine.

Admittedly, disciplines vary in the extent to which a personal response is expected of students. In poetry, it is the student's direct response which is called for. Any response which is offered as a result of reading it in a work of literary criticism would be unacceptable. In medicine, however, it is precisely the current thinking in the field that one is after. But these differences mask more important underlying similarities in student learning.

Take English literature, and recall Leavis' point to which I have referred before. In offering his or her response, the student should be doing so in a spirit of 'this is so, isn't it?' Students should stand ready to explain and to defend their views; and to listen to counter views and take up a further position if the balance of the contending positions points that way. That, as we saw in Chapter 4, is the nature of truth: it is a continuing discourse, in which rival views are taken forward. So, in the humanities, students' views are neither the beginning nor the end; they are based on evidence and understanding, and are subject to assessment by the students themselves and by others.

Move back now to medical education. Even though we want the judgements of young doctors to be securely based on the evidence, we want to feel that they have not just assiduously acquired the necessary knowledge, but also have immediate first-hand understanding of it in practice, having conducted patient examinations, observed relevant operations, and so forth. When more or less alone at night in the casualty ward, the doctor needs to be able to make up his or her own mind, and exercise judgement about the particular features presented by the accident victim just wheeled in. There has, then, in the higher education curriculum, to be major elements of immediate experience and personal responsibility even in the fields where students are having to work extraordinarily hard simply to acquire formal knowledge. All these elements can be found in the best of medical education, most notably in McMaster University in Canada, where students pose their own problems and use the resources of the university to solve them.[3]

What does all this amount to? Simply that in higher education, we expect students to go beyond the material they encompass and to form their own affinity with it. Learning that x is not sufficient – simply being able to recall a Shakespearean play, or a formula for a chemical compound, or the artists who were members of a particular school of painting, is not what higher education is about. We want students to show that they have entered into what they have learned. Insight, involvement and reflection are called for, not learning as such. The learning has to be transcended. Students have to show that they understand what has been learned so deeply that they are able to look down on it and assess it critically for themselves. Even if the student is not able to come up with alternative offerings of his or her own, at least he or she can say with some honesty: 'I believe that to be the case, and this is why.'

What bearing does this have on practical parts of the curriculum? It cuts in opposing directions. Whether we have in mind the student teacher, or the art student in the studio, or the student nurse, practical experience necessarily calls for a degree of personal involvement by the student and to that extent it is desirable. But practice can mean going through the motions just as much as accumulating factual knowledge. Admittedly, not all practical activities are as routine as many laboratory techniques; they often have a degree of openendedness built into them, demanding a personal response from the student. Even so, the student can respond in a relatively unthinking or unreflective way. For that reason, the model adopted in medical education where the student is continually asked to articulate his or her experience and give reasons for acting in a certain way is particularly valuable. It is an approach now being taken up increasingly, too, in teacher education;[4] and could be countenanced much more in other practically oriented curricula.

The general point is this. Whether we have in mind the student learning that such and such is the case, or learning how to do such and such, we look to the student to rise above the learning. There is the learning, and there is the critical evaluation of it. Logically, critical reflection is 'higher' because it calls for a state of mind reflecting on that learning. And it is to that higher-order state of mind that learning in higher education must lead. Given these observations, 'higher learning' may appear an attractive term. But it is full of snares, for it can all too easily lead us to think that the learning characteristic of higher education is a sub-set of conventional learning.

I have tried to show in this discussion that higher learning is not learning at all in any familiar sense. Ordinarily, learning allows us to go on in the same way, to repeat what has been learned, whether it is a matter of fact (that London is the capital of England) or an action (driving a car in familiar circumstances). The question is whether the student can go on in unfamiliar circumstances, can exercise judgement, can be his or her own person.

Some who follow this line of thinking argue that if there is a form of learning wrapped up in 'higher learning', it is learning how to learn. There is truth in this, but it needs to be construed correctly. It is misleading if it means simply that students learn how to acquire conventional encyclopaedia-like knowledge for themselves. It is an acceptable shorthand if we understand by it that students learn how to form a relationship with what they learn. For the learning which students acquire is learning how to respond to what they encounter. They learn not to take things on trust, but to make sure they fully comprehend in order to make their own assessments. They learn how to form informed critical evaluations. And they learn how to place their learning in a wider context. All these forms of learning are not *learning that* such and such is the case, but *learning how* to do such and such. In short, to borrow a voguish term, they acquire the competencies which are characteristic of higher education.

On this reading of higher learning, it is no accident that philosophy, fine art and the humanities generally are feeling the need to justify themselves. It is there, above all, that we see these independent intellectual capacities encouraged, and it is there that the gaze of the state is felt most keenly. One consequence of the bleak winds sensed is that the advocates of these disciplines turn to showing just how useful they really are; or could be, with a little tinkering of the curriculum, with a little information technology here, an element of 'transferable skills' there. Such manoeuvring, though, is symptomatic of the distrust which they face, and reflects less on them than on the dominant culture of the age. It needs to be firmly said that these essentially non-instrumental disciplines do not constitute a dilettante add-on to higher education, unnoticed if lost. Precisely because they promote higher-order capacities from the students, where the students are expected to place their experiences in a wider context of values and social affairs, these studies contribute vitally to the expansion of the collective consciousness of society. Any diminution in their role within higher education is bound, therefore, to have the effect of 'closing the British mind'.[5] But to make that observation is nothing less than to point to one way in which the UK is becoming a less open society.

Authority

Surely, in higher education if nowhere else, we find people who are rightly termed authorities. They have demonstrated publicly, through close scrutiny by their peers, that they know what they are talking about. They have mastered some corpus of knowledge, however small, and have probably made some contribution of their own to its development. In turn, so it might seem, they are rightly in authority when it comes to teaching. That, after all, is part of what we mean by 'professor': x is so on top of his or her subject that he or she has something to profess, to convey, to teach.

Even if the premiss is sound, the conclusion does not follow. If we recall the earlier section on knowledge, the idea of a single individual reaching a secure position of authority in relation to knowledge is dubious to say the least. But put aside the question-begging character of the premiss, and turn instead to the conclusion.

It by no means follows from the fact that x is a recognized authority in a discipline or professional field that x has authority to teach. Richard Peters once distinguished between a teacher being an authority and being in authority.[6] I would put the distinction I am making slightly differently. The authority which x derives from his expertise in a particular subject – as granted by his peers in the academic community – and x's authority to teach are different kinds of authority. In higher education, students are present normally of their own volition, whatever the pressure felt from parents and their own social circles. Also, as the 18-year-old cohort dips, students become a valuable commodity: institutions of higher education are increasingly conscious that students could up sticks and transfer to another institution. And students are, after all, adults, with many entering higher education for the first time in their middle age, or even beyond.

All this brings out that teachers in higher education teach partly on sufferance. If the students do not value their learning experience, they can go elsewhere. As a matter of fact, their programme of studies is a legal contract with their institution, the institution being required to provide a reasonable quality of course. But irrespective of the legal position, the character of the teaching process is such that higher education teachers have to pay attention to the expectations and perceptions of their students.

What is so special about higher education as opposed to any other part of the educational system? In one sense, there is nothing special about it. Whether primary, secondary or adult education, the teaching situation is a human transaction, an interchange between persons. For any teaching to be effective, learning and understanding have to occur on the part of the pupil or student. This in itself is a salutary reminder that x's authority in a discipline is not sufficient to generate her authority as a teacher. For that, there has to be some evidence that the pupils or students are responding to what is put before them. In all educational settings, authority as a teacher has to be earned in one's effectiveness as a teacher.

There are additional dimensions to the authority of teachers in higher education. There is the point already implied. Higher education students are adults. They have minds of their own and will form their own views on what is put before them. This means that lecturers and tutors will have to find ways of connecting with their students' outlooks. Any falling short in doing so reflects more on the teaching than on the students' preparedness to respond. The onus of making that interpersonal connection between their differing maps of the mind must rest in the first place with the staff, not with the student.

There is an even more telling reason why, in higher education, the teacher's authority has to be won and cannot be presumed. This connects with my earlier account of truth. I have said that for a student to make a truth claim, whether original or not, the student has to own it. He or she has to believe it, and to be able to back it up with reasons which he or she also believes. Commitment and sincerity both enter into truth claims. This is so whether we have in mind the validity of a propositional truth claim, or the satisfactoriness of an action in the domain of professional education. But if this is to occur, the teaching relationship must be sufficiently open for students to invest something of themselves in what it is they say or do.

It follows that authoritarian teaching relationships and the passive assimilation of knowledge can have no part in higher education. And the fact that we have a particular vocabulary of 'tutor', 'lecturer', 'professor' and indeed 'student' is testimony to the particular character of the teacher–learner relationship. There is, however, a difference between teacher and taught. Recognizing the non-absolute character of knowledge does not mean that the lecturer and the student are equal in their epistemological authority. But if students are to be encouraged to weigh things up for themselves, to form their own views, and to articulate them with their own reasons, then it is also incumbent on their lecturers and tutors to offer their own truth claims to their students in the spirit of 'this is so, isn't it?' (to use again Leavis' central question). To borrow an important phrase from Paulo Freire, there has to be a 'dialogic relationship' between tutor and student.[7]

Admittedly, the epistemological weight of the relationship will almost always rest with the lecturer. However, with open learning and project work in undergraduate work, and with postgraduate work, the relationship will often approximate to one of equality.

The conclusion to be drawn from this discussion is that, in higher education, authority has a reciprocal aspect. And in two senses. First, the authority of the lecturer in the teaching relationship has to be to some degree granted by the student. Students have to be willing to work under the direction of the lecturer. They have to agree that what they hear and see is meaningful to them, connects with their universe of meanings, and is offered in an acceptable way. To this extent, the teacher's authority is conferred by the student; the student can always say 'no thanks'. Secondly, students have to make their own connections in understanding what they experience on their programme of studies. The student has to be able to say: I understand this for myself; I can assent to this, but not that. In other words, students have to reach a position of some authority themselves.

These are not just nice philosophical points. They have practical importance. In Chapter 9, we saw how expertise in research is different from expertise in teaching. This discussion has confirmed that view, though from another angle. Teaching effectively in higher education calls for the extraordinary ability on the part of the teacher to bring students to the point where they can distinguish sense from nonsense for themselves, where they can say and do things for themselves and give reasons for so doing which are full of insight, and where they have the intellectual resources to take off under their own steam. This means that whatever a lecturer's status as an authority in his or her own epistemic community, the lecturer also has to possess as a successful teacher the authority to manage effectively his or her students' learning.

Stages of higher learning

One of the exciting occurrences in higher education is seeing students becoming 'hooked' (in Marjorie Reeves' evocative terminology) on something of lasting value. Where it occurs, we see students wanting to be immersed in a body of knowledge on their own account and in their own way. This has both positive and limiting aspects.

From a positive standpoint, that kind of happening brings with it an educational experience with a particular degree of vitality. Words we might employ to describe that experience would include authenticity, first-handedness, liveliness and immediacy. In a higher education curriculum, second-handedness is eschewed. Whether in performing experiments, or in being directed to primary sources of evidence in history, or in becoming acquainted with the journal literature, or in designing artefacts to meet a design problem, we encourage students along the path of their own immediate experience.[8]

All this is desirable and, indeed, essential; but higher education cannot rest there. A genuine higher learning is subversive in the sense of subverting the student's taken-for-granted world, including the world of endeavour, scholarship, calculation or creativity, into which he or she has been initiated. A genuine higher education is unsettling; it is not meant to be a cosy experience. It is disturbing because, ultimately, the student comes to see that things could always be other than they are. A higher education experience is not complete unless the student realizes that, no matter how much effort is put in, or how much library research, there are no final answers. Indeed, the realization should come that there are all sorts of rival positions, and that there is no absolute way of choosing between them.

Some observers describe this process as one of 'cognitive dissonance'. The term is certainly helpful, conveying something of the psychological unsettling that can occur, but it does not capture the full extent of what might take place. The notion of cognitive dissonance suggests the countering of one entrenched view of the world with another; so the student is faced with a difficult choice. That happens. But even more, the student should come to understand that there are an infinite number of frameworks with which to describe the world; and that none has any binding claim over the others. In short, knowledge is 'relative'.

Again, though, higher education cannot rest there. The student may come to appreciate that each concept, or theory or professional practice is set within a particular framework of thought or action. The student may be able to stand back and to relativize his or her own learning. But it is crucial that the student is not, as a result, paralysed into inaction.[9] The student has to be able to take yet a further step, and to be able to take up stances, hold to particular theories, or simply to act. There has to be a moment of personal insight, in which critical evaluation is not put aside but is transcended. In that moment, the student is freed to make decisions, to make judgements about the balance of the evidence, or to opt for a particular course of action. Far from being insipid, fence-sitting or unduly critical, a fully effective graduate student is able to choose, to believe and to act with 'authoritative uncertainty'.[10]

This sketch of a student's intellectual development has followed the student through the stages of assimilating encountered knowledge; deep understanding; recognition of its provisionality and contested character; exercising critical judgement; being sensitive to other knowledge forms, and relativizing one's own experience; and taking a personal stand. There is here a progressive intellectual maturity,[11] whereby the student gains but breaks through relativism and critical thinking, to attain a position of creative independence. This conception of progressive intellectual maturity has emerged from the philosophical argument of this book, but it is far from being a purely philosophical viewpoint. It bears a close affinity to the work of W. G. Perry, whose detailed analysis of student development is based on considerable empirical work in the USA.[12]

A deep learning experience

Admittedly, not every student passes through all the intellectual stages I have just identified. Also, courses in some subjects are perhaps more prone to arrest their students' development. The evidence is unclear as to whether there is a science–humanities divide here. It would not be surprising if there were; if science courses tended to act as a brake on students' intellectual formation. Science courses are overpacked with factual material which students cannot evade. Those courses also tend to confine students' reading to purpose-written textbooks, which contain applications of currently espoused theories. Those texts are *not* intended to promote students' engagement and critical thinking but, instead, are intended to initiate students into the culture of the scientific discipline in question. As Kuhn describes it:

> science students accept theories on the authority of teacher and text. What alternatives have they . . . ? The applications given in texts are not there as evidence, but because learning them is part of learning the paradigm at the base of current practice.[13]

However, other subjects may not be immune from corresponding limitations. Courses in the humanities may encourage a personal response from the students, but do they always open up a full range of rival positions? Courses in the technologies and the professions may encourage action but, again, is it always action based on an awareness of the alternatives, their value positions and their social consequences?

Arguably, the most productive area of research into higher education over the past 20 years is that concerned with student learning.[14] It has been an international effort, with key work conducted in England, Scotland, Sweden, the USA and Australia. The conceptual framework it has produced is particularly pertinent to the discussion here. The research has focused on students' learning strategies, and has developed a typology of them. Two pairs of concepts have been elaborated in the light of empirical work conducted in actual curricular settings. Learning strategies are described within a *surface–deep* axis, depending on whether students simply attempt to cover the ground, routinely assimilating and reproducing what is put before them; or whether they are interested in gaining a deep understanding of the material. Learning strategies are also characterized along a *holistic–atomistic* axis, corresponding to attempts by the student to form a view of a programme of study as a whole; or to an approach geared merely to understanding each element as it is encountered.[15]

This research programme is of fundamental importance for higher education. It has practical significance, because much of the work within the programme has shown how the total curriculum experience – of which teaching methods are a part – affects the strategies which students adopt. Their learning strategies are not just personal responses, but partly predictable and rational responses to the situation in which they find themselves. Talk by lecturers of students developing their critical abilities is just cant when students are obliged to adopt atomistic and surface approaches just to assimilate and reproduce the course content, and where they are expected to spend many hours every day in the laboratory or to complete an essay every week, and to sit ten or more 3-hour papers in 2 weeks.

The deep and holistic approaches adopted by students to their learning are very much implied by the conception of higher education developed here, which has stressed the importance of personal understanding and critical insight. What is regrettable, though, is that the research programme has continued to describe such a wide range of student responses under the same term – 'learning'. Describing both passive assimilation and critical reflection as 'learning' – and therefore all student efforts as 'learning' – overlooks the wide gulf between the responses students can make. This has two unfortunate results.

First, the conception of what might pass under the heading of 'learning' falls short of the possible process of intellectual development. The range of student 'learning' strategies explored covers only some of the lower and intermediate stages of intellectual growth I have just outlined. The work of Perry, with his stages of cognitive growth, is acknowledged within the research programme, but justice is hardly done to it. Gaining and breaking through a relativized understanding of knowledge requires a conception of human intellectual independence and an epistemological sophistication which the term 'student learning' cannot sensibly be stretched to cover.

Secondly, the use of the single term 'learning' fails to suggest the radical change in approach and attitude required of staff in institutions, if students are to be enabled to pass through all the possible stages of intellectual growth. For what is being implied is nothing short of a paradigm shift wherein students and their intellectual capabilities come to occupy the central ground. We need to move from the concepts of knowledge, teaching and learning to the idea of students making their own journey ultimately to a position of intellectual independence. Knowledge, teaching and learning are only justified in so far as they contribute to that much more ambitious end.

Theory, practice and competence

In Chapter 2, we saw that the tension between liberal education, with knowledge considered 'as its own end', and a more utilitarian conception of higher education was central to the nineteenth-century debate. That tension is still with us, but overlaid on it are two others. The first is that of the relationship between theory and practice, about which much has been heard since the Second World War as higher education has been used more and more as an entry route by professions seeking higher status.

The second is more recent still. It is the growing clamour from industry for the graduates it employs to have more work-related skills, and the ensuing tension with the mainstream curriculum. The demand is not always expressed in consistent terms. Sometimes, occupation-specific skills are called for; on other occasions, more diffuse skills are sought. A number of national or quasi-national bodies have entered the arena, each with its own vocabulary. We have seen that, in the UK, the Training Agency has initiated a major Enterprise in Higher Education scheme. Other comparable UK initiatives are taking place: the Royal Society of Arts is sponsoring a Higher Education for Capability programme; the National Council for Vocational Qualifications, with its ideas on a competency based curriculum, is beginning to turn to higher education; and the Council for Industry and Higher Education talks of developing the students' personal transferable skills.

These are signs of what may turn out to be a dramatic, if almost unnoticed, revolution in the higher education curriculum. We are long past the stage where talk about the curriculum could be left to the academics; beyond the stage where the views of the professions and the wider society had to be sought. Now we have reached the situation where, in effect, external agencies are having a major and virtually direct impact on the curriculum. I argued in Chapter 5 that the image of the ivory tower in no way describes the contemporary position of higher education. These recent developments are testimony to that view.

How can we make sense of these developments in terms of the student experience? First, it should be clear that the idea of higher education being developed here is not opposed to a curriculum oriented to the worlds of action, of work and of the professions. From its medieval origins, when it provided an intellectual grounding for those intending to earn their living in the law, the church and medicine, higher education has been ready to acknowledge the wider society which sustains it. So the development of skills, whether relatively broad or occupationally specific, is not an issue in itself. The state is now determined to move the curriculum further in that direction, and it may well have to be accepted as a fact of life, of sheer survival.

The question, though, and this is the second point, is the relationship of those utilitarian elements with the curriculum. The medieval student's studies included rhetoric; and today we see institutions preparing to develop 'self-presentational' skills in their students.[16] But the practical components of the curriculum, whether in the medieval university or in courses of professional education as they developed after the Second World War, have been subsidiary elements in a much wider programme of studies; *and* they have an internal connection with the general programme of theoretical studies. We might expect students of dance or music to engage in practical activities, but their theoretical studies are, by and large, directly related to those activities.

The danger of the current developments is two-fold: that they are likely to lead to the curriculum becoming dominated by technique; and that the techniques in question are imported from the outside world, and are imposed arbitrarily upon, and unconnected with, the curriculum.

One polytechnic has resolved that all its humanities degree students shall acquire some appreciation of computers and information technology. This makes perfectly good sense, *provided* that that understanding is organically linked to their studies. This may well be possible: there is hardly a field of study in which computers do not have a valuable role to play. But if it were simply a matter of providing skills to make their students more employable, that would be a much more dubious enterprise. The UK polytechnics have performed a signal service to higher education by showing how professional education can be developed, with practice being placed firmly in a framework of systematic intellectual exploration. Now, though, a tendency is developing in which the idea of 'polytechnic education' is being reduced from 'many arts, many skills' to simply 'many skills'.[17] 'Practice' need not be eschewed as part of higher education; but its presence in the curriculum must be justified in terms of the opportunities it affords for the student's critical reflection. Some of the present developments seem to be running counter to that fundamental principle.

The student as reflective practitioner

Over recent years, in the field of professional education, Donald Schon (1983) in the USA has developed an idea bearing the name of 'the reflective practitioner'. The idea has become both powerful and productive, but is in essence simple. It is that, in their various fields, professionals rarely act through any explicit theory or articulated principles governing professional practice, and much more on the basis of tacit principles and knowledge which are embedded in their professional behaviour. In Schon's terminology, if you want to find out how professionals act, look not to their 'espoused theories' but to their 'theories-in-use'.

This way of conceiving of professional practice has profound implications for professional education. It implies that a curriculum which first offers students theoretical components, and then expects them to put the theory 'into practice' in the practical situation, is misconceived. Instead, it suggests that the balance of curriculum elements should be reversed, with the student learning how to practise as a professional, and that the 'theory' should be derived by inviting the student to reflect on the practice to tease out the principles embedded in it.[18]

This way of looking at professional education is having a considerable impact on many fields. For example, both student teachers and student nurses are being expected to spend more time in the professional setting, and are being encouraged to appraise their own actions and to be explicit and articulate about what they are doing and why.

The point of mentioning this development is not to launch on a digression about professional education, important though that is. Its presence here has a different purpose. The argument of this chapter amounts to the proposition that *every* student is or should be a 'reflective practitioner'. The student has his or her subject field with its own knowledge corpus, and is, it is to be hoped, sufficiently interested to become immersed in it. But the promise of the student's higher education is realized when the student is able to raise him or herself out of that state of 'delight' (to borrow again from Marjorie Reeves) and to reflect on what he or she is doing and thinking.

Only in that moment of self-reflection can any real state of intellectual freedom be attained; and then only to a limited degree. Only through such a position of critical self-evaluation can the restricted epistemological validity of one's position, and its possible ideological strains, be recognized for what it is. Only through becoming a continuing 'reflective practitioner' can the student – and graduate – avoid succumbing naively to conventional 'wisdom'. And only in that way will the student gain a measure of personal integrity.

Conclusions

There are welcome signs that teaching and learning are being taken more seriously in improving the quality of higher education.[19] Staff development, focused on teaching effectiveness, is now undertaken systematically by many institutions of higher education. There are signs, too, of an interest in the character of student learning. Two qualifications are needed, though. 'Learning' has always been, and continues to be, subservient to 'teaching', in higher education debate and action.[20] Sometimes, to show that learning is not forgotten, the two terms are run together in the phrase 'teaching and learning', as if they are the same kind of activity with similar aims. That assumption, as we have seen in this chapter, is illegitimate. The other qualification is that the manifold capabilities which fall under the umbrella term 'learning' are not sufficiently understood.

These are not accidental oversights on the part of the academic community. For if learning was put ahead of teaching in the discourse of higher education, and if the independence, creativity and personal endeavour which are part of learning were addressed; if both were taken on board seriously, what would be implied would be a major challenge to the power relations in higher education, between those who teach and those who are taught.

The learning that is characteristic of higher education is not all of a piece; some of it is not properly described by the limited concept of learning. Each student should be embarked on a journey involving succeeding stages of intellectual maturity and independence. For that to happen, students have to be given some space in which to develop intellectually in their own way. From time to time, curricula should be reviewed and, if necessary, pruned even of so-called necessary material. If students are to exercise personal judgements, they have to be given a measure of personal responsibility for their work. And if they are to develop critical abilities, and to see their work in a wider perspective, that too must be built into the curriculum and not just expected to happen. Serendipity is no substitute for the exercise of self-denying decisions on the part of those who see themselves as being paid to teach.

12

A Critical Business

Introduction

If there is a single key concept in the idea of higher education, it is 'criticism'. That, by itself, is not saying very much. Almost everyone these days seems to be in favour of developing students' critical abilities, from the students themselves, through the academic community, to the government, employers and professional bodies.[1] The reason that so many different interest groups, with their contrasting standpoints, can apparently unite in this way is obvious enough. The notion of 'critical abilities' is susceptible to a wide range of interpretations. As with most things of interest, it depends what we mean by critical abilities.

It could mean students developing a flexibility of mind and attitude that is appropriate to their future careers in the worlds of commerce, industry and the professions. Given the challenge of competitive international markets, the corporate world, at least in its rhetoric, is keen to recruit bright graduates who as managers will be able to turn a critical eye on established practices.[2] Many professions, too, are very ready to affirm their weddedness to the value of the critical attitude: there is a growing sense, at least among the senior echelons, that tradition is all very well, but it can act as a brake on necessary change.[3] A third perception of 'critical abilities' comes from the disciplines of the academic world. There, an awareness exists that the critical attitude is fundamental to the growth of academic knowledge.[4] A further formulation might come from those who hold to a wider sense of the mission of higher education. For some, the development of the student's critical abilities is central to liberal education, with its emphasis on developing the student's autonomy.[5] Finally, there are those of a Marxist persuasion, who look to higher education enabling students to form a critical perspective on society and social affairs, and on that basis to effect radical social change.[6]

So, there are a range of senses which attach to the idea of the student's critical abilities, reflecting different value positions. However, in this chapter, I do not want to tackle any of those perceptions head on. Instead, I want to try to develop a further view of what it means to see criticism as a significant feature of higher education.

Despite their manifest differences, all five views that I have just sketched out are united in that none of them hangs or falls on the notion of critical abilities. While, for each, the idea of critical abilities is important, it is one feature among others. For example, in professional education, professional competence is equally important, if not more so. In the Marxist idea of education, attention is also given to open access, and to combining theory with practice for all students with a view to effecting social change. And in the liberal idea of education, equal account might be taken of student choice and breadth of study. Here, the argument I want to make is more than that critical thought is an important feature of higher education. I want to develop the stronger thesis that criticism is the essence of higher education.

The idea of criticism

One cannot be critical in the abstract: one has to be critical of some *thing*. And the act of criticism takes place in the context of standards.[7] So much so, that in the conventional use of the term, 'being critical' has come almost exclusively to mean that the object or action in question has fallen short of the standards in question. This is as much unnecessary as it is undesirable; critical evaluation can lead to positive assessments, just as much as to negative ones. The assumption that criticism has to lead to a negative evaluation is particularly unfortunate in higher education. For students all too easily feel that they have to come up with negative assessments if their appraisals are to be worth anything. They fail to grasp that what is required is their own detailed response to what is before them.

Granted a context of standards, what is the logic of appraising something? Why, in higher education, do we tend to associate this kind of intellectual activity more with the performing arts, the humanities and the social sciences, and with professional education, than with the pure sciences and the technologies? There is a logic to this differentiation, for critical evaluation only makes sense where the object in question could be other than it is. The standards we bring to bear in the act of appraisal have their purchase precisely because the act, or artefact, or creation, or social institution is not fixed, but has a degree of mutability about it. For that reason, the exercise of critical abilities in the sciences is bound to be more restricted than in the arts and the humanities. But it is far from being absent. While it makes little sense to talk of criticism of the physical world, it makes every sense to talk of criticism turned on to the theories and concepts which science has produced to explain the external world, for they could certainly be other than they are.[8] Unfortunately, we sometimes give the impression in science and technological education that the current models, terms and theories of science are given and have merely to be assimilated by students. There are, then, no fields of knowledge or endeavour where critical thought does not have a purchase.

Criticism has application, therefore, in a relatively open situation where things could be otherwise, but there is more to it than that. Language is a social institution of a kind; and self-evidently it is open to all sorts of change. It is also subject to all kinds of criticism; not just listeners to Radio Four, but the employers of graduates speak disapprovingly of the way the English language is spoken. But the deep grammatical structure of language, as revealed by Chomsky for instance, is not susceptible to criticism in quite the same way.[9] Why is this? The answer is that it lacks human agency or human intention. This suggests that critical evaluation has point where the object in question is attributable to some person or group of persons. That is why we find it employed in relation to an action, a belief, a theory, a performance, or an artistic creation. For in all those cases, human agency is clearly at work.

Let us go back to the point about criticism taking place against a background of criteria. Often, the criteria – even in the academic world – are assumed, and are hardly brought out into the open. Polanyi, we saw earlier, has drawn attention to the 'tacit' knowledge by which even scientists with their supposedly elaborated codes proceed in their work. Look, too, at the process by which students are assessed: very rarely do examiners in higher education try to identify explicitly the criteria by which they are going to examine. Evaluation, then, may require prior criteria against which the evaluation can be made; but that does not mean that we can give a full and detailed account of those criteria.

Another way of putting it is that even though the academic community is founded on a culture of critical discourse (see Chapter 7), normally it gives little thought to the criteria by which its critical judgements come into play. Why is that? The answer is that the criteria are built into the traditions of the separate disciplinary communities. And being part of the tradition, they are part of the way of going on in those sub-cultures. Physicists and historians do not, by and large, spend much time reflecting on their own criteria, the criteria by which their form of thought moves on. They just get on practising their trade. It is only in embryonic forms of thought, or professional fields trying to establish themselves (paramedical areas), or subjects where there is a lot of infighting (sociology), where the standards of critical judgement come up for much review.

Two concepts of criticism

This leads us to a fundamental distinction in the character of critical judgements, a distinction between what I shall call internal and external criteria of judgement. For the most part, criteria of critical reasoning are internal to disciplines or professional fields, and rightly so. They may vary even within branches or specialisms. The tests of acceptability of the durability of a physical structure for a civil engineer may not be the same as those for an electronics engineer; the criteria in assessing human activity used by an experimental psychologist will contrast with those employed by a Jungian psychotherapist. But the key point is that the criteria by which academics approach theories, or artefacts or human actions, are criteria which are part of the discipline itself. In higher education, we naturally believe that a fundamental aspect of the student's programme of studies consists of getting the student on the inside of just such internal standards of reasoning in the discipline he or she is studying.

But in higher education, we hope that students will not just beaver away, in however committed a fashion, at their chosen discipline or profession. We also hope that, by the end of their course, students will be able to stand back, to see their core subject in a wider context, to have a sense of its development and how it relates to other subjects, and to have a due sense of its contribution to the world.

For that level of critical reasoning to be reached, criteria of evaluation which are internal to a discipline are inadequate. Whether the students (or the staff, for that matter) realize it, external criteria have to be taken on board. There is nothing extraordinary in this: it is a feature of any course which invites students seriously to reflect on whatever is in front of them. It could involve a civil engineering student considering the social effects of a new construction – in other words, taking on a sociological perspective; it could be a student of English trying to answer the question 'What is literature and why do we assume that it is a good thing?' – and so embracing the thinking of moral philosophy; it might be a student in the performing arts trying to understand how and why a particular tradition had evolved – so embarking on a historical study; it could be a chemistry student being invited to consider the effects on the natural environment of industrial or agricultural chemicals – so adding a biological approach to the subject; or it might be a social science student keen on human perspectives being encouraged to look at underlying statistical patterns.

There is nothing *outré* in any of this. All these examples are part and parcel of what we can encounter in higher education courses. In one sense, it simply reflects the notion of getting students to read widely in *and* around their subject. But the examples all have this feature of getting the student to appreciate that it is possible to approach the objects of interest within their subject – chemicals, human behaviour, literature, technology – from the perspective of an external discipline, and that it can be illuminating to do so.

How far external evaluation of this kind is introduced into a course must be a matter of judgement. The student has a legitimate interest in pursuing his or her own cognitive or practical interests, and in getting to grips with the internal demands of the core discipline. It is understandable if the core discipline(s), with their internal forms of evaluation, constitute the majority of the student's course. But a course which only consisted of getting the student on to the inside of one or more disciplines would not count as a course of higher education; it would merely be a training in those disciplines. The training, however high-level, is converted into higher *education* only when the student is able to form an independent evaluation of what he or she has learned or mastered, is able to put it into some kind of perspective, and is able to see not only its strengths but also its limitations.[10]

What is the justification for this claim? How can the essence of higher education lie in those elements of the student's course which may well form a minority of his or her studies? The answer has two connected elements. First, the status of this kind of critical evaluation by the student: it is literally a higher form of cognitive perspective, in which the critical reflection enables the student to form a view of his or her learning. Secondly, there is a fundamental connection between critical reasoning of this kind, and the idea that the process of higher education can bring with it a new level of intellectual freedom for the student. In Chapter 2, I argued that the emancipatory conception of higher education – as I termed it – is to be found historically in the deep structure of the concept of higher education (and I developed the idea in Chapter 8, in discussing emancipation as the highest form of rationality). What, though, are the connections between criticism and this sense of intellectual freedom embedded in higher education?

At the basic level, of criticism internal to a discipline, the connection is straightforward. The first requirement in getting students to adopt a serious orientation to knowledge is that they come to care about truth.[11] Actually arriving at truth is more complicated than staff and students normally recognize (see Chapter 4). The requirement, though, is for the effort to be made, so that students come to appreciate the standards of truth and evaluation internal to the discipline. In being able to discriminate truth – or something approximating to it – from falsehood or nonsense, the student enters a state of intellectual freedom in relation to that portion of the world which is the focus of his or her studies.

The idea that the acquisition of truth brings with it freedom from dependency on naive perceptions, falsehoods and ignorance is a key ingredient in the liberal conception of education.[12] This is retained in the critical approach to knowledge. But the critical approach to knowledge goes further for, through it, the individual is even freed from uncritical acceptance of the intellectual view of the world. The graduate, for the rest of his or her life, will not be tied to glib or unsupported statements which might be encountered in the discipline. The graduate will not even be tied to the current set of accepted truths about the world in the discipline. He or she will be sensitive to the negotiated status of those truth claims; and will be aware that the truth claims are *claims*, subject to dispute by the disciplinary community in its continuing conversations.

In the critical approach to knowledge, both the commonsense view and the academic view of the world are seen as *views* and not as an absolute account of the world. The critical approach to knowledge brings with it a state of intellectual freedom, in which the individual is freed from unquestioning faith in *any* view of the world.

I have also pointed to external critique, where we try to get students to form a view of the object of their studies, employing a perspective other than their home discipline. The connection between this form of critique and freedom is more far-reaching still. Whereas the basic orientation of internal critique (of theories, propositions, practices, artefacts) is truth, the basic orientation of external critique is freedom itself.[13] For external critique is intended to show up the limitations of a form of thought as such. Specifically, it can uncover disciplinary partiality, ideology, hidden interests, professional skullduggery, deception and illusion.[14]

The examples of external critique I gave earlier show how this works in practice, but other more pointed examples can easily be identified. For instance, Gellner's attack on analytic philosophy from an anthropological perspective;[15]

the exposure of eugenics in 1930s psychology;[16] the connections between certain kinds of research in chemistry and the agricultural and food industries; the models of human motivation – often little more than employee manipulation – to be found in management studies;[17] Illich's critique of medicine;[18] and the underlying interest in control over the natural environment within the physical sciences. All these indicate the kind of critique that is possible when we employ a perspective other than that provided by the immediate discipline.

External critique is absolutely educative. It imparts a fresh way of seeing the familiar. It can also amount to a fundamental critique of the student's core discipline and, therefore, has to be handled with care, as it can be unsettling. In practice, this is seldom a worry. The more immediate concern is that the student's lecturers, who are themselves practitioners of the discipline, are hardly likely to mount a penetrating attack on their own intellectual home. They are not normally going to bite the hand that feeds them. The question for an institution of higher education, therefore, is how such an external perspective can be built into the curriculum. Built in – in some way – it must, if the full emancipatory promise of higher education is to be achieved. For, through that form of criticism, students can be freed from dependence on their own discipline, being able to see it for what it is, warts and all. It is through this form of critique that the student will reach the highest level of intellectual independence. And that, after all, is the ultimate point of higher education.

Critical thinking

Particularly in the USA, but also in the UK, we can see the signs of a movement developing around the belief in the value of critical thinking.[19] That movement is highly suspect, for two reasons.

First, at its core is the idea that critical thinking is a particular kind of intellectual activity in its own right. This is correct; but its adherents then go on to assume that critical thinking consists of a set of intellectual skills that can be exercised by themselves. We have, accordingly, a 'critical thinking' industry, with books and exercises intended to improve individuals' critical thinking; and other individuals who profess expertise in the field, and who claim to be able to teach it. But this is a non-starter. Any serious kind of criticism, as we have seen, is about something. There has to be something already in existence – a theory, a practice, an artefact – for criticism to have any purchase. As Richard Peters once remarked, 'Critical thought is vacuous without anything concrete to be critical about.'[20]

This leads to the second point. The belief that critical thinking can be practised meaningfully by itself, far from promoting critical thinking, as its proponents assume, only results in emasculating it. When turned on the major achievements of humanity, it can help to illuminate them, and can carry our understanding of the world forward. If kept in a small cul-de-sac by itself, it will be utterly benign.

That much may be granted, that critical thinking has to have something to work on if its impact is not to be marginalized. But a further response is sometimes encountered from those who seem to fear its potential power. This is the view that, because criticism works by being directed on existing knowledge claims, it follows that nothing *in general* can be said about criticism. The form that criticism takes has to be specific to its object. The kind of criticism that is appropriate in the performing arts is quite different from that in technology, which again differs from the nature of criticism in philosophy. In each field, the criteria are specific to the discipline in question.[21]

There is some truth in this argument, but it should not be pushed too far. Obviously, the first requirement in developing students' critical abilities is to get them immersed in the disciplines they are studying, and bring them to appreciate and to respect the internal criteria of evaluation – the kinds of evidence, criteria and values that are particular to each discipline. But the kind of criticism which I termed external critique is much less conditioned by the object under review and its conventional disciplinary home. Indeed, that is its point, that it draws on other criteria of evaluation.

The key tools of critique

So, external critique is both open and structured. We encourage students to draw on whatever disciplines will shed new light on the topic before them. In principle, any discipline can be called on in this way, as an intellectual resource which has the power of showing hidden ways of perceiving the object in question. There are, though, two disciplines in particular which are especially powerful in generating an external critique of a discipline: philosophy and sociology.

They are the most powerful because they can most effectively expose the discipline for what it is. Again, this need not be a destructive exercise. Philosophy can, for example, bring to light a discipline's tests for truth, and the criteria by which truth claims are normally evaluated. Sociology, especially if coupled with a historical perspective, can help reveal the positive social interests which lie behind the effort invested by society in the discipline and the inclusion of the discipline in courses in institutions of higher education. In gaining those insights, students may well develop an enhanced appreciation of their home discipline; they will certainly gain an improved understanding of its inner composition.

In suggesting that philosophical and sociological perspectives be added to the curriculum, I am not proposing that discrete packages of philosophy or sociology be introduced. On no account should that happen, for it would simply bring additional corpuses of closed knowledge into the course of study. Nor is it being suggested that students become embryonic philosophers or sociologists, adroit in handling the concepts and techniques of those disciplines. Students can be introduced to epistemological issues without ever using the term 'epistemology'. What *is* required is that students are helped to see beneath the surface appearance of their core discipline; and that the concepts and perspectives of philosophy and sociology are valuable in bringing about that exposure of the discipline.[22]

Philosophy has value in two ways: first, in helping the student to form an understanding of the character of knowledge claims in the student's discipline; and, secondly, in giving the student a framework in which to pose value questions of the course of studies. The types of question a philosophical perspective could prompt might include:

1. What is the dominant mode of knowledge within the discipline? Is it propositional or non-propositional? If it is rooted in a view of man interacting with his environment, what is the character of those interactions? Or is it a more contemplative picture of man?
2. What are the criteria or values by which the student's home discipline 'progresses'? To what extent are they inconsistent? Are there examples of favoured theories which reflect some criteria, while other – perhaps discarded – theories reflect others? Are there examples of successful theories which have not done justice to any of the espoused criteria?
3. To what degree is the knowledge corpus of the discipline 'objective'?
4. What are the modes of reasoning of the particular epistemic community?
5. What are the tacit presuppositions of the discipline? Do they assist the progress of the discipline, or act as an undue constraint?

The value of the sociological perspective is that it enables students to see why society believes in the discipline in question. The student can understand that the discipline is not given in any absolute sense, but has been socially formed and reflects interests both of rival factions within the disciplinary culture and of the wider society.[23] Typical of the questions a sociological perspective might prompt are:

1. How extensive across the world is the discipline? What different forms does it take in different societies? What is its place in the social hierarchy of knowledge?
2. To what extent is it an open discipline? How many journals does it have? What are their editorial policies? Can individuals with a distinctive point of view get a hearing?
3. What are the rival viewpoints within the discipline? Are the competing views purely academic debates, or do they also reflect wider social interests?
4. What are the fundamental social interests of the discipline? To what extent is it one of control (whether of the natural environment or of the human environment)?

There are three points to be made about these examples. First, the questions are at least as important as the answers. Simply in being posed, and their force understood, the students' education is advanced. At the same time, students are freed from a blind faith in their home discipline, and their intellectual perspectives are broadened. (To borrow a metaphor from Chapter 2, they come out of Plato's cave.)

Secondly, these are critical questions in two senses. On the one hand, the questions are oriented towards exposing the discipline, bringing into the open its hidden character. On the other hand, the student comes to realize that the discipline could be other than it is (and, indeed, historically has been wedded to different values and presuppositions).

Finally, introducing inquiries of this kind into the curriculum has to be accomplished by being thoroughly integrated with the student's core studies. It is not that students will get turned off by being given unconnected dollops of philosophy and sociology, and it is not that bringing in specialists in philosophy and sociology will lead to an incoherent curriculum, although both are true. It is that such questions can only be properly pursued in the company of the disciplinary studies. The critical questions have to be turned on to the discipline and relevant examples furnished from within the discipline. For that reason, too, such investigations should be directed by the mainstream staff themselves. It will be said that many lack the competence, or the vision, or the self-confidence (for such critical inquiries turned on one's own discipline can be unnerving). That would be a pity, for here is an area of study in which the staff can share and learn with the students, all working collaboratively together, perhaps on carefully designed mini-projects.

It turns out, then, that we can say something in general about critical thought after all. Our critical strategies do not have to be bound by the nature of the object of our attentions; they do not have to be discipline-specific. Our critical strategies can range far wider, and in doing so can take on a general character. Some critical approaches have application across all disciplines. It is perfectly proper to raise *aesthetic* questions in courses in biological sciences or (in courses on occupational therapy) on the aesthetic quality of aids given to patients; or to ask *moral* questions about work in nuclear physics or (in legal studies) about sentencing policy in the courts; or to find out the *historical* development of any subject. Many disciplines can be called up to impart a critical perspective, and questions and strategies can be mounted which have use across a wide variety of courses of study. My own preference has been made clear. Where time is short, and choices have to be made, philosophical and sociological perspectives are likely to prove to be the most valuable in developing the critical approach to knowledge. They can provide the makings of a common framework for a critical understanding of knowledge which any student on any programme of study should have at least some acquaintance with.

The exercise of critical reason

What is going on when we get our students seriously to reflect in this way? How can we conceptualize this process? In essence, it is quite simple. What we have is a critical discourse, constituting the core of the student's studies. Then we have the student's critical reflections on that discourse. Those critical reflections take their bearings from a discourse of their own, whether it be epistemology, moral philosophy, sociology, aesthetics, history or whatever. We have here a critical discourse operating on another critical discourse – in a word, metacriticism. If the idea of higher education being argued for in this book can be summed up in one word, that is it.[24]

Exercising critical reason in this way, and at that level, is not a luxury, a mere add-on to the student's programme of studies. Nor is it a sheer intellectual exercise, a modern form of the *Glass Bead Game*, as depicted by Hermann Hesse in his novel. What is at issue here is nothing short of a genuine educational process, in which the student's perception of his or her studies is transformed. The familiar is suddenly seen in a new way; the student's core discipline is illuminated under a different cognitive perspective.[25] The student comes to appreciate that the hold on the world offered by the immediate discipline is simply *one* hold on the world. There is no absolute way of describing or engaging with the world; only an infinite number of ways of doing so.[26]

But, as we have seen, there is more than the student's gaining a relativized sense of the knowledge encountered on a course. The critical attitude affects not just one's perception of knowledge out there (Popper's world III), but also one's perception of one's own knowledge (world II). The critical approach to knowledge leads to a critical perspective on the knowledge acquired, so that the individual comes, as it were, to put brackets round it. Criticism leads to critical self-reflection, where students are able to stand back and place their knowledge and accomplishments in a larger perspective. This is the hallmark of a genuine higher education: the ability to conduct a critical dialogue with oneself. The student acquires knowledge, understanding and a range of competencies in a particular domain. But the student also comes to the point of being able to look continually over his or her shoulder and ask critical questions of his or her own position. This internal dialogue will not be confined to technical questions framed within the discipline. The properly educated student will ask of him or herself: not only 'is that so?', but also 'what is the point of it?'

In principle, there is nothing strange in this. The ability to keep an eye on oneself – a critical eye, at that – is the taken-for-granted *sine qua non* of a higher education. We assume that graduates will do and say things in a considered way and not proffer the first thing that occurs to them. We expect them to have some degree of self-awareness, and self-regard, in their knowledge claims. This means, for instance, that they will admit the limit of their understanding, and forbear to offer a view in an area beyond their competence. We so much take these matters for granted that we forget that these abilities are constitutive of what we mean by 'higher education'. So, at one level, all the idea of 'metacriticism' does is to remind ourselves of what we ordinarily take higher education to be. In suggesting that the idea of higher education is hinged on self-criticism, I am not so much developing a personal concept of higher education, therefore, as drawing to the surface our common (though largely hidden) understanding of higher education.

At another level, I am pointing to the hidden potential in the idea of critical self-reflection. In Chapter 8, I sketched out three different levels of rationality: groundedness, enlightenment and emancipation. Critical self-reflection does not have to be confined to self-questioning over the grounds of one's beliefs and actions. We can take our students beyond that stage of technical feedback and on to the levels of self-enlightenment and self-emancipation, through encouraging ever-wider and higher levels of self-criticism. And, as we have seen, for that to happen, the student has to transcend the confines of his or her own discipline, to take a dispassionate view of it from the outside.

I have been examining the exercise of critical thought, but the account up to now has largely concentrated on critical thinking by the individual student. There is good reason for this, because the internal dialogue is by definition a dialogue within the individual; and that, I am arguing, is the essence of higher education. But the internal dialogue is greatly aided by dialogue with others.[27] This means that the student's learning has to be an interactive affair, the student working together with other students. Criticism from one's lecturer is one thing; criticism from the student's peers is quite another. However open it might be, the social relationship in the teaching situation is bound to produce a natural deference in the student. The real question is, how does the student respond to critical evaluations of his or her work from other students? It is entirely right, therefore, that we are beginning to see the signs of peer assessment being employed as part of the formal assessment procedure in some institutions of higher education.[28]

In concluding this section, let me tackle a potential criticism. The argument just offered may gain agreement in principle, but it could be said that in practice it is unworkable. For what is being implied is that graduates should be able to internalize the whole universe of knowledge, because in theory all knowledge is interconnected and critique can draw upon any domain of knowledge in the act of placing or evaluating a discipline. Nothing short of the resurrection of Renaissance man seems to be on the cards, in command of all knowledge. This criticism is misplaced. What is being called for is that graduates should have gained the beginnings of the ability to stand back from their studies and to take a view of it. This will require some widening of their studies, and that needs to be handled with care in ways connecting with their interests. In a 3- or 4-year programme of studies, and with the broadening elements occupying a minority of time and probably concentrated towards the latter half, graduates will have only just begun on this voyage of critical reflection. But they will be on the way.

Criticism and society

Within liberal thought, institutions of higher education have long been held to offer an independent source of critical commentary on society. In a democratic society, the academic community is the location of a dissenting voice. The 1960s saw a disenchantment with this view, academia being seen instead to be an accomplice in the mainstream projects (industrial, military, political) of society. For a brief moment, the liberal belief in unconstrained *thought* was hijacked by the radicals and converted into the idea that higher education should become the base for mounting social *action*. That frenzied period has passed and, if anything, the pendulum has swung in the other direction. By and large, the academic community seems content simply to accommodate to the instrumental needs of post-industrial society.[29] It is time that the idea of higher education as a critical commentator on society was restored because, without it, higher education is itself impoverished.[30]

This claim has to be justified in a way which maintains the internal integrity of the process of educating students. Students have their courses to follow, courses which are often set in disciplinary frameworks that have little or nothing, on the surface, to do with society. Can any kind of social critique be inserted into those courses without being superficial, jejune and irrelevant to the students' interests?

The answer has already been implied. Forms of knowledge, even the most pure and theoretical, do not exist in a vacuum. They have emerged in, and been sustained by, society, and are on offer in institutions because they reflect certain kinds of social interest. Their objects or products are useful to society. Astrology and witchcraft, as we noted earlier, are not available. If students really want to understand a form of thought or a professional domain, they ought not to graduate without some inkling of those wider connections.

The social dimensions of knowledge can come through in various ways. It might be that there are technological, industrial or military products or processes associated with a discipline. Social affairs may also be the actual object of the inquiry – as in the social sciences or humanities. Or social activities and institutions may be an important adjunct of study – as with many professional courses. Or there may be ideological elements worth teasing out, either in the object of study (in the social activity or institution brought into purview) or in the corpus of knowledge itself.

For example, it would be wrong to allow a chemist to graduate without an understanding of the uses and misuses of chemicals in the modern world, both on the natural environment and on the human body (anabolic steroids used by athletes, for instance). Or for a civil engineering student not to appreciate the environmental implications of large-scale works such as the channel tunnel. Or, following Chernobyl, for physics students not to develop a sensitivity to the biological and environmental dimensions of their studies. Or for a student studying literature not to grasp a wide range of 'readings' of the works of Jane Austen, for instance (including Marxist, feminist and post-structuralist readings). Nor can it be assumed that professional courses always tackle the social aspects: How much do accountants or pharmacists consider the professional–client relationship?

Why is this social dimension important? There are two reasons. First, it is important to the student's intellectual well-being. The idea of higher education as 'liberal' turns into a fiction so long as courses are determined solely by the introverted stance of the student's core discipline. For the student will be in no position to understand the way in which the knowledge corpus impacts on the world. And, in that case, the student will be unfree, unable to form a coherent critical assessment of the social uses of his or her own knowledge in the wider society. Graduates, after all, pass into society and take up significant posts of managerial or professional responsibility. The question is whether they are going to fall in line uncritically with the dominant interests of the sectors in which they work, or whether they are going to act constructively with a larger view – a view with a grasp of the general public interest.

Secondly, and even more importantly, knowledges in modern society are becoming increasingly separated from each other, with experts unable to communicate with each other. Under those conditions, the ability of society to understand itself and democratically to direct its own future is being diminished.[31] It is vital, therefore, that graduates are able to connect their cognitive and professional interests with those of other networks and to begin to develop genuine communicative structures in society. 'The knowledge society' requires new forms of dialogue between professionals and citizens, if society is to comprehend and effectively confront the problems facing it.

So the idea of higher education as a fulcrum for critiquing society can be resurrected – *must* be resurrected – and still allow us to do justice to the internal integrity of students' programmes of study.[32] By subjecting the curriculum contents of higher education to criticism, we subject much of society's cognitive structure (and thereby much of modern society itself) to criticism. This is no self-indulgent intellectual luxury: it is a condition of the maintenance of an open society in the modern age.

13

Redrawing Interdisciplinarity

Introduction

The reader will have gathered that, on the argument being presented here, academic disciplines are a major impediment to the realization of a liberal conception of higher education. A liberal conception cannot be sustained amidst barriers to the student's intellectual inclinations. We cannot be serious about maintaining a liberal approach to higher education if we allow the student's mind to be 'cabin'd, cribb'd and confin'd'. But academic disciplines do just that. They are bounded packages of knowledge and experience, each with its own internal character. They stand for narrowness and limitations on the development of the mind. Admittedly, they encourage – indeed, demand – that the student follow a developmental path; but they do so at the cost of corralling students into groups, hedged in by definite boundaries. Disciplines are anathema to any real, open and liberating educational experience.

The formation and maintenance of separate disciplines have repercussions which go well beyond the educational experience of the individual student, important though that is. First, students taking courses in different academic areas are unable to talk to each other in academic terms. Perhaps even more seriously, they have no sense of sharing in a common endeavour. Academically, their loyalties are to their academic department. Any sense of community with students in other departments – even on the same corridor in a hall of residence – will come from common leisure and social activities, rather than from a common language spanning their disciplines.

Secondly, and parallel to the first point, there is now hardly any sense of a common discourse among academics. We looked at this phenomenon in Chapter 7, where I argued that one possibility of recovering the sense of a genuine academic community lay in institutionalizing a culture of critical discourse.

But there is a third problem, which I touched on earlier. It is that this carving up of the academic world, this division of labour, reduces the possibility of a genuinely participatory democracy. Modern society becomes fragmented, with decision making being the result of a conjunction of power élites, pressure groups and 'experts' drawn on *ad hoc*. And yet, as the ecological problems of the world accumulate, and as policy issues pile up, the need for all citizens to have an informed understanding of complex matters is paramount. It is not just a matter of democratic decision making, of accountability and of understanding the decisions made by the planners, the bureaucrats and the politicians. It is that we are all responsible for many of the problems facing us, and for understanding the implications of our actions. This includes the effects on the atmosphere of the CFC sprays used in the home, and the problems of disposing of domestic waste; but it also includes making links between the damage to the rainforests of Brazil and the economic relationships between the developing and the developed worlds. There is a connection between the lifestyle of the Brazilian peasant and that of the Western worker.

Two general points can be made. First, the problems of the world do not come in simple disciplinary containers. There are interconnections between ecology and economics, for example, and between both of them and politics. In the end, all knowledge is connected, and anything we do in our educational transactions to convey a different picture is damaging. Secondly, the upshot of a discipline-driven research enterprise is that researchers talk mainly to themselves; and, even then, the so-called peers cannot always understand each other.[1] As a result, culture generally is fragmented, and communication in society is thwarted. Society itself unravels, at a time when it is most needed.

Can anything be done to address this situation in higher education? The signs are not good. When they were established in the 1960s, amidst much talk of 'redrawing the map of learning',[2] the new green-field universities represented a major attempt to combat disciplinarity, both in research and in the curriculum. 'Schools' of study were founded, bringing cognate disciplines together. Students were required to take a broad programme in their first year, and a joint honours programme in their subsequent years. The 1970s saw added interest in interdisciplinary programmes across the Western world, following the student movement of the late 1960s with its demand for more socially 'relevant' curricula.[3]

However, over time, the conventional disciplines have re-established themselves as the building blocks of the curriculum.[4] Joint honours programmes have been reduced largely to independent programmes run alongside each other; and because of the reluctance of academics to think through their objectives for a non-standard programme, the students find themselves doing 120 per cent of the work. Many institutions in the public sector have developed multidisciplinary courses. But precisely because they offer students a wide menu from which to choose their subjects, and because the students taking a course unit will be following many types of programme, any integration of the different components is left to the students. Multidisciplinary courses tend to be just that: a collection of units, with vertical relationships within disciplines, but with few horizontal connections made across the disciplines.

On disciplines

If past attempts to go beyond discipline-bound courses have met with mixed success, why was that? Is it just a matter of inadequate organization, a failure to inject sufficient resilience against the preponderant power of the disciplines (from which academics derive their professional livings and identities)? Or is it a reflection of the structure of knowledge; a consequence of the different logics inherent in the separate disciplines, such that following more than one discipline is like riding two or more horses at once – in the end, the rider finds himself on just one of them? Is the situation essentially an empirical or a logical matter?[5]

It is obviously both. But the success of any approach to an interdisciplinary format will be a matter of how we conceive 'interdisciplinarity'. In this chapter, I want to argue for a particular kind of interdisciplinarity, which as a shorthand I shall call 'critical interdisciplinarity'. This will amount to a substantiation of the critical strategies sketched out in the previous chapter. Before I do that, let us look briefly at the idea of 'discipline' itself, for we can hardly work towards interdisciplinarity unless we have a reasonably clear idea of the more basic building blocks. Disciplines cannot be wished away, even if we wanted to do so. The question for the educator is: How do we deal with them, and bring them into some kind of relationship?

Disciplines are aptly named. Pursuing them, getting immersed in them, demands discipline, whether on the part of the student or the researcher; disciplines call for rules of engagement to be mastered and kept.[6] Competence is a matter of knowing how to go on (in Wittgenstein's terminology). The individual has to learn the central concepts and theories, certainly; but also the tacit rules of reasoning, and the unspoken criteria for making inferences. To borrow from Kuhn, the governing paradigms and their exemplars have to be understood, and accepted as the way of doing things.

But then, educationally, a problem arises: How can we get students to see that disciplines contain this large element of sheer convention, that things should be done in this way rather than that because this is simply the accepted way of behaving? How can we bring them to the point of seeing through these conventions, of understanding that even though the conventions act as bars round a cage, the bars are rubber, not iron? If their higher learning is to be fully educational, students have to realize that those bars can be bent and escape is possible, even if they do not seek to flee from the security of the accepted customs themselves.[7] Indeed, it has to be admitted that where teachers do encourage such creativity (e.g. a completely unfamiliar form of essay writing), students often turn out to be resistant to change. They can be particularly conservative in their approach. And not surprisingly, for disciplines provide identity and security (the 'I am a psychologist' syndrome).

So, a key curriculum question in higher education is this: Can a discipline-based curriculum fulfil the wider educational objectives, objectives which call for individual disciplines to be transcended? Can a programme of studies which is organized around a particular discipline engender an understanding of its limitations, and indeed its particular place in the total map of knowledge?

The basic problems posed by disciplines in higher education are more complicated than this, however. As Hirst has pointed out, in higher education the term 'discipline' is used to cover different kinds of activity and complexes of knowledge, and – within those clusterings – stands in various relationships to research and teaching. We might call home economics, philosophy, international relations and medicine all 'disciplines', but the internal structure of each is distinctive in terms of its unifying concepts, tests for truth, institutionalized research practices, and so on.[8]

Disciplines in higher education being such different entities, it would seem that any attempt to make general statements about bridge-building between disciplines must be doomed from the outset. It is difficult to see that any rules could be established for bringing disciplines together in a way which would amount to 'interdisciplinarity' and which would hold for all such interconnections. Bernstein has suggested that the integration of two or more disciplines requires their subordination to a relational idea.[9] But given the different kinds of entity which pass for disciplines, relational ideas could be themselves driven by a range of interests: they might be research driven, or dictated by the epistemological logic of the disciplines, by professional considerations, or by matters concerning their organizational effectiveness within departmental structures.

The result is that beyond rather vague talk about rule-following and standards, we can say very little that is general about the character of 'disciplines' in higher education. We can say still less *in general* about possible relationships between them.[10] In fact, the suspicion begins to form that, because many so-called disciplines are themselves nebulous clusterings of topics and activities (both academic and professional), interdisciplinarity is something of a chimera, a mythical conglomeration, which we would not like very much if we came across it.

The aims of interdisciplinarity

These comments will be irritating to many. It will be said that a large number of undergraduate programmes in fact range far wider than single discrete disciplines. A significant proportion of courses are either explicitly multidisciplinary, or are joint honours; or they are built around professional areas of interest (pharmacy, leisure studies, business studies and the like) which, of their nature, are again multidisciplinary and indeed interdisciplinary in character. Well, let us look at this claim – that many courses are already multidisciplinary and interdisciplinary in character – in a little more detail. What are the different aims and motivations underlying such broadly based programmes and what kind of educational experience do they offer? (In the survey that follows, both multidisciplinary and interdisciplinary examples are interwoven; nothing would be gained by rigidly restricting the discussion to one or the other.)

Educational

The essential aim here is that multidisciplinary programmes should offer a broadening dimension to the undergraduate's experience. There is a sense, particularly in the UK, that undergraduate courses are too narrow and that greater breadth is worthwhile in itself. When pressed further, there is an added demand that the package of experience should be 'integrated' and not just be a collection of unconnected elements. The approach favoured by some universities in the USA for students, whatever their discipline, to have some initiation into the 'Great Books' of Western civilization, or even the approach of the former colleges of advanced technology and of the polytechnics in the 1960s for a separate element of liberal studies, would not pass muster under the 'integration' requirement.

The 'educational' aim can sometimes have a further target, with the student's programme of studies being expected to have some carry-over into the student's life-world.[11] Just this aspiration can be found in the educational aims of the Council for National Academic Awards, which looks to the student appreciating 'the nature of attitudes, modes of thought, practices and disciplines *other than those of his or her main studies*', but also sets down the expectation that 'the student must be encouraged to develop the ability to see relationships within what he or she has learnt, and to *relate what he or she has learnt to actual situations*'.[12]

What is at issue here, in the educational set of aims, is the broad development of the student's mind through breadth of study and making connections between the various elements.

Epistemological

Here, the focus is on the internal logic of different disciplines and areas of inquiry. There is a recognition of their contrasting conceptual frameworks, truth criteria, levels of objectivity and methodologies; and from that recognition spring various considerations. The main idea is that through an appreciation of the conceptual frameworks offered by other domains, the student will be better able to stand back and to understand the conceptual framework of the core subject in which he or she is interested.[13] There is also a sense that the intermeshing of different forms of thought will increase the chances of new kinds of thinking emerging. The clash of different logics is likely, so it is felt, to spark off creativity by the student.

Communicative

The drive here is to see if any kind of common discourse can be developed across the numerous disciplinary sub-cultures.[14] With Latin as the language of the medieval university, scholars were able to move remarkably easily between the universities of Europe (both as individuals and, at turbulent times, in great migrations). In the early to mid-Victorian age, classics was the dominant – though by no means universal – means of recognition among academics. It seems that if there is a lingua franca for higher education today, it is to be found in information technology.[15] To think in these terms is to mistake technique for language. The archaeologist, the graphic designer and the engineer may all use the computer; but this does not by itself mean that their ability to understand each other is in any way increased.

Pedagogical

The pedagogical orientation to interdisciplinarity is concerned with trying to improve teaching and learning. One consideration on the teaching side is that interdisciplinarity encourages more cooperation among the staff responsible for a course. This is, in itself, worthwhile: it opens up the 'secret garden' of the classroom or laboratory, with staff being obliged to be more open about what they are trying to do. At the same time, students are exposed to a wider set of teaching strategies, and are likely to adopt a more varied set of learning styles. And if the programme is genuinely interdisciplinary (rather than simply being multidisciplinary), the hope is that the students' learning will be more self-directed, as they are encouraged to form their own connections between the various elements of their learning.

Preparation for the labour market

Increasingly, employers are looking for graduates who are 'adaptable' and 'flexible', and who have a range of 'personal transferable skills' to offer. Traditional discipline-bound courses may have developed students' abilities to communicate within their chosen discipline – though employers are not even sure about that – but they do not promote students' wider abilities to make themselves understood by others in the working environment who do not share their specialist expertise. There is a suspicion, too, that the bookish, individualistic ethic of the academic community is unsuited to developing graduates' wider abilities to work with others in the pragmatic decision-making culture of the workplace.[16] Accordingly, there comes a plea from industry (e.g. in the UK, from the Council for Industry and Higher Education) that courses in higher education should offer a much more varied diet of experiences.[17] This form of interdisciplinarity, therefore, is driven by forces external to higher education and has an explicitly instrumental motivation.

Technocratic

This motivation behind interdisciplinarity has similarities with the general 'labour market' demand. It, too, is external and instrumental. But it needs to be distinguished. For while employers are saying that the subject studied by their graduate intake is often immaterial (provided that the students have the right set of attitudes to the workplace), the modern post-industrial society is also calling for particular kinds of highly qualified expertise. Higher education is seen as the vehicle for producing the corps of planners, engineers (in the broad sense), information gatherers, managers both of production and of the cultural industry, and professionals of all kinds. There is the further thought that these experts, in order to function effectively, need to have their studies grounded in an understanding of many subjects, including law, sociology, psychology, economics, statistics and even history, politics and other fields of inquiry.

Managerial

Multidisciplinary work has a particular attraction for the managers responsible for the allocation of resources in an institution of higher education. If the course work of an institution can be carved up into discrete units, and if students' programmes of study can be built on a cross-disciplinary basis, the power relationships in an institution are altered in favour of management. For the most expensive resource is the academic staff. If their ownership of a 3-year single-discipline course can be ended, much more flexibility can be injected into institutional management.[18]

Informatory

There is an instrumentalism at work, too, in this set of motivations, but it can at least be claimed that it is trying to do justice to an original conception of higher education. This orientation to interdisciplinarity springs from a concern that the growth of separate disciplines has brought with it a heightened inability of higher education to communicate with society. We do not have to go back to the medieval universities: in early and mid-Victorian Britain, both scientists and men of letters saw it as part of their duty to communicate their findings or thoughts to the wider society.[19] Now, as academics have their livings firmly in discrete sub-communities in academic life, that sense of responsibility is lost. So those who are sensitive to that earlier age wonder if, through some kind of interdisciplinarity, the academic community might be helped to recover its mission to communicate with the wider public.

Normative

The normative approach notes with some disdain the labour market and technocratic programmes for a broader curriculum explicitly oriented to social considerations. However, its proponents consider that there is no neutral space available to higher education in the modern state, as perhaps the informatory conception implies. Either one succumbs to the dominant forces of the modern state, or one works actively to confront them. Accordingly, here, interdisciplinarity is seen as a vehicle for putting knowledge into the service of deliberately chosen social ends, contrasting with those of the dominant culture. The work at

Bradford University in peace studies follows this model: it is an attempt to inject particular ethical dimensions into the pursuit of knowledge.[20]

Rational

This motivation has connections with the normative. It, too, sees a lack of reason in the curriculum today, driven blindly as it seems by external forces. But instead of injecting particular ethical motives, the rational orientation glimpses the chance of generating a curriculum out of the knowledge enterprise itself. The belief here is that by bringing the disciplines into a tight relationship with each other, an overarching system of reasoning will emerge – a supra-rationality, in fact. By organizing an institution around a unifying interdisciplinary theme, the claim is that higher education will assist in the achievement of positive social ends. The work of the European Centre for Educational Research and Innovation (CERI) has been pushed in this direction, and it has offered – as examples of such interdisciplinarity – international relations and 'anthropology considered as science of man'.[21] But going down this path leads on to the task of persuading the academic community of the universality of the proffered framework. That CERI has found it impossible to get its programme off the ground suggests that the universality is somewhat limited.

Critical

The final approach to interdisciplinarity that I want to disentangle stems, as with the previous two, from a sense that the discipline-based curriculum offers students an over-narrow experience, with limited educational benefits. It also shares with those two the belief that knowledge reflects wider social interests, and that it is incumbent on higher education to work out the interests it wants to sustain itself: there is no neutral position available. Where it parts company with them is over their determination to use higher education to drive through questionable social programmes, however well-motivated. For that replaces one ideology (the technocratic and market) with another. Instead, the critical approach to interdisciplinarity is founded on a belief that by taking criticism seriously, ideology can be neutralized to a significant degree, although never eradicated. The central idea is that widening the student's curriculum beyond a core discipline or area of inquiry can help to make explicit and therefore more challengeable the central presuppositions and interest-structure of that core discipline. Through critical interdisciplinarity, truth claims can be upheld more fully in the awareness of their limitations and their implications. It is this conception of interdisciplinarity which I began to outline in the last chapter, and which I wish to defend here.

Before spelling out a little further what, in practice, 'critical interdisciplinarity' might mean, it is worth seeing the relationships between the different kinds

Table 1 Relationships between different kinds of
interdisciplinarity

	Conservative	*Radical*
Personal	Educational Epistemological Communicative Pedagogical	Critical
Social	Labour market Technocratic Managerial	Informatory Normative Rational

of interdisciplinarity I have just outlined. They can be summarized as in
Table 1.

There are just three points I want to make about this analysis. First,
'interdisciplinarity' stands for so many disparate and competing aims and
educational programmes that the term by itself does hardly any conceptual
work. We can deduce very little about a programme of studies from the fact that
it is described in the institution's prospectus as 'interdisciplinary'. The term is
as much a piece of rhetoric as it is a description. Many so-called interdisciplinary programmes do not warrant the description. The programmes may – as in
most areas of professional education – draw in concepts and perspectives from
several domains but, precisely because they are drawn in, those different
perspectives become part of the discipline itself. The student is not given a
separate disciplinary framework from which to view the central discipline.[22]

Secondly, the different purposes behind interdisciplinarity have tensions
between them. They may even be logically exclusive and the educational
programmes they spawn can be mutually incompatible. The technocratic
approach will tend to avoid value issues in the curriculum; the normative and
rational approaches are intended explicitly to raise value questions. That said,
the programmes are not as watertight as they may appear. There are obvious
overlaps, some of which I have mentioned. But more than that, it may be
perfectly possible to pursue different kinds of purpose at once, within the same
interdisciplinary programme. As is usual for curriculum designers, the question
will be: How much give-and-take can there be? A programme may have to fill
technocratic or labour market ends, but are there educational or other kinds of
social purposes that can be accomplished at the same time?

Thirdly, genuinely interdisciplinary programmes represent an attempt to
import values into the curriculum which transcend those of a particular
discipline. Resistance will be felt from the disciplinary interests. This is no bad
thing: it obliges parties to be explicit about the ends and values for which they
stand. It then becomes possible to see if a coherent interdisciplinary programme
which does justice to different sets of values, possibly in tension with each other,
can be brought off successfully.

Critical interdisciplinarity

In Table 1, critical interdisciplinarity is shown as the only form of interdisciplinarity to be both personal and radical in motivation. How can we understand this double aspect?

In Table 1, 'personal' is contrasted with 'social'. Critical interdisciplinarity is personal before it is social because it is rooted in the development of mind. I say '*before* it is social' because critical interdisciplinarity also incorporates a social aspect. It recognizes the social bases of higher education, that higher education has been established as a key institution in modern society, and that the knowledge made available to students is itself a social institution of sorts, with social origins. A critical interdisciplinarity will, therefore, be conscious of the social character of higher education and some of the critical elements of a student's programme of studies will be directed at those social components. So there is no sharp break between the personal and the social aspects of critical interdisciplinarity; they are interwoven. But the starting point is the student's mind, and its development.

What about the other dimension in Table 1: In what way is critical interdisciplinarity radical? There are two linked points. The first can best be put negatively: critical interdisciplinarity refuses to take an uncritical stance towards knowledge. In interdisciplinary programmes which are critical in a thoroughgoing way, the student is encouraged to appreciate that the knowledge which is being acquired does have its limitations. Objectivity and truth cannot be taken on trust. There may even be hidden ideological influences at work, whether of the wider society or of the disciplinary community. In this way, the student comes to adopt an arm's-length relationship with the knowledge encountered. Yes, it is learned and understood; but it is also held at bay. The student comes to realize that given different historical circumstances – different societal pressures, different academic in-fighting – things could be very different.

The other sense in which critical interdisciplinarity is radical is that this particular educative process has the potential to exert a transforming effect on the student. Long after all the discrete pieces of knowledge have been forgotten, many graduates come to feel that their studies have had the effect of changing the way they look at the world. What they have taken on, with everlasting value, is a particular cognitive perspective, the framework of a discipline. That effect often arises out of a conventional subject-based education; and it is a relatively narrow kind of cognitive change, for the graduate has normally adopted an uncritical stance to that perspective. Critical interdisciplinarity, I am suggesting, offers the chance of effecting a more significant change. With critical interdisciplinarity, the student comes to see how his or her favoured subject stands in relation to other fields of study, and comes to see the limitations in his or her field of study. The graduate is able, as a result, critically to deploy that field of study as a resource, is able to see how far it is useful, knows when to turn to other fields of study, and is generally independent of the knowledge which has been acquired. In other words, critical interdisciplinarity offers the prospect of a significant degree of intellectual freedom for the student. In this sense, too, it should be seen as a radical programme.

Towards an interdisciplinary curriculum

Admittedly, this is all very abstract. Can we fill out the general picture at all? In one sense, no. Precisely because critical interdisciplinarity does not accept that a student's programme of studies should be bounded by the knowledge boundaries of academic disciplines, the total field of knowledge available to a genuinely interdisciplinary programme is limitless. Consequently, the interconnections that might be drawn in such a course of study are infinite, and no ground-rules can be given for their identification.

The discussion in the last chapter about critical approaches to knowledge did, however, begin to map out a framework. If we are to do justice to the promise of higher education and enable students to reach a state of complete intellectual freedom, there can be no restraint on the intellectual resources we draw on to mount our critical strategies. From where do we derive those intellectual resources? From the disciplines themselves, for there is no other source available. The general picture is shown in Fig. 2.

We have to accept that, things being what they are, both teachers and students will tend to have joint interests in pursuing a particular subject or professional field. I take that as a fact of academic life. What I am arguing for is

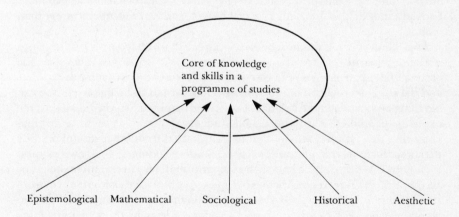

Figure 2 The structure of critical interdisciplinarity.

that we should try to ensure that the programme of studies is, nevertheless, to some degree open; that the light of other disciplines can come through. The knowledge that the student is keen on acquiring is called to account by other disciplines. The disciplines which act as interrogators – history, aesthetics, ethics, empirical science, mathematics or whatever – are chosen where they can do genuine critical or illuminating work. Their critical power does not come from any intrinsic characteristics, because, in principle, any discipline may be called on in this way. Their force comes rather from the fact that, by being used as critical weapons, they show the limitations of the discipline under attack. Their force comes through critique as such.

In Fig. 2, I have highlighted a wider range of perspectives which are likely to prove valuable in illuminating a discipline.[23] In the last chapter, I suggested that epistemology and sociology are likely to prove to be most potent as critical interrogators. I repeat, however, that in theory any discipline can exert critical insight of this kind. How might this work in practice?

A course in music, for example, could include an examination of the effect of sound-waves on the ear, and so lead on to physics or to anatomy (i.e. drawing in the empirical mode of inquiry). It could also lead to an examination of other forms of music in other societies, or to an inquiry into its social relationships such as patronage and audiences (the sociological dimension). It could stimulate an examination of the forms of music over time (the historical dimension). It might examine the conceptual relationship between music and sound, and perhaps relate different musical styles to other contemporary forms of aesthetic style (so developing an aesthetic dimension). It could look at what is meant by music as a language, and by musical knowledge (the philosophical and epistemological dimensions). And it could investigate the ideological underpinnings of different forms of notation: Do they carry a sense of harmony or conflict, and have they helped to sustain certain kinds of social arrangements rather than others?

This kind of programme could be extended to all courses. It develops interdisciplinarity organically by building on the student's interests. The outline I have just given is not prescriptive. It would be a matter for the teacher and the students to agree on the direction and format to be followed. Nor can anything be said about the balance of the interdisciplinary studies as against the mainstream studies. The point is that students should be brought to a realization that their studies are not hermetically sealed from other disciplines and that other forms of thought can shed much understanding on their own studies.

Nor am I trying to argue how such an interdisciplinary programme should be accomplished. Overarching themes or topics – perhaps drawn from the environment – might be one way. Or key concepts might be examined from different points of view. For example, students taking courses in the humanities, the sciences and the social sciences might be asked to compare 'perception' from a psychological, philosophical, sociological, biological and literary point of view.[24] The task would be not just to understand in an analytical way the comparative differences in the disciplinary frameworks, but to go further and actually appreciate that none of the points of view are reducible to any of the others. For such a project, students could work in teams, even drawn from across courses in various subjects. And part of the project would be activity based, with creative tasks which gave an illuminative insight into perception in the different fields.

Other examples can be cited. Students in the natural sciences can be encouraged to consider the aesthetic dimensions of their work (cosmologists, molecular biologists and nuclear physicists have all, in recent years, shown just such an awareness). Students taking courses in professional education should be given an understanding of the inevitably narrow epistemological bases of their disciplines, as well as an insight into the limited applicability of their disciplines to human behaviour and social institutions; an insight into, in other words, the technocratic gulf between their acquired formal knowledge and their interactions with their future clients.[25]

More than making connections

So, critical interdisciplinarity can be applied in an infinite variety of ways without doing an injustice to the core programme being followed. The aim behind this form of interdisciplinarity has to be kept in focus, however. It is not for the purpose of making connections between different kinds of knowledge; still less is it for producing 'breadth' of mind for its own sake (worthwhile as these ends are). It is rather the emancipatory aim of reducing the hold that *any* form of knowledge has on the student, and of so enabling the student to be free from knowledge as such.

The 'inter' in 'interdisciplinarity' is important. Simply allowing students – in a multidisciplinary, credit-based course – to pursue a number of course units drawn from different subjects will not do. Indeed, it could do positive harm. For they may end up with an unconnected potpourri of elements. As a result, students may be hoodwinked into thinking that they have more understanding than they possess of the different fields. They may, instead, have acquired a 'Mastermind' grasp of things or an integrated mush of facts and ideas, an easy familiarity with disparate entities but lacking any real critical insight.[26] The rhetoric accompanying interdisciplinarity is often couched in terms of the penetrating experiences it makes available; but in practice its effects may be just the reverse.

Rather, the way forward lies in developing programmes of study which provide for students to pursue their interests in some depth, but which also have elements of permeability so that students can grasp the limitations of their own field(s) of study. By bringing other forms of inquiry to bear on students' interests, the programme of study remains integrated but is opened out. In the process, students are put in a position to be more critical of their learning, though in a constructive way.

This form of interdisciplinarity has a number of positive characteristics. It is inescapably educative: it extends the student's range of vision, allowing him or her to see where the studies fit in the general framework of knowledge. It gives meaning to the idea of an inquirer after truth, where truth is potentially all truth and not just a minute portion of it. It offers a unity to the efforts of students on all courses of study, enabling them to talk meaningfully to each other in academic terms; and so regains part of the meaning of 'university' as a single universe of knowledge. Critical interdisciplinarity is, simply, a modern embodiment of the idea of 'a community of scholars'.

An interdisciplinarity of this kind will have an even wider value. Within the academic community, it will help to build bridges between the academic disciplines. First, it will lead to more cooperation, dialogue and even team teaching across departments in an institution. Secondly, it is likely to inspire cross-disciplinary research projects. Thirdly, if it were to take off, it would enable the academic community to recover a sense of itself *as* an academic community, with an interest and a discourse which transcend particular disciplines. It is an interest and a discourse grounded in a culture of critical discourse (see Chapter 7).

Even beyond this, critical interdisciplinarity can begin to unify academic discourse with the problems and perceptions of the wider public. Graduates will have begun to see that the problems of the world and the problems of the academic community coincide, and that bridges can and must be built between them. This is not to pretend that a romantic common culture is recoverable: it is not. But a genuine critical interdisciplinary culture within the academic world will perhaps help to reduce the isolation of academics and to open them more to the will of the general public, and so bring to knowledge a more democratic accountability.

14

A Liberal Higher Education Regained

Introduction

'Did the liberal university ever exist?' The scepticism implied by Peter Scott's question is entirely justified.[1] But, as I have tried to show in this book, the modern prospect of a liberal higher education today is especially problematic, and on two counts. First, the possibility of securing objective knowledge and of pursuing truth in a disinterested way can no longer be assumed (the epistemological undermining). And, secondly, the social independence of institutions of higher education has evaporated, through their being swept up into the apparatus of the modern state (the sociological undermining). Because the idea of a liberal higher education carries just this two-fold sense of freedom – freedom in the domain of knowledge and freedom in terms of social autonomy – the idea appears to be merely the plaintive rhetoric of another age. Can a form of liberal higher education be recovered? Should it?

I shall duck the second question for the moment. To the first, I can say that I have tried to show that a liberal higher education can be restored, not entirely but to some degree. The ideological interests of the wider society and the internal interests of particular disciplinary communities can never be eradicated (there is no prospect of it, at least). But those constraints on a liberal higher education can be neutralized, to some extent, by giving attention to learning rather than teaching, and seeing 'learning' as including capabilities which call for genuine intellectual independence; by taking the idea of criticism seriously; and by opening the curriculum to the claims of other disciplines. In this final chapter, I want to suggest that to these three strategies should be added a fourth, that of open learning, understood as giving students responsibility for their own learning. Before that, however, let us distinguish two different ideas of liberal education.[2]

Two concepts of liberal education

We can term the first concept of liberal education a 'conservative' concept. The key word signifying the sense of 'liberal' under this concept is 'liberty'.[3] The general idea is that all individuals have the seed of liberty within themselves, and the task of the educator is to help it grow. Education is a matter of allowing to unfold those characteristics of reason and independence which lie naturally within the individual.[4]

In this conception, there is a sense that the constraints preventing that unfolding are relatively weak. The individual has it naturally within himself or herself to be free, and to achieve the state of liberty. On this view, the best course of action for the educator to take is to ensure that the curriculum puts as few constraints in the way as possible. The task, in other words, is to so arrange the educational environment that the liberty of the individual will show itself and naturally develop.

Against this, I want to put a second conception of liberal education, which I shall call the 'radical' concept.[5] Here, the key meaning of 'liberal' is given by the idea of 'liberation'.[6] In this conception, there is a heightened sense of the constraints acting on the individual. The constraints are seen as binding unless something is done about them. Essentially, they are social and psychological in character. On the one hand, social institutions and social arrangements are seen as exerting constraints on the individual which cannot be simply shrugged off. And, on the other, inner problems of the psyche are also seen as having hidden but real impact on individuals, which again cannot easily be overcome.[7]

On this view, education becomes a process of 'liberation', helping individuals to understand the forces acting on them in such a thoroughgoing way that they are enabled to undergo a self-transformation. By allowing them to see those forces for what they are, individuals go through a cycle of self-reflection, self-understanding and seeing themselves in a new way. The educational process is dramatic, and therefore radical, but essentially it is achieved by the individuals for and by themselves.[8]

Now, in so far as there has been any real sense of a liberal education in British higher education, it has been almost entirely the conservative concept at work. The radical concept reared its head briefly in 1960s, but in such an inchoate and ill-thought out way that its short life was inevitable and, frankly, justifiable. Today, it is evident in the field of adult education, but this has so far made little impact on higher education.[9] Where has the conservative concept been apparent? Most obviously of all, in the two ancient English universities, in the educational freedom given to the students especially in the non-science subjects.[10] The one-to-one tutorial system of those two institutions is a symbol of this independence: essentially, it is a form of accountability, in which the student as an individual is able to demonstrate that the time available to him or her over the past week or so has been used profitably. This, though, is not the only form of liberal education in UK higher education.

Mind and body

In charting the murky waters of liberal higher education, there is another distinction worth observing. It is whether higher education is seen primarily in terms of the development of the mind, or of the whole person. For those who see higher education essentially as a matter of the individual's cognitive achievements, a liberal higher education is one which holds to the value of truth-seeking.[11] The central idea, as we have seen, is that of being freed from error; the mind is brought into the light and is able to see the world as it really is. (The metaphors of Plato's cave and of Newman's intellectual enlargement may be recalled from Chapter 2.[12])

This idea can be mapped on to the conservative–radical distinction which has just been made. In its conservative formulations, there is a strong belief in objective knowledge having been obtained through the research endeavours of the academic community, and it becomes the task of higher education to transmit it. This leads to a relatively passive learning situation, with the student largely on the receiving end of prepackaged knowledge, which is often of a second-hand character. In its more radical version, though, a sceptical view of knowledge is taken. Accordingly, the student is expected to come to a personal view of the knowledge encountered, and to take up a critical stance. In its most radical form, this view is also accompanied by the idea that the knowledge so won, through personal involvement by the student, can lead to a higher level of self-empowerment. Where knowledge is entered into vividly and claimed as his or her own by the student, the student is freed – intellectually, at least – to determine his or her cognitive options him or herself.

In an analogous way, the idea of liberal higher education centred on the whole person also has conservative and radical interpretations. The conservative version looks to providing a higher education which is characteristic of those who are socially free persons. This idea is essentially the product of a stratified society, and carries the implication of a selective system of higher education.[13] It also tends towards defining higher education in terms of character formation'.[14] This is an idea of higher education characteristic of elements of Victorian university orthodoxy.[15] Its remnants, though, can be seen today in the UK system, in the preponderance of full-time students, and with the service functions of higher education concentrated in the polytechnic sector, leaving the universities to sustain the wider social and cultural functions of higher education.

The radical conception of a person-centred liberal education amounts to nothing less than a total transformation and emancipation of the individual student. It consists of a coupling of theoretical and practical elements, but in a way which promotes a thoroughgoing and lived appreciation of modern society and the different perspectives of the different social groupings. Nothing like it exists in the UK, although some programmes of professional education approach it, particularly in the public sector. Even there, it is *ad hoc* rather than a matter of implementing a general conception of higher education.

The concept of polytechnic education could have been developed something along those lines, adapting the original institutional version of Eastern Europe to Western culture.[16] But the concept has been emasculated. Far from undergoing a personal transformation, with individuals being brought to understand the constitution of the society in which they are to act as graduates, most of the products of the system are put into the position merely of being functionaries; middle-ranking technicians and managers preserving the societal framework rather than making fully informed, constructive interventions within it.

It is tempting to put these two axes of liberal higher education – conservative/radical, mind/person – against each other in a grid. All varieties of liberal higher education would then find their spot somewhere in the four quarters of the space thus created. But it would be a superficial analysis. It would miss the subtle ways in which claims of liberality enter the inner life of institutions of higher education.

Consider access, for example. Those who look to the development of the mind, but who hold the conservative concept of liberal education, will opt for a selective system of entry based on a formal demonstration of prior cognitive achievements (typically, in England and Wales, the applicant's performance in A levels). On the other hand, those who see liberal education in terms of an education of the whole person will be more likely to take extramural accomplishments into account, whether in sport or in some other domain.[17] In either form, selection will tend to have a class bias.

Compare that with a more radical approach to access. Where the focus is the development of the mind, and where the possibility of personal growth during the course is recognized, an attempt will be made to go beyond or even be dismissive of formal entry qualifications. Instead, an attempt might be made to assess the extent to which the applicant has a generally inquiring, open and critical outlook; or even more radically, no attempt would be made to impose criteria of admission (as with the Open University).[18]

Where, instead, the transformation of the whole person is hoped for, an attempt might be made to assess the total accomplishments of the individual *and* the extent to which he or she has learned from them. The assessment of experiential learning, now being imported into the UK from the USA, does just that.[19] Here, admitting institutions place the onus on the applicants to reflect on and document their own achievements. This process of self-reflection and self-appraisal may be lengthy and may require guidance; but it is also self-developmental for the applicants concerned. This procedure is particularly valuable for mature students who lack formal entry qualifications but who can come to recognize their own past learning and so develop an increased sense of their own worth.

This analysis of access could be extended to other aspects of higher education. However, the details of that analysis are less important than the general point: the two concepts of liberal education – conservative and radical – are not just concepts, but have an impact on the elements of the internal life of higher education institutions.

Open learning: Perhaps not so liberal

We have seen that all kinds of ideas and practices pass under the banner of liberal education. And some barely warrant the title 'liberal'. This paradoxical nature of liberal education – that on examination, pretensions to liberality turn out to be pretty vacuous – is readily apparent in the alternative interpretations given to open learning. Within open learning, independent study (as at the University of Lancaster and East London Polytechnic[20]) is the most striking example: for there the student's programme of study is under the student's control, with the student being accountable under the terms of a pre-agreed contract. Learning contracts in general,[21] the facility to learn at one's own pace using learning resources, distance learning, and project work are other examples of open learning which promote the student's liberty, and fall under what I term the conservative idea of liberal education.

Open learning in this form falls under the 'conservative' concept because it simply provides students with elements of liberty for their natural development to unfold. The onus is on the students to be responsible for their own development. The assumption is that, given sufficient freedom (to work on what they want, or when they want, or where they want, or in the way they want, or at a pace they want), a genuine educational development is assured. 'Conservative' is sometimes a pejorative term: it implies things are falling short of possibilities. This is precisely the case with open learning. For while it can be well-intentioned, lessening unreasonable obstacles to effective learning, it does not guarantee any kind of 'liberation' of the student's mind.

Indeed, it is not accidental that open learning is encouraged for managerial reasons from within institutions; and it is also being supported for utilitarian purposes from outside. Employers and others see in it the possibility of developing 'personal transferable skills', 'group skills' and even 'enterprise skills'. This is hardly surprising; for open learning, *if not coupled to other educational aims*, can leave students largely where they start from. There can be no assurance that their general cognitive and moral perspectives, their self-perception, or their fundamental values, are going to be changed. For many, open learning appears to be a radical programme for higher education; actually, it may well be a piece of thoroughgoing conservatism.

Certainly, open learning does not have to have such limited outcomes. But the danger is always present of the forces of conservatism, if not inertia, reasserting themselves. Indeed, on one reading (Robbins 1988), precisely this has happened with the Independent Study programme at East London Polytechnic.[22] Some of the staff saw in it possibilities for radical personal development, in fact the kind of self-transformation outlined under the radical concept of liberal education. But, on Robbins' account, those radical aspirations have been disappointed as the Independent Study programme has turned in the direction of realizing more down-to-earth aims.

In the same way, the Higher Education for Capability initiative – recently relaunched in the UK by the Royal Society of Arts – is, Janus-like, facing in two directions at once. Some of the drive points in the direction of the individual student achieving self-transcendence, with a new level of inner integration and self-understanding. But other forces are at work which see in it a vehicle for combating the anti-industrial ideology of the academic world (as it is seen), and here 'capability' means enhancing the capacity of UK Inc. So again, in an initiative designed to develop open learning, we see the forces of radicalism and conservatism contending with each other.

General education

General education offers another approach to liberal higher education. Open learning focuses on teaching methods and outcomes. General education, in contrast, speaks directly to the curriculum, its main concern being to build curricula which transcend disciplines.

Underlying moves towards general education are three identifiable strands of reasoning. First, there is a determination to counter the excessively narrow undergraduate curriculum (particularly so in the UK). Secondly, there is a wish to use the curriculum as a means of unifying the disciplinary sub-cultures of the academic community. And, finally, there is a desire to see the curriculum promoting civic virtues and an appreciation of the common good (this is a strand particularly characteristic of the USA).

It will be apparent that these are very different aims, and we can justifiably conclude that general education is a confused concept. This also leads to uncertainty in its application. For some kind of content is going to be required to fulfil the aims; but then, on what basis is the selection to be made? The Carnegie Foundation in the USA has attempted to identify key themes addressed to 'those experiences, relationships, and ethical concerns that are common to all of us'.[23] Six themes are proposed, including language and communication, and shared membership of groups and institutions (to take the first two).[24] There can be little to quarrel over in their selection; after all, the themes are intended to be merely illustrative. But if this approach to general education is taken, if it is a matter of providing contextual studies wider than the student's core programme, what is to be the relationship between the core and the contextual studies? If no connection is sought, if the general studies are separate from the students' main interests, what likelihood is there of the students' attention being captured? Or, indeed, that of the staff who teach them?

This line of questioning, it might be said, invents a straw man. General education, it might be argued, should not be about general content. There are, on this view, no general concepts or theories worth the name; any enquiry pursued in depth will end in some particular discipline or other. Instead of content, therefore, the 'general' in the term refers to general intellectual powers of the mind; that is to say, intellectual qualities which transcend particular disciplines. For some, it is precisely in the development of general intellectual abilities that a genuine higher education – as distinct from a technical education – is to be found. (This is the view contained in the Robbins report of 1963.[25])

In other words, we need to distinguish general abilities from general ideas.[26] But what sort of general abilities are to be invoked? There is no absolute consensus, but a typical catalogue is offered in the general educational aims to which the Council for National Academic Awards (CNAA) subscribes (and which it expects every course to reflect). There we find intellectual and imaginative skills and powers; an enquiring, analytical and creative approach; independent judgement; critical self-awareness; rigorous approach to data, demonstration and argument; clear communication; seeing relationships between what is learned, and relating what has been learned to actual situations; and appreciation of modes of thought, practices and disciplines other than those of the student's main studies.

Now, lists of this kind are not uncommon – especially in the USA – and there is nothing wrong in them.[27] The questions are: What does such a list amount to? What does it or should it add up to in practice? It is answering questions like these that leads to difficulties. The underlying assumption of such espoused general educational aims is that a level of intellectual development is attainable which warrants a common description, irrespective of the discipline studied. It makes sense to talk of the attainments of the individual studying physiotherapy, physics and philosophy in the same terms. If this view could be translated into general guidelines for action, then indeed we would have a powerful means of combating the narrowness of a discipline-bound curriculum. And we would have a means of encouraging lecturers designing different courses to employ a common educational vocabulary in working through the objectives of those courses.

But this prospect remains just a hope. Even a national validating body like the CNAA has been unable to state the cash value of its general educational aims, leaving it to the good sense of those in the disciplines to realize them through the design of individual courses. The result is that lip service has been paid to CNAA's general educational aims. In turn, as the aims have come up for review over the past 20 years, they have been progressively reduced in status, length and scope. In the CNAA's latest edition of its handbook, they are almost lost, taking up one very brief three-line paragraph.

There is a genuine difficulty here. Is it, in fact, possible to give a general description to the work of students in all the different fields of study and activity? Or are, say, the analytical, communicative, imaginative or critical abilities of students in physics, physiotherapy or philosophy only given real cash value in terms of the specific demands that their separate disciplines place on them? Is the idea of general intellectual development above and beyond particular disciplines just a unicorn concept: a nice thought, but nowhere to be found? We should not give up the hunt just yet.

The idea of emancipation

One of the purposes of this book has been to restore the liberal idea of higher education through what I have termed the emancipatory concept of higher education. I want to bring out an aspect of this concept in preparing the ground for my final suggestions on liberal higher education.

Jurgen Habermas – whose work has formed a backcloth for this book – has strenuously argued that there are two distinctive forms of human formation: one through labour or work, and the other through communication. Neither has supremacy; and neither is reducible to the other.[28]

In this book, I have *not* argued that seeing higher education as a preparation for work is wrong. What I have tried to do is to show that, by itself, such preparation cannot be a sufficient approach to higher education. The emancipatory promise of higher education will go unfulfilled. Action, skill, performance and work itself are entirely acceptable elements of higher education, *provided* that they are accompanied by understanding, self-reflection and self-appraisal. For that, there has to be communication, for two reasons. First, the student has to be able to give an account of what he or she is doing, *and why*. Secondly, giving an account means being willing to enter into a dialogue. Meaningful action must not be allowed to degenerate into technique.[29] It must be accompanied by communication, by the willingness to give reasons – in short, by a preparedness genuinely to share a form of life with others rather than impose (action or thought) on them.

We hear much about communication in higher education today. But it is almost always defined as a need to improve communication skills. Of understanding and mutual dialogue, we hear virtually nothing. The suspicion remains that 'weak communication skills' is a code for either 'this graduate won't accept what we tell him', or 'how can I get the workforce to accept my instructions?' I have tried to show that there are signs that higher education is in danger of accepting this one-dimensional perspective: technique driving out real communication.

Technique, as distinct from understanding and communication, is not only present in higher education in those elements of courses which are demonstrably activity-based. Technique can enter the very heart of the curriculum itself, namely the students' grasp of knowledge and their relationship to it. We have entered a climate where institutions of higher education are evaluated by performance indicators. And, in so far as they are addressed to educational matters at all, these indicators are predominantly concerned with input and output measures;[30] in other words, how many students the institutions can 'process'. In an age such as this, it is not surprising if staff and students conspire together to do the minimum to satisfy the examiners. Students become adept at being 'cue-conscious', in identifying just what has to be done to pass the examinations.[31] As a result, knowledge becomes 'commodified'. It takes on the guise of an inert package of facts, passed between the lecturer, the student and the examiner. Assimilating and demonstrating an easy familiarity with the package are the requirements, the student duly wrapping up its re-presentation so as to be just a little different from fellow students.

To describe higher education in these terms with any degree of plausibility is in itself to show how acquiring knowledge has, for the student, taken on the character of work rather than communication.[32] There will be doubters at this suggestion. But consider: with work comes the possibility of a set of conditions which is imposed, rather than genuinely negotiated; and in its wake, alienation, as forms of life and thought are demanded. This is precisely the case in higher education, evidence for which comes in the form of high non-completion rates on many courses. Indeed, it is a wonder that so many of our students complete their courses at all, given the limited extent to which their educational experience can really be called their own. But there is, we have just observed, a mutual interest between staff and students in manipulating the system, so that as many as possible pass through whatever the quality of the learning experience.

Therefore, communication, understanding and the rational life are in danger of being squeezed out of higher education, to be replaced by sheer labour and technique. (To say as much is only to say that higher education is falling into line with the wider society.)

It follows that the emancipatory dimension of higher education will not be recovered by any strategy which deals only with the content or with the educational processes to which the student is subject. *Both* work, in the form of the content of the curriculum, and communication, in the form of the opportunities for self-expression and critical self-reflection in dialogue with others, have to be confronted.

A truly liberal higher education will not be restored, therefore, simply by altering the relationships between teacher and taught, by recognizing students as centres of consciousness in their own right. Nor can it be accomplished just by recognizing that students can rightfully claim a stake in framing the curriculum by, for example, developing the use of learning contracts or widening the opportunities for open learning. Nor can it be achieved solely by giving encouragement to students to be critical, by formulating and expressing their own view of the knowledge or experience encountered.[33] Nor, finally, can it be pulled off purely by opening the boundaries of the curriculum, by showing students connections between their immediate interests and other disciplines. No – the fact is that *all* these strategies are required to be adopted together.

Higher education as emancipation

Earlier in this chapter, we left open the issue of whether general education resides in general ideas or general methods. In these closing remarks, I want to offer the suggestion that it resides in both. General methods are relatively straightforward: they lie in making greater use of open learning, so that students can exert a significant degree of control over their own learning; and in more collaborative work, so that students can engage with each other in genuine 'communicative' dialogue. General ideas are more problematic. In previous chapters, I have argued for critical thinking and a curriculum which is permeable to disciplines other than the student's core studies, particularly to the perspectives of philosophy and sociology. But is there anything that can be said to justify these ideas so as to raise them above polemic?

I believe there is. If we are really interested in assisting students in becoming masters of their own thinking and development – in taking liberal education seriously, in other words – then we should begin by focusing some attention on the key areas of constraint. In this book, I have suggested that there are two such dimensions of constraint on students' educational development; and, at this point, a brief re-statement of them may be helpful.

The first is that the student's core discipline or professional field contains its own view of knowledge. Not only is the student offered just a slice (or two) of the total picture of knowledge; more perniciously, the discipline contains its sense of what counts as knowledge and truth. The hold on the world that the student gains has a particular character, with its own tests for truth, its own criteria for a valid experience, and its own sense of what can and should be communicated to others in the field. Seen in this way, objective knowledge turns out to have a large element of closure in it; and truth turns out to be partial. (I termed this the epistemological undermining of higher education.)

The second area of constraint arises from the fact that the student's programme of studies is not a disinterested bundle of experiences plucked from thin air, but represents a number of social interests. In addition to the interests of the academic community, higher education accommodates the wider interests of society, including industry, commerce and the professions. The higher education curriculum can no longer pretend to be autonomous, provided by social institutions which are independent of society, for higher education is itself now part of the total apparatus of the modern state. (I called this the sociological undermining of higher education.)

It was in response to these two characteristics that I have argued for the importance of developing the student's critical abilities, together with incorporating a range of disciplinary experiences into the curriculum. I have also argued that, while illuminating connections are possible between all kinds of discipline, it is to philosophical and sociological perspectives that we should look for the greatest critical insight. We can now see why these two approaches to evaluating knowledge are likely to prove the most effective.

If, as I have argued, the curriculum is facing two dominant sources of limitation, then any recovery of a liberal education – with its implication of freedom of thought – has to tackle them head on. The epistemological and sociological underminings are the key threats to a liberating curriculum. Accordingly, they have to be confronted, with philosophical and sociological insights playing a significant part in opening up the curriculum. The student must be encouraged to ask questions about the character of knowledge claims and their implicit values: he or she should embrace a philosophical perspective. The student must also be expected to get to grips with the formation of the discipline or professional field, its underlying interests and its social implications: there should be elements of a sociological perspective.

It is worth repeating that courses in philosophy and sociology are not being proposed. It is a matter of bringing students to become aware of the kinds of questions that, centrally, they need to ask of their learning experience. It is a matter of giving 'critical self-reflection' an adequate interpretation, without leading to self-indulgence or dilettantism.

Nor, again, am I saying that the philosophical and sociological perspectives are the only 'critical' perspectives. As we saw earlier, different perspectives will shed light on different programmes of study. But while we must be flexible enough to allow students to take off in any direction, to follow through the interdisciplinary connections that they identify for themselves, the philosophical and the sociological perspectives must be present somewhere. For the epistemological and sociological underminings are universal and require continuing vigilance if they are to be checked.

In this chapter, I have tried to draw out a radical conception of liberal education, linking it to the idea of emancipation. Key elements in 'emancipation' are self-understanding and self-empowerment. The philosophical and the sociological perspectives present themselves so forcefully precisely because they make possible self-understanding and self-empowerment in a particularly striking way. It is because it is in those dimensions that the limitations on the student's experience are strongest that the educational offensive has to be mounted there. They may not always be sufficient, but they are a necessary weapon in arming for critical insight into one's educational experience. They are an essential condition for the student to reach a state of intellectual independence.

Prospects

The prospect of a liberal higher education is being threatened by the combined interests of the academic community and the wider society. The one promotes an undue disciplinary narrowness, and limited conceptions of knowledge; the other promotes an unreflective assimilation of knowledge, turning it into mere technique. It happens, though, that moves are afoot, prompted by social interests that are also acting to open up the curriculum. Open learning, distance learning, credit accumulation and transferable personal skills are all obliging the academic community to look critically at its educational offerings, and to break away from traditional curricula. At the same time, broader curricula are being demanded, as industry looks to graduates who are not steeped in individual disciplines, but can take a larger view and exhibit more 'flexible' attitudes of mind. The question is: Will the academic community respond to this agenda and give it an educational imprint, or will the narrowness of discipline-bound curricula be exchanged for the narrowness of an industry-led competence-bound curriculum?

Historically, I have tried to show that higher education has contained a radical programme of personal development and, indeed, liberation. At its core, the idea of higher education incorporates the idea of an individual gaining personal intellectual freedom through his or her encounter with knowledge. This emancipatory conception of higher education, as I have called it, does not have to be given up. At least, it should be fought for. We should have a larger vision of what higher education stands for, over and above the contending forces. And it may just be possible for the academic community to come to an accommodation with the interests of the wider society.

The signs are not entirely comforting that the academic community cares sufficiently about such wider educational matters. Yet there are some hopeful indications that a *rapprochement* between liberal aspirations and socioeconomic requirements is possible. In earlier chapters, I commented on the anti-liberal character of courses in professional education, but the best of them are illustrative of a *modus vivendi* between emancipatory and instrumental aims. There is a willingness to rethink professional education, to realize educational ends which are wider than conventional discipline-based curricula and which are also critical of professional practice. And this preparedness is showing signs of becoming an international movement, taking place, for example, in the UK, in the USA and in Sweden.[34] The best programmes in engineering, medicine, nursing and teacher education are interdisciplinary, integrate theoretical and practical activities, call for independent learning and problem-solving, encourage the students to formulate and articulate reasons for action adopted, ask the students to work in groups, and draw the students into considering wider ethical or social issues.

Perhaps, too, as student demand is being allowed to play a larger part in determining the shape of the system, the students themselves will exert this kind of educational influence. But again, the signs are limited, for the students are primarily instrumental in their thinking too. Perhaps an organization like the Council for National Academic Awards could take an initiative, and launch a new 2-year pass degree award for broad interdisciplinary programmes of study, which also demonstrably fulfil its general educational aims (mentioned earlier). But unless the UK universities also participated, such a scheme would be likely to remain marginal to the total system.

In the end, all the parties have to accept their share of responsibility in the matter. But the examples of professional education I have mentioned do suggest that a genuine negotiation of interests is possible and that out of it may come an improved curriculum, doing justice both to 'operational' values[35] and to the emancipatory values embedded in the idea of higher education. It is perhaps just possible to build bridges between the world of work and higher education. In the process, a curriculum may result which is a legitimate expression of liberal values in the modern age.

Conclusions

Review

The discussion in this book has moved on three levels, corresponding to the three tasks set out at the beginning. First, I have tried to show that the term 'higher education' has a conceptual weight of its own. It is not simply a sub-set of the concept of education, and it should not be assumed that our thinking about education in general automatically holds for higher education. Nor is higher education to be identified with any of its institutional forms. It certainly makes sense to explore the idea of the university; and it also makes sense to work out a concept of polytechnic education. But higher education is worth exploring in its own terms. And it is so, not just for the sake of higher education itself, but for wider reasons.

One of the central matters addressed in this discussion has been the fragmentation of the academic community into continually proliferating sub-communities. This development is so entrenched and so pervasive in its effects that it is misleading to talk of a single academic community. But this increasing differentiation in knowledge structures needs to be seen as part of the wider fragmentation of the culture of modern society (Lyotard 1984; MacIntyre 1985). It is doubly vital, therefore, to see if higher education can be conceptualized in an overarching way as a unitary enterprise. Or, on the contrary, to see whether we have to accept that the academic community is just a collection of contrasting language games, each going its own way, with its own view as to what counts as truth, with its own relation to the wider society, and with its own sense as to what is important in the development of the individual. An inquiry into higher education, then, is important not just because it helps us to understand higher education, but also because it helps us to see whether there is any prospect of bringing about a common means of communication across the cognitive cultures of modern society.

On a second level of discussion, this book has tried to map out the key themes that any attempt to offer an overarching educational theory of higher education has to tackle. For one of the motivations behind the book is the sense that our current practices in higher education are too little supported by an examination of fundamental educational issues and of the relevant philosophical and sociological assumptions. In effect, this inquiry has amounted to a sketch of an academic field, which is largely undeveloped in the UK. The nearest name that we could give to it would be the philosophy of higher education. As outlined here, though, that would be slightly misleading, for this project has gone beyond the framework of the philosophy of education as it has been practised over the past 20 years, to embrace social theory and critical theory. What has been developed here is the outlines of a philosophy of higher education conceived as social philosophy and conducted with a practical intent.

It is worth reiterating a point made at the start. Even if the specific argument offered here is not fully accepted, I would still hope that the general topics raised will be acknowledged as establishing much of the framework for any attempt to develop a substantiated educational perspective on higher education. No educational theory of higher education deserves to be taken seriously unless it recognizes the central philosophical problems (of knowledge, rationality, academic freedom, and so on) *and* is sensitive to the social dimensions of higher education, both the external relationships with the wider society, and the internal social dynamics of the academic community and the student experience.

The third level of debate in this book has focused on the meaning of the term 'higher education'. The central claim made here is that 'higher education' is essentially a matter of the development of the mind of the individual student. It is not just any kind of development that the idea points to. An educational process can be termed higher education when the student is carried on to levels of reasoning which make possible critical reflection on his or her experiences, whether consisting of propositional knowledge or of knowledge through action. These levels of reasoning and reflection are 'higher', because they enable the student to take a view (from above, as it were) of what has been learned. Simply, 'higher education' resides in the higher-order states of mind.

This kind of developmental process can take place in any type of institution of higher education – or none. For, conceivably, individuals (autodidacts, as some call them) can undergo this experience through their own activities. As an idea, therefore, 'higher education' has an independence of any institutional form it may take. Indeed, it emerged in Chapter 11 that, strictly speaking, 'higher education' is conceptually independent of both teaching *and* learning. Institutions, though, can be, and usually are, helpful in bringing about 'higher education'.

Criteria of higher education

At the beginning of the book, I said that a test of any educational theory of higher education was this: Does it suggest a set of necessary conditions that an institution has to meet in order to justify the appellation 'institution of higher education'? I believe that we are now in a position to do that.

An institution of higher education justifies the title when it fosters educational processes of the appropriate kind. The analyses in this book suggest six conditions, which together constitute such processes. *Higher* educational processes promote:

1. A deep understanding, by the student, of some knowledge claims.
2. A radical critique, by the same student, of those knowledge claims.
3. A developing competence to conduct that critique in the company of others.
4. The student's involvement in determining the shape and direction of that critique (i.e. some form of independent inquiry).
5. The student's self-reflection, with the student developing the capacity critically to evaluate his or her own achievements, knowledge claims and performance.
6. The opportunity for the student to engage in that inquiry in a process of open dialogue and cooperation (freed from unnecessary direction).

These are the minimal educational conditions for an educational process to justify the title 'higher education'. They are logically necessary, in the sense that they follow as a matter of logic from the idea of higher education. To the extent that an educational process falls short of these conditions, it also falls short of achieving the promise of higher education. They are, therefore, the essential conditions an institution has to uphold if it is to deserve the title 'institution of higher education'.

Combating the double undermining

Apart from these general arguments, I have also sketched out a specific view of higher education. I have argued that, historically, higher education has contained an emancipatory dimension, promising a freeing of the mind so as to empower it to be master of its fate. I have tried to show that this liberal idea of higher education can make sense today, despite the double undermining that it faces.

On the one hand, it is confronted with an undermining of its epistemological base, because the assumption of securing objective knowledge and truth has been placed in doubt in the wake of modern philosophical and theoretical developments. On the other hand, the assumption that the guardianship and dissemination of knowledge should be conducted in an institutional setting relatively independent of social interests has proved vacuous, because higher education has become a pivotal institution of the modern state. This sociological undermining has been further compounded as the academic community has developed into a multitude of sub-communities, each imposing its own stamp on our representations of the world.

My argument has been that by recovering the emancipatory content of the idea of higher education, it is possible to some extent to neutralize the effects of this double (epistemological and sociological) undermining, even though it is impossible to remove it. Specifically, I have suggested four strategies: critical perspectives, directed at the core of the student's curriculum; opening the curriculum to allow in elements of interdisciplinarity; particular attention being paid to philosophical and sociological perspectives; and open learning, including self-directed learning and group work. These four strategies should be adopted together; otherwise, there is a danger of any of them being narrowly conceived and becoming just one more technique.

Through a curriculum of this kind, a liberal higher education is possible. It will not be liberal in the sense of either being divorced from the world of affairs or inhabiting a world of knowledge freed from social interests; the graduate comprehends that neither kind of purity is available. Instead, the kind of higher education sketched out here is liberal in the sense of cognitive self-empowerment. The graduate is able, intellectually, to stand on his or her own feet, although aware of the predicament of the essential uncertainty (cognitively or morally) of any position taken up or action performed. The well-educated graduate is able to keep an eye on him or herself, continually looking over his or her own shoulder on the essential insecurity of any stance adopted.

This is not a completely satisfactory situation. But it is the best available, given the double undermining that higher education faces.

Critical reflections

Finally, there are three potential criticisms of the position I have taken which deserve some response. First, it could be said that *the* idea of higher education worked out here is simply *an* idea of higher education. I have not, in other words, escaped the accusation 'that's only your view', a potential charge I mentioned in the first chapter. There are two responses. First, I have tried to show that the emancipatory conception of higher education does in fact have its roots in the whole history of the thought and practice of higher education. It is part of the conceptual archaeology of what is meant by higher education. My other response to this criticism is to point out that there is an inherent openness in the emancipatory conception of higher education; and so, characterizing this concept as simply one of several partial alternatives is misleading. The emancipatory concept of higher education is founded on the student's growing self-insight and self-evaluation: the student comes to see that his or her thoughts and actions could be other than they are, and that there is no final resting place. The curriculum processes promoted by the emancipatory conception of higher education are themselves open-ended. Staff and students work together, appraising them and modifying them in the light of experience.

It follows that this idea of higher education will lead to states of mind, curricular arrangements and institutional processes which allow for questioning about themselves. The reflective processes prompted by the emancipatory concept even provide for critical evaluation about the concept itself. There is no question, therefore, of the emancipatory concept being imposed arbitrarily, or of predetermining in any detailed way the character of the curriculum. If it is to be genuinely emancipatory, it will offer space for staff, students and all involved to determine their own fate collectively.

A second commentary on this idea of higher education might be to suggest that it is excessively intellectual. Talk of self-reflection and higher-order states of mind is sheer academicism. Quite apart from the need to supply qualified personnel in a host of professional settings, the world has major problems of poverty and the environment, and individuals want to find their own personal fulfilment. All this points to a higher education geared towards action, social contribution and involvement. But nothing said here runs counter to these points.

Indeed, I have argued that our conceptions of knowing in higher education are unduly limited, and that knowing through action (as in professional education), through performance (as in the performing arts), and through collective activities, should be much more embraced in the curriculum. Developments of that kind, though, can and should still be tested against the criteria of higher education. Do they lead to independence of thought and action? If responsible action is being encouraged, is the student asked to give an account of his or her actions? If performance is expected, is the student expected to be able to demonstrate that this movement or technique was adopted deliberately, and that alternatives could have been chosen?

A final criticism of the view of higher education set out here might be that, morally, it takes an overly neutral position. In apparently not wishing to impose a value position, it runs the risk of opening the way for all kinds of morally undesirable attitudes to find a home in higher education. How, for example, might it fare in the face of a student who is an avowed member of the National Front? For does the emancipatory conception not imply that students should follow their own inclinations?

There are two responses. First, higher education should not be expected to contribute to every facet of an individual's personality. As Marjorie Reeves has commented, 'education cannot "make a person": it has a more limited role'. Secondly, and even more significantly, the objection misses the point. The emancipatory conception of higher education *is* value-laden. It is founded on a belief in the life of reason; and on the assumption that (whether through words or action) structured discussion aimed at advancing understanding matters. The loss of absolute foundations of knowledge and values (marked by relativism and post-structuralism) does not mean that 'anything goes'. On the contrary, it means that we have to accept personal responsibility for any truth claim or value judgement we espouse. Consequently, in so far as our National Front student brings behaviours which violate those underpinnings, he is liable to be excluded from the community of higher education. In the face of unreason, the reasoned life cannot be silent.

It may be further rejoined that, in that case, what we have here – under the label of the emancipatory concept of higher education – is an ideology, albeit the ideology of the Western liberal enlightenment. To the extent that by ideology is meant a cluster of beliefs with its inherent set of values, the charge must be accepted. But if by ideology is meant a tightly bounded outlook, representing narrow interests and brooking no criticism or dissent, the charge must surely be rejected. For, as we have seen, the emancipatory conception of higher education is ultimately founded on the right to criticize, and on the right to dissent even from the idea itself.

Notes and References

In these notes, most references are given in full. Where only a partial reference is provided, the full reference is to be found in the selective bibliography.

Chapter 1   The Missing Element

1. *Student Numbers in Higher Education – Great Britain 1975 to 1987*, DES Statistical Bulletin, March 1989, 4/89.
2. Niblett, W. R., 1979, Review of Brubacher's On the Philosophy of Higher Education, *Higher Education*, **8**(3) 349–350. Professor Niblett might be forgiven for omitting to add that (in 1979) there was no university chair of higher education in the UK. This is still the case. Professor Niblett was the last holder of an established chair of higher education, in the 1960s at the University of London Institute of Education. A personal title of Professor of Higher Education was conferred on Professor Lewis Elton, by the University of Surrey, in the 1980s. (Professor Elton has since retired.) This historical point underlines the lack of effort put into understanding higher education in the UK.
3. Allen, M., 1988, *The Goals of Universities*, Milton Keynes, Open University Press; Nuttgens, P., 1988, *What Should We Teach and How Should We Teach it: Aims and Purposes of Higher Education*; Birch, W., 1988, *The Challenge to Higher Education*.
4. Minogue (in *The Concept of a University*, 1973) goes so far the other way, in defending the intrinsic character of the university against external forces, that for him, even 'the survival of universities is not an academic concern of universities' (p. 99). For reasons I explain in the text (especially Chapters 2 and 5), this implied separation of the university from the world of practical affairs is not a tenable position, either.
5. An exception to these observations is Tony Becher's *Academic Tribes and Territories*, 1989.
6. McMurrin, S. M. (ed.), 1976, *On the Meaning of the University*, Salt Lake City, University of Utah. Additionally, e.g. Kerr, C., 1972, *The Uses of the University*; Nisbet, R., 1971, *The Degradation of the Academic Dogma*; Wegener, C., 1978, *Liberal Education and the Modern University*; and Derek Bok's works, 1982, *Beyond the Ivory Tower*, and 1986, *Higher Learning* – a title very similar to Hutchins' small but important book half a century ago (1936), *The Higher Learning in America*, New Haven, Yale University Press.

   However, American books are not immune to the tendencies noted here: the (1984) collection edited by Burton Clark, *Perspectives on Higher Education*, Stanford, California, University of California Press, contains no chapter on either educational or philosophical perspectives.

7. To give just one example from each country: Bergendal, G., 1984, *Knowledge Policies and the Traditions of Higher Education*; Cameron, J. M., 1978, *On the Idea of a University*; Chambers, J. H., 1981, *Knowledge, Authority and the Administration of Tertiary Education*, Armidale, University of New England. Also, in Australia, J. P. Powell has written in academic journals over the past 20 years on the idea of higher education.

8. Peters, R. S., 1969, What is an educational process?, in R. S. Peters (ed.), *The Concept of Education*.

9. Except for a small amount of degree work in technical colleges offered under the auspices of universities, especially the University of London through its external degree system. See Robinson, 1968, ch. 1.

10. DES Statistical Bulletin, 4/89, op. cit.

11. Gallie, W. B., 1955, Essentially contested concepts, *Proceedings of the Aristotelian Society*, **56**. See also Aspin, D., in *Metaphor and Meaning in Educational Discourse*, W. Taylor (ed.), 1984, p. 27. My argument is that higher education is a contested concept so far as its peripheral goals are concerned, but that in terms of its core, it is not. In other words, it is not *essentially* contested.

12. DES Statistical Bulletin, 4/89, op. cit., table 6.

13. Cf. Taylor, C., Neutrality in political science, in P. Laslett and W. G. Runciman (eds), 1969, *Philosophy, Politics and Society*, 3rd series. Oxford, Blackwell.

14. Conceivably, it might do so as a research project, or even as a student project (in economics, sociology or game theory). (I owe the point to Leslie Wagner.) Whether it would be permissible for an institution of higher education to make a profit from such an enterprise is a further matter.

15. DES, Cm. 114, 1987, *Higher Education – Meeting the Challenge*, p. 7, para. 2.11.

16. Lawson and Appignanesi, 1989, pp. xi, 51, 57.

17. Witness 'academic freedom', chosen as the theme of the 1988 annual conference of the Society for Research into Higher Education.

18. The distinctions within liberal education that follow draw on Peters, R. S., Ambiguities in liberal education and the problem of its content, in his collection (1980).

19. Ker's edition of Newman's work, *The Idea of a University*, 1976, p. 99. Newman's reflections on the university and education were made in 1851–2 and delivered in the form of *Discourses on the Scope and Nature of University Education*, given in Dublin on the founding of the Catholic university there.

20. The idea of a theoretical undertaking with a 'practical intent' borrows from Habermas, who uses the term in describing his own work. For example, *Habermas: Autonomy and Solidarity* (1986, p. 55, interviews with Jurgen Habermas, edited by Peter Dews, London, Verso). He adds an interesting rider, in commenting that 'not even a theory with practical intent can provide any more or anything other than, in the optimum case, a set of plausible hypotheses'. That is, too, what I have tried to do in this book.

21. His essay, Falsification and the methodology of scientific research programmes, in I. Lakatos and A. Musgrave (eds), 1977, p. 157.

Chapter 2   A Contested Concept?

1. The phrase 'the idea of the idea' refers to the widespread assumption that there can be a single idea of higher education, whatever its actual form (an assumption which this book shares). For a sceptical examination of the idea of the idea of higher education, see Rothblatt, S., 1988, *The Idea of a University and its Antithesis*, a paper presented to the seminar on the sociology of culture, La Trobe University, Australia.

2. For example, among individuals who have had a definite view of higher education, Mark Pattison in the nineteenth century: see his 1969, *Memoirs*, Sussex, Centaur; Sparrow, J., 1967, *Mark Pattison and the Idea of a University*, Cambridge, Cambridge University Press; or Walter Moberly in the twentieth: see his 1949, *The Crisis in the University*, London, SCM Press.

   Among historical developments, where institutional forms embody particular conceptions of higher education, the following would also count as testimony to the ubiquity of the emancipatory *idea* being argued for here: the development of the Scottish universities – see, for instance, Stone, L., 1983, Social control and intellectual excellence: Oxbridge and Edinburgh, 1560–1983, in N. Phillipson (ed.); von Humboldt and the formation of the German universities at the end of the eighteenth and beginning of the nineteenth centuries – see Gellert, C., 1981, *A Comparative Study of the Changing Functions of English and German Universities*, University of Cambridge, PhD thesis; and the new universities of Great Britain in the 1960s – see Sloman, A., 1964, *A University in the Making*, London, BBC; and Daiches, D. (ed.), 1964, *The Idea of a New University*, London, Deutsch.

3. Plato, 1971 edition, *The Republic* (edited by Cornford), pp. 227ff.

4. Ibid., pp. 232 and 231.

5. Ibid., p. 252.

6. Ibid., p. 225.

7. Ibid., p. 182.

8. As does Hirst, P., Liberal education and the nature of knowledge, in R. S. Peters (ed.), 1973.

9. For the background to this section, see Rashdall, 1895, *The Universities of Europe in the Middle Ages*, Oxford, Clarendon Press; Mainsbridge, 1923, *The Older Universities of England*, London, Longmans, Green and Co; Hackett, M. D., 1970, *The Original Statutes of Cambridge University*, Cambridge, Cambridge University Press; Gellert, C., op. cit., note 2; Brooke, C. and Highfield, R., 1988, *Oxford and Cambridge*, Cambridge, Cambridge University Press.

10. Cameron, J. M., 1978, pp. 26–7.

11. Newman, J. H., 1976, in *The Idea of a University*, I. T. Ker (ed.), p. 103. Oxford, Oxford University Press.

12. Ibid., p. 30.

13. Ibid., p. 103.

14. Newman's emphasis, ibid., p. 145.

15. Ibid., p. 104.

16. Ibid., p. 131, my emphasis.

17. Ibid., p. 111.

18. Ibid., p. 123.

19. Ibid., p. 125.

20. Ibid., p. 118.

21. Ibid., p. 105.

22. Ibid., p. 110.

23. Ibid., p. 112.

24. Ibid., p. 118.

25. Jaspers, K., 1965, *The Idea of the University*, London, Peter Owen, pp. 51ff.

26. Ibid., p. 25.

27. Ibid., pp. 25–7.

28. Ibid., p. 25.

29. This idea of Jaspers is remarkably similar to that of the contemporary social theorist,

Jurgen Habermas (and doubtless reflects something of the German philosophical outlook – see Chapter 4).

30. Ibid., pp. 28–9 and 45.
31. Ibid., p. 63.
32. Ibid., pp. 64–5.
33. Ibid., p. 48.
34. Ibid., p. 66.
35. Ibid., p. 41.
36. The discussion has been shifting to and fro between talk of 'the university' and of 'higher education'. In this chapter, not much hangs on the distinction. Here, we just need to remember that a certain degree of translation and updating is required when we encounter the term 'the university' when used in relation to higher education prior to its expansion in the 1960s and the formation of the polytechnic and college sector.
37. Collier, K. G., 1982, Ideological influences in higher education, *Studies in Higher Education*, **7**(1) 13–19.
38. Edwards, E. G., 1982, *Higher Education for Everyone*, Nottingham, Spokesman, pp. 28–36.
39. See Crosland, D., the then Secretary of State for Education, in speeches given at Woolwich (since renamed Thames) Polytechnic, 1965, *The Role in Higher Education of Regional and Other Technical Colleges Engaged in Advanced Work*, DES, Administrative Memorandum, 2 May; and at the University of Lancaster, *The Structure and Development of Higher Education*, 1967, reprinted in Robinson, E. 1968. On the 'service' functions of the new sector, see Burgess, T., 1977, *Education after School*, London, Victor Gollancz.
40. See Marcuse, 1968, *One Dimensional Man*, for perhaps the most forthright statement of this kind.
41. Pateman, T., 1972, *Counter Course*, Harmondsworth, Penguin; Roszak, T., 1973, *The Making of a Counter Culture: Reflections on the Technocratic Society & its Youthful Opposition*, London, Faber and Faber.
42. Avorn, J. L. *et al.*, 1968, *University in Revolt: A History of the Columbia Crisis*, London, Macdonald; Weaver, G. and Weaver, J. H. (eds), 1969, *The University and Revolution*, Englewood Cliffs, NJ, Prentice-Hall; Nagel, J. (ed.), 1969, *Student Power*, London, Merlin.
43. Cockburn, A. and Blackburn, R. (eds), 1969, *Student Power*, London, Penguin; Marcuse, H., 1973, *An Essay on Liberation*, London, Penguin. Marcuse saw the students as a catalytic agency. It was their task to help bring about the change in consciousness of the workers, a precondition of any structural revolution.
44. Minogue, 1973, p. 71.
45. Ibid., p. 77.
46. Ibid., p. 76.
47. Ibid., p. 80.
48. Cf. Gellner, E., 1969, *Thought and Change*, pp. 105ff.

Chapter 3   Witchcraft, Astrology and Knowledge Policies

1. See Barnes, 1974, p. 117; Feyerabend, 1978, pp. 296–9, 304–305; 1982, pp. 91–5, 134ff.
2. Kuhn, in I. Lakatos and A. Musgrave (eds), 1977, p. 8.
3. Santinelli, P., 1988, Winning status by an arm and a leg, *Times Higher Education Supplement*, 2 September, p. 6.

4. Ashby, E., 1958, *Technology and the Academics*, London, Macmillan, p. 56; Nuttgens, 1988, ch. 1, note 3; Heyck, 1982, *The Transformation of Intellectual Life in Victorian England*, pp. 172–3. The 1852 Royal Commission, in looking at Oxford, found that – with subjects being limited to those taught by the Fellows – 'Students have had not motive whatever supplied by the University to induce them to study Physiology, Chemistry, and other Natural Sciences', quoted in Sanderson, 1975, *The Universities in the Nineteenth Century*, London, Routledge and Kegan Paul, p. 95.

5. On the way 'knowledge policies' affect the curriculum in higher education, see Bergendal, 1984.

6. Ayer, A. J., *The Problem of Knowledge*, Harmondsworth, Penguin, 1956, p. 35; Scheffler, I., *Conditions of Knowledge*, Glenview, Illinois, Scott, Foresman and Co., 1965, p. 65.

7. A point made most forcefully by Karl Popper in his assertion that 'Knowledge in the objective sense is *knowledge without a knower:* it is *knowledge without a knowing subject*' (Popper's emphases), 1975, p. 109.

8. Of which the young A. J. Ayer was an articulate spokesman: *Language, Truth and Logic*, London, Victor Gollancz, 1936.

9. See Gellner's essay, The crisis in the humanities and the mainstream of philosophy, in J. H. Plumb (ed.), 1964, *The Crisis in the Humanities*, Harmondsworth, Penguin, criticizing the effect of Wittgensteinian philosophy on philosophy in general: 'Forms of life are a problem, not a solution' (p. 67).

10. Gellner, 1974, p. 170.

11. Ibid., p. 194.

12. Popper, 1975, p. 164.

13. Ibid., p. 185. Precisely because it looks to be an account of learning and acquiring knowledge that holds across all disciplines, the Popperian epistemology has been invoked as an underpinning to the cross-disciplinary Degree programme in Independent Studies (Burgess, T., 1977, *Education after School*, London, Victor Gollancz; Robbins, D., 1988, *The Rise of Independent Study*, Milton Keynes, Open University Press).

14. Popper, in his essay Reason or revolution?, in T. W. Adorno *et al.*, 1977, *The Positivist Dispute in German Sociology*, London, Heinemann, pp. 289ff.

15. Popper, 1975, p. 108; see also his essay on The logic of the social sciences, in Adorno *et al.* (op. cit.), where we find such remarks as 'The method of the social sciences, like that of the natural sciences . . .'.

16. Feyerabend, op. cit., note 1; also 1987.

17. For the conceptual background to much of this section, see Gellner's writings, op. cit.; also 1969 and his essay, Concepts and society, in D. Emmet and A. MacIntyre (eds), *Sociological Theory and Philosophical Analysis*, London, Macmillan, 1972. But, interestingly, Gellner does not accept the logic of his own arguments and ends up by offering us a selector philosophy of his own (1974).

18. As we saw in Chapter 2, Newman associated the idea of 'university' with 'universal knowledge' (1976, p. 5) or 'universal learning' (p. 95). Though, on Cameron's assessment, Newman knew 'this is not historically accurate', p. 75; Cameron, J. M., 1978, op. cit. (ch. 1, note 7), p. 25.

19. For a more formal philosophical example, note Gellner, 1964, op. cit., note 9, on Logical positivism, which for him 'always somehow had rather an inexpungable aroma of Christ Church, Oxford'. He (1969) compares Ayer's *Language, Truth and Logic* unfavourably with Snow's *The Two Cultures*: 'Snow's essay is as much a piece of philosophy as the other . . . but the superiority of Snow's formulation arises from the

fact that the problem of the relation between that which is science and that which is not, is a problem about "cultures", ways of life, . . . and not about some strangely atomic . . . entities such as "propositions" or statements or whatnot' (p. 209).

20. This discussion has been using the term 'knowledge policies'. The term is generally unfamiliar in the UK, where the academic community has a significant degree of freedom to determine which areas of knowledge are taught in academic institutions. Other more centralized systems of higher education have had to confront the issue as a matter of deliberate policy (e.g. Sweden: Bergendal 1984). The use of the term does, however, bring out the point that even though it might not have been accompanied by any explicit deliberation, the inclusion or exclusion of a form of knowledge in the curriculum is in part a reflection of presuppositions about knowledge: tacit conceptions exist about the character of acceptable knowledge. Knowledge policies are at work, whether we realize it or not.

21. See the discussions, from the quite different perspectives of Gellner, 1969, ch. 3; 1974, chs 3 and 4; Feyerabend, 1987, ch. 3; Lyotard, 1984, *passim*, but see p. 26.

22. By 'humanities' here, I mean all those forms of awareness and structured creativity which express our humanness; that is to say, I include fine art, where too we see signs of a sense of self-doubt, and a willingness to incorporate business studies and information technology in an effort to demonstrate their 'relevance'.

23. Gellner, Feyerabend, Lyotard, op. cit. See also Habermas, 1976 and 1978; and his essay, Technical progress and the social life-world, in his collection (1972). These connections between knowledge and the legitimation of modern society in Habermas' thought are brought out in the commentary of Kortian, G., 1980, *Metacritique: The Philosophical Argument of Jurgen Habermas*, Cambridge, University of Cambridge Press.

24. A similar perspective comes through in Hamlyn, D. W., *The Theory of Knowledge*, London, Macmillan, 1971, that is also far from being simply a defence of science-based varieties of formal knowledge: different forms of life with their own forms of knowledge are recognized as a logical possibility. But it is still, in the end, a restrictive epistemology that we are offered, for '[knowledge] presupposes that the person who knows has the relevant concepts or ideas, concepts that might conceivably be formulated in verbal terms' (p. 54).

25. As R. S. Peters implies, 1966, p. 30. On this general point of knowledge-through-activities, see Feyerabend, 1987, p. 106 *et seq*.

26. Barnes, 1977, p. 9.

27. Hampshire, 1970, p. 93. The point, in the context of higher education, is borne out by the fact that while the term 'experiential learning' has become part of the vocabulary of higher education over the past decade (Evans, N., 1980, *The Knowledge Revolution*, London, McIntyre Grant; Weil, S. and McGill, I. (eds), 1989, *Making Sense of Experiential Learning*, Milton Keynes, Open University Press), we still lack a worked-out epistemological theory of it.

28. This phrase of Wittgenstein's has been taken up by Lyotard, who points to the fragmentation of modern cognitive life with (so it seems) approval (see former references).

29. Admittedly, this result is precisely what Feyerabend at least is trying to prevent; for it is the power of science as an ideology that he is trying to reduce.

30. Bergendal, 1984, p. 71 *et seq*.

31. In not attempting more seriously to offer an epistemology which speaks to our own age, are the philosophers not guilty, perhaps, of contributing to their own demise?

32. See work in the sociology of science, e.g. Bloor, 1976; Barnes, 1974 and 1977; Barnes,

B. and Edge, D. (eds), 1982, *Science in Context*, Milton Keynes, Open University Press. See also the work of Robin Horton, African traditional thought and Western science, in M. F. D. Young (ed.), 1971, on the comparability between Western science and primitive thought.

33. Or the 'intersubjective' character of knowledge, as many describe it (Hamlyn, 1971, op. cit., note 24; Peters, 1966, p. 54; Bernstein, 1983, p. 226; Rorty, 1989, in H. Lawson and L. Appignanesi (eds), p. 11).

34. Habermas, 1979, p. 61: 'the essential presupposition for the success of an illocutionary act consists in the speaker's entering into a specific engagement, so that the hearer can rely on him'.

35. On promoting personal involvement by the student, see Reeves, 1988.

36. See Rorty, 1980, ch. viii, on the quest for truth as 'edification' (since '*Bildung* sounds a bit too foreign', p. 360); Habermas' inaugural lecture, 1978, p. 301, on the Greek conception of the link between theory and the conduct of life.

37. Gellert, 1981, op. cit., ch. 2, note 2; Svensson, L. G., Actors and structures in the selection of knowledge, in Bergendal (ed.), 1984, p. 91; see also Rorty, op. cit., Note 36.

38. The point is made by Habermas, 1978 and Bergendal (ed.), 1984.

39. Cf. the conclusions of Bernstein, 1983, pp. 223–6, which are not totally dissimilar.

40. The phrase is that of Feyerabend, though he points out that this is not the only methodological principle which he advocates (1982, p. 39).

41. The concept of openness is perhaps most associated with Popper. The idea comes through in another way in Popper's work, when he points out that while our knowledge claims have to be made within a framework, it is always possible to step outside the framework – a position which leads him to talk of 'the myth of the framework', Normal science and its dangers, in I. Lakatos and A. Musgrave (eds), 1977, p. 56.

42. For more on institutions and communities as being characterized by their 'practices', see MacIntyre, 1985.

43. Maxwell's *From Knowledge to Wisdom* (1987), comes close to this position. For example, 'It is only insofar as we can act successfully in the world, and can propose and assess possible actions, that we can be in a position to possess or to acquire propositional knowledge' (p. 174). This view leads him to distinguish 'truths' in terms of their value to humanity (p. 104).

Chapter 4   The Truth, the Whole Truth . . .

1. Lukes, S., 1973, On the social determination of truth, in R. Horton and R. Finnegan (eds), *Modes of Thought*, London, Faber and Faber. For a critique of the general idea that there are universal rules of thought, see Winch, Understanding a primitive society (esp. p. 100), in B. R. Wilson (ed.), 1970. Lukes' rejoinder, Some problems about rationality, is contained in the same volume. See also Barnes, 1974, pp. 34–41.

2. Peters provides an example of this way of thinking when he says that 'science is the supreme example of reason in action . . . because of the agreement in judgements which it permits by means of its testing procedures. These guarantee objectivity and the escape from arbitrariness'. Subjectivity and Standards, in W. R. Niblett (ed.), 1975, p. 149.

3. See, for instance, the analysis of the movement of thought within mathematics offered by Bloor, 1976 (I discussed this in Chapter 3).

4. Habermas, 1978, p. 362.

5. Ibid., p. 150.

6. In making these observations on structuralism, no judgement is intended on those structural theories themselves.

7. Hamlyn, D. W., *The Theory of Knowledge*, London, Macmillan, 1971, pp. 255–7.

8. Gellner, 1969, pp. 86 and 184.

9. Bloor, 1976, p. 87.

10. Ibid., p. 86.

11. The terms 'world I' and 'world II' are taken from Popper, *Objective Knowledge*, 1975, p. 74.

12. Leavis, 1969, p. 48, where he talks of a 'third realm'.

13. Popper, op. cit., p. 73.

14. Ibid., p. 73.

15. See also, Popper's essay, On the sources of knowledge and ignorance, in J. N. Findlay (ed.), 1966, *Studies in Philosophy*, Oxford, Oxford University Press.

16. For different versions of relativism, see Margolis, J., 1986, *Pragmatism without Foundations*, Oxford, Blackwell.

17. Popper, 1975, pp. 60–61.

18. Becher, 1989; Gouldner, 1976.

19. A view implicit in Barnes, 1974.

20. For example, Pitcher, G. (ed.), 1964, *Truth*, Englewood Cliffs, NJ, Prentice-Hall.

21. If the natural sciences favour the correspondence theory of truth, it could be argued that the professionally oriented courses support the pragmatist theory of truth, and the humanities and the social sciences the coherence theory of truth. (I owe the point to Tony Becher.)

22. On 'theory-ladenness', see Harris, 1979, pp. 39–40; Bloor, 1976: 'We never have the independent access to reality that would be necessary if it were to be matched up against our theories' (p. 34); Gellner, 1974, p. 74; Kuhn, 1970, p. 206.

23. Feyerabend, 1978, pp. 43–4.

24. Kuhn, 1970, p. 35.

25. Feyerabend (in I. Lakatos and A. Musgrave (eds), 1977) argues that Kuhn's view of science provides solace for those happy to work in a routine and specialized groove; whereas he would rather wish us to adopt a principle of theory proliferation.

26. Feyerabend (1978) also draws similar educational implications from his anarchic view of scientific progress.

27. William James, quoted in Scheffler, I., *Conditions of Knowledge*, Glenview, Illinois, Scott, Foresman and Co., 1965, pp. 44–5.

28. For Nazi Germany (and its universities), 'the sole criterion of the truth of an idea [was] whether it will serve the German race, or rather the Nazi Party . . .' (p. 117). The new chairs established in universities included those in 'folk doctrine', 'race politics', 'race hygiene' and 'spiritual history' (p. 119). Nash, A. S., 1945, *The University and the Modern World*, London, SCM Press.

29. Marjorie Reeves (1988) offers perhaps the best defence of this view.

30. On the weakness of textbooks in science, see Kuhn, 1970, pp. 80 and 136–8.

31. Gadamer, H. G., 1975, *Truth and Method*, London, Sheed and Ward, p. 169.

32. Ibid., p. 168.

33. Ibid., p. 163.

34. Leavis, 1969, e.g. p. 43.

35. Kuhn, 1970, p. 147ff. Though compare Feyerabend, 1982, pp. 65–70, where he argues that theories might be incommensurable in terms of their content, but they can still be compared on more subjective grounds (such as simplicity or coherence). But this involves turning theory choice 'from a rational and objective routine into a

complex decision involving conflicting preferences and propaganda will play a major role in it, as it does in all cases involving arbitrary elements'.

36. In his writings, Feyerabend has conducted a running debate with Lakatos' account of theory appraisal (e.g. Feyerabend, 1978, 1982). For an assessment of Lakatos' views from an educational perspective, see Harris, 1979, pp. 41ff.

37. The phrase 'deep subjectivity' is that of Roger Poole (1972), who offers a brilliant defence (against objectivism) of a subjective acquisition of knowledge. One of the attractions of the framework he develops is its flexibility. As he says, 'Each and every human concern has to develop a subjective method in its own terms and for its own purposes, and it is obvious that what suits one discipline or art will not suit another in exactly those terms or in exactly the same way' (p. 132).

38. See Habermas' work on 'universal pragmatics' (1979). A good secondary account of this aspect of Habermas' thought is given in Roderick, 1986, chs 3 and 4.

39. See Roderick, 1986, pp. 78 and 85. See also Geuss, 1981, pp. 66 and 70. (Geuss' little book contains a more critical – though still very accessible – account of Habermas' work.)

40. Habermas, 1978, Postscript, p. 374. In his 1982 essay, he describes and defends it as the 'discourse theory of truth', A reply to my critics, in J. B. Thompson and D. Held (eds), *Habermas: Critical Debates*, London, Macmillan.

41. Bernstein, 1983; Habermas' inaugural lecture, reprinted 1978, MacIntyre, 1985.

Chapter 5   Ivory Tower?

1. The general point, that in clarifying our conceptual options, we have to engage in sociology, has been made by Gellner (1969) and MacIntyre, A., 1971, *Against the Self-Images of the Age*, London, Duckworth.

2. On universities' income patterns, see *University Statistics*, Vol. 3, table 4, Cheltenham, UGC.

3. Galbraith, J. K., 1969, *The New Industrial State*, Harmondsworth, Penguin, p. 372.

4. Roizen, J. and Jepson, M., 1985, *Degrees for Jobs: Employer Expectations of Higher Education*, Guildford, SRHE/NFER-Nelson.

5. Though, as Peter Scott points out, with the computers producing increasing amounts of data, much of the knowledge base of the post-modern society is likely to be sheer information rather than analyses and reflections that count for knowledge, *Times Higher Education Supplement*, 18 August 1989.

6. Habermas, 1972, ch. 6, p. 101: '. . . society and the state are no longer in that relationship that Marxian theory had defined as that of base and superstructure'. Gorz, in Young and Whitty, 1978, p. 132: '. . . developments . . . rather lead to the conclusion that the productive forces are shaped by the capitalist relations of production'. This modified view of the base–superstructure relationship also comes through the work of Althusser: see Abercrombie, N., 1980, *Class, Structure and Knowledge*, Oxford, Blackwell, p. 95. This theme and its implications for our understanding of higher education was one of the central issues facing a Swedish international conference (Bergendal, 1984, pp. 10ff. and 122).

7. Bell, 1976; Lyotard, 1984; Bohme, in Bergendal, 1984.

8. Habermas, 1972, ch. 6, pp. 113–14.

9. Habermas, 1976. This is also a point which comes through the work of Gellner, for whom we are 'ineluctably wedded' to this form of civilization (1969).

10. Peter Scott points out that there has been a jostling for supremacy within the humanities (classics, philosophy, history and English all in turn securing the leading position); none the less, together they provided the core of the liberal university in its

custodianship of an intellectual tradition 'derived from the culture of an elite' (1984, pp. 30–31).

11. Castles and Wustenberg, 1979. See also Gorz, op. cit., note 6.

12. Althusser, 1969. See the discussions in Abercrombie, op. cit., note 6, pp. 122ff.; Giroux, 1983, pp. 79ff.

13. For example, 'Sydney has one opera house, one Arts centre, one zoo, one harbour, but two philosophy departments. The reason for this abundance is not any over-whelming demand for philosophy . . . but the fact that philosophy has party lines' (Feyerabend, 1982, p. 154).

14. Shaw, 1975; Habermas, 1976; Barnes, 1977.

15. See the descriptions of the proposals from the 11 successful universities and polytechnics, *Enterprise in Higher Education: Key Features of the Enterprise in Higher Education Proposals*, heffield, Training Agency, 1989.

16. The term 'personal transferable skills' has come into common use in the UK recently. It is, though, ill-defined and without any proper philosophical grounding, reflecting its use by so many different groupings. *Transferable Personal Skills in Employment: The Contribution of Higher Education*, London, National Advisory Body, 1986.

17. *Contracts between the Funding Bodies and Higher Education Institutions.* Consultative Paper, London, DES, 1987.

18. For the background to this paragraph, see Gouldner, 1976, ch. 8, p. 185, but throughout, and 1979; Giroux, 1983, ch. 3; Scott, 1984, ch. 2; Bergendal, 1983, 1984; Aronowitz and Giroux, 1987, ch. 8.

19. Bowles and Gintis, *Capitalism and Education in the United States*, in Young and Whitty (eds), 1978. This amounts to a repudiation of their 'correspondence' thesis, made elsewhere. See also O' Keeffe, D., 1979, Capitalism and correspondence: A critique of recent Marxist analyses of education, *Higher Education Review*, Autumn, pp. 40–54; Giroux, 1983.

20. Julian Symons, 1957, *The General Strike*, London, Cresset Press, pp. 67–9.

21. Habermas' inaugural lecture, p. 309; and p. 135 (1978).

22. Habermas' insistence on this logic of the empirical sciences was one of his points of disagreement with Marcuse, who had felt that a different kind of science was a possibility (1972, ch. 6).

23. This is a point on which there is general agreement, both across the conservatives (Gellner, 1969, pp. 69–70; Popper, 1975, ch. 6, pp. 240ff.) and the radicals (Marcuse, 1968, ch. 1; Habermas, 1972, ch. 4; Feyerabend, 1987, ch. 12; Mendelsohn, in Bergendal (ed.), 1983).

24. Rose and Rose (eds), 1976. See especially the essays by Rose and Rose, Cooley, Ciccotti *et al.*

25. Dr Sydney Brennar, molecular biologist, University of Cambridge, talking on a television documentary on genetic research, 1988.

26. Peacocke (ed.), 1985, especially his own essay; Bergendal (ed.), 1984, his essay Several dimensions or one?

27. Habermas, 1972, ch. 6, p. 112, leading to what he has termed 'decisionism' (1976, pt. III, ch. 1), i.e. without rational argument.

28. See Barrett, 1979.

29. Ziman, J., 1980, *Teaching and Learning about Science and Society*, Cambridge, Cambridge University Press.

30. Goodlad, S. and Hirst, B., 1989, *Peer Tutoring: A Guide to Learning by Teaching*, London, Kogan Page, ch. 5. It is possible for the students to opt to produce an

analytic report of their tutoring experience, which would count towards their degree award.

31. The lack of critical self-reflection within empirical science, and the consequent impoverished self-understanding, is one of the main thrusts of Habermas' early work (1978).

32. Gellner, 1974, p. 171; Peacocke, 1985; Wallen, in Bergendal (ed.), 1984.

33. Shaw, 1975.

34. In Peter Scott's useful distinction, are they to contribute (science-like) to knowledge as product, or (humanities-like) to knowledge as process – a process of educating students (1984). See also his essay in Bergendal (ed.), 1984.

35. The point is made by Basil Bernstein, in pointing out the implications of an academic structure reflecting a collection code and exhibiting high classification, with a rigid vertical division of subjects (in Young (ed.), 1971, pp. 60–62).

36. Bernstein, ibid.

37. Shaw, 1975.

38. A total of 29 per cent of students registered on courses in polytechnics and colleges include periods of supervised work experience, *CNAA Annual Report, 1987–88*, London, CNAA, 1989.

39. For an analyis of different models of professional education, see Barnett, R., Becher, R. and Cork, N., 1987, Models of professional preparation: Pharmacy, nursing and teacher education, *Studies in Higher Education*, **12**(1) 51–63.

40. Schon, 1983, *The Reflective Practitioner: How Professionals Think in Action.*

41. Witness Plumb, J. H. (ed.), 1964, *Crisis in the Humanities*, Harmondsworth, Penguin.

42. Gellner in his essay in Plumb, ibid., pp. 72–3. Also, Gellner, 1969, ch. 8; 1974, pp. 147–8 and 193–4.

43. All humanities students at the Polytechnic of North London are expected to gain experience of using computers, and of information technology. On the general take-up of computers in the humanities, see the study by a group at the London School of Economics: Hirscheim, R. A., Smithson, S. C. and Whitehouse, D. E., 1988, *A Survey of Microcomputer Use in the Humanities and Social Sciences: A UK University Study*, London, London School of Economics.

44. It was, though, a restricted form of critique, involving a limited view of knowledge and society, producing in Leavis an outright hostility to philosophy and to Marxism. There are signs, too – in Leavis' debate with Snow – of an awkwardness with the social sciences as well. With his aggressive stance towards the industrial society, and his disdain for science and technology, we find Leavis identifying the university – at least, Cambridge – with English: 'We were in fact that Cambridge' (1969, p. 18). See Perry's commentary on the conservatism in Leavis' thought (in Cockburn and Blackburn (eds), 1970, *Student Power*, Harmondsworth, Penguin, pp. 268–276); and for a more sympathetic account, which points up the sociological elements in Leavis' work, Filmer (in Jenks (ed.) 1977).

45. See the essays by Morris and Black in Niblett (1975).

46. The structuralist approach to literature is arguably one manifestation of this impotence, an impotence which reflects the lack of vision of contemporary work in the humanities of an alternative set of possibilities in modern society.

47. For the range of responses actually being made by UK academic institutions to the external forces acting on them, see Boys, C. J. *et al.*, 1988, *Higher Education and the Preparation for Work*, London, Jessica Kingsley.

Chapter 6   Living with Ideology

1. General texts that I have found helpful on the sociology of knowledge are: Abercrombie, N., 1980, *Class, Structure and Knowledge*, Oxford, Blackwell; Berger, P. L.
and Luckmann, T., 1971, *The Social Construction of Reality*, Harmondsworth, Penguin;
Hamilton, P., 1974, *Knowledge and Social Structure*, London, Routledge and Kegan
Paul.

    On the sociology of academic knowledge – though normally confined to the
sociology of knowledge in the school setting – useful texts are Young (ed.), 1971;
Young and Whitty (eds), 1978; Hopper, E. (ed.), 1971, *Readings in the Theory of
Educational Systems*, London, Hutchinson.

    Valuable work has also been accomplished in the sociology of science, e.g. Barnes,
1974 and 1977; Bloor, 1976; Barnes, B. and Edge, D. (eds), 1982, *Science in Context*,
Milton Keynes, Open University Press.

2. Bloor, 1976. See the important debate of this proposed programme in Hollis and
Lukes (eds), 1982.

3. For works on the general matter of ideology, key primary sources are: Karl Marx's
classic statement, *The German Ideology* (reprinted 1977), London, Lawrence and
Wishart; Karl Mannheim's work, 1936 (reprinted 1976), *Ideology and Utopia*,
London, Routledge and Kegan Paul; and Louis Althusser, 1969, *For Marx*,
Harmondsworth, Penguin.

    Helpful overviews are: Plamenatz, J., 1971, *Ideology*, London, Macmillan;
Larrain, J., 1979, *The Concept of Ideology*, London, Hutchinson; Mepham, J. and
Ruben, D.-H. (eds), 1978, *Issues in Marxist Philosophy*, Harvester, Brighton; Thompson, J. B., 1985, *Studies in the Theory of Ideology*, Cambridge, Polity; McLennan, D.,
1986, *Ideology*, Milton Keynes, Open University Press.

    On ideology in the context of education, see Apple, 1979 and 1985; Giroux, 1983;
Aronowitz and Giroux, 1987 (one of the few such works to contain any discussion of
higher education).

4. The metaphor is Gellner's, in Breaking through the bars of the rubber cage, *Times
Higher Education Supplement*, 9 May 1980.

5. On the notion of interests as reflected in cognition, see Geuss, 1981, section 2;
Barnes, 1977; Habermas, 1978; R. Bernstein, 1983, pp. 216 *et seq.*

6. Habermas, 1972, pp. 99 and 111 *et seq.* The point is picked up by Gouldner, 1976,
p. 31. See the comment by Minogue, 1973, pp. 178–9.

7. Perhaps the person who has done most to encourage the inclusion of values as an
explicit topic in the curriculum, through specific examples and developmental work,
is Gerald Collier, though his work remains mostly in journal articles. See, for
instance, his 1988, Higher education and the critique of values, *Journal of Moral
Education*, **17**(1) 21–6; 1989, Culture clashes, value conflicts and professional
education, *Higher Education Research and Development*, **8**(1) 59–68.

8. Thompson, op. cit., note 3; also Stuart Hall's essay, in his collection, 1978, *On
Ideology*, London, Hutchinson.

9. Gellner, 1969, p. 25; though he points out that it by no means follows that 'as we
cannot opt out of this world, our judgements must be its judgements'. See also pp.
107–108: 'We cannot divest ourselves of our conceptual clothing and stand bare and
receptive to the world "as it really is".' I do not find helpful, therefore, Althusser's
(1969) notion of 'an epistemological break' between an ideological form of thought,
and the pure science that is supposed to arise in its place.

10. On the idea of an educational class, see especially Gouldner (1979). See also the
useful discussions in Bergendal (1984) and Bjornsson, A., 1984, *Intellectuals and Power*

or the Power of Intellectuals, Swedish Research on Higher Education Report, Stockholm, National Board of Universities and Colleges. The idea was also suggested by Ralf Dahrendorf, 1978, The rise of an educational class, *Times Higher Education Supplement*, 14 July.

11. The ideological character of science is argued from within Marxist critiques (Rose and Rose, 1976), from within Critical Theory (Marcuse, 1968; Habermas, 1972) and from within the philosophy of science (Feyerabend, 1978, 1982).

12. Lyotard, 1984, pp. 53ff. See also Bloor, 1976.

13. For another, though to my mind unsatisfactory, rebuttal of the self-refuting argument, see Bloor, ibid., p. 13. The problem is that Bloor seems unnecessarily to follow the general view that to say belief (b) is relative to situation (s) is to say something about the truth of (b).

14. Bertrand Russell once fastened on this idea of a hierarchy of languages (1940, reprinted 1965, *An Inquiry into Meaning and Truth*, Harmondsworth, Penguin, pp. 59 –60). More recently, in the context of confronting ideology, see Gouldner, 1976, p. 53.

15. For example, Habermas, 1979, p. 120.

16. Ch. 4, note 39. See also Connerton, 1980, pp. 102–108; Kortian, G., 1980, *Metacritique: The Philosophical Argument of Jurgen Habermas*, Cambridge, Cambridge University Press, pp. 118–20.

17. On reflexivity, see e.g. Jenks, 1977, pp. 4 and 78; Giroux, 1983, pp. 154 and 203; Habermas, 1978, esp. postscript; Gouldner, 1979, pp. 47 and 59.

Chapter 7   Culture

1. Robbins, 1963, para. 28, p. 7.

2. Leavis, 1969, p. 58; Williams, R., 1958, reprinted 1966, *Culture and Society 1780–1950*, Harmondsworth, Penguin, pp. 304ff.

3. Williams, ibid., p. 285.

4. Clark Kerr, 1972, p. 20.

5. This is not a proper interpretation of the term, but it is an appealing interpretation: 'The original sense of universities – a community of teachers and students – is just as important as the unity of all studies' (Jaspers, 1965).

6. See Chapter 3.

7. Writers from whom this analysis has been developed include: Hirst, 1974; Gouldner, 1976, 1979; Becher, 1989; Polanyi, 1966; Peters, 1966; Kuhn, 1970. In each view of academic knowledge, we can see signs of conservatism *and* revising (even revolutionary) tendencies. We see signs too of tacit, taken-for-granted ways of going on, and a determination to make matters explicit.

8. Gouldner's *The Future of Intellectuals and the Rise of the New Class* (1979). I regard this as the key text on the culture of critical discourse of academics (or CCD, in Gouldner's own acronym). See also Gouldner, 1976.

9. Cmnd. 9501, 1985, *Academic Validation in Public Sector Higher Education*, Report of Committee of Inquiry, chaired by Sir Norman Lindop, London, HMSO; *Degree Courses in the Public Sector: Quality and Validation*, The Government's Response to the Lindop Report, written reply to House of Commons question, March 1986, House of Commons Library.

10. That could not seriously have been maintained by any informed observer. It was only in parallel to Lindop that the Reynolds Working Party began to draw up codes of practice on the maintenance of standards in universities. Those codes of practice have encouraged universities to examine their own procedures for sustaining

'quality' (UGC/CVCP Working Party, 1986, 87, 88, 89, *Academic Standards in Universities*, London, Committee of Vice-Chancellors and Principals.)

Yet the practices that universities are being urged to adopt are highly restricted, and could not be said to offer the opportunity for systematic self-critical examination. In the code of practice focused on course 'validation' and review, there is no mention of a peer review system. The process of course review urged on to universities is limited to a mechanical course monitoring procedure, focused on numerical indicators. Nowhere is there any mention of a genuine critical dialogue between those responsible for teaching a course and their peers.

11. Lawton, D., 1982, *The End of the Secret Garden? A Study in the Politics of the Curriculum*, London, University of London Institute of Education.

12. Note that the performance indicators picked out by the UGC/CVCP Working Group on performance indicators are purely numerical in character, and are largely efficiency indicators focused on inputs and outputs. Assessment of institutional performance on this approach is purely a matter for the bureaucrat or accountant: it requires no academic or educational judgement (CVCP/UGC, 1987, *Performance Indicators in Universities*, Second statement, London, CVCP). See also Cave *et al.* (eds), 1988, *The Use of Performance Indicators in Higher Education: A Critical Analysis of Developing Practice*, London, Jessica Kingsley.

13. *Report of the Steering Committee for Efficiency Studies in Universities* (Jarratt Report), 1985, London, CVCP.

14. Ibid. These developments are reversing the drift towards excluding lay elements over the past decades. See Moodie, G. and Eustace, R., 1973, *Power and Authority in British Universities*, London, George Allen and Unwin.

15. The best account that I know of is, unfortunately, unpublished: Gellert, C., 1981, *A Comparative Study of the Changing Functions of English and German Universities*, op. cit., ch. 2, note 2.

16. Although Newman denied any pretensions to social superiority in talking of the development of the 'gentleman', it was in the context of the wider social formation of the student that his idea of the university was set out.

17. Admittedly, the Humboldtian conception of the university held an idealist view of the interconnections between knowledge, the mind and the state. See Scott, D. F. S., 1960, *Wilhelm von Humboldt and the Idea of a University*, inaugural lecture, 1959, Durham, University of Durham. But, in practice, it was an education far removed from the common culture.

18. Carswell, J., 1985, *Government and the Universities in Britain: Progress and Performance, 1960–1980*, Cambridge, Cambridge University Press.

19. Snow did go on in a subsequent formulation to suggest that the social sciences had become a separate cognitive culture: Snow, C. P., 1964, reprinted 1978, *The Two Cultures and a Second Look*, Cambridge, Cambridge University Press. Gellner (1969), by the way, considers Snow's book to be superior to Ayer's *Language, Truth and Logic* (1936, London, Victor Gollancz), as a view of the cognitive options open to modern society.

20. Leavis, 1969, pp. 171ff. See also Hirst, 1974, ch. 11; Habermas, 1972, ch. 4; and Bantock, G., 1968, ch. 9, *Education, Culture and the Emotions*, Bloomington, Indiana, Indiana University Press.

21. Gellner, 1969, ch. 8.

22. Bernstein developed the concepts of 'elaborated' and 'restricted' codes, to distinguish the different registers of language in use in the school setting and in the children's homes. Bernstein, B. B., 1971, Language and socialization, ch. 11 in N.

Minnis (ed.), *Linguistics at Large*, London, Victor Gollancz. In the context of higher education, I think the conceptual distinction is useful, but needs to be treated with care, for arguably disciplinary languages are *both* restricted (available only to those in the know) and elaborated (fully transparent, and available for systematic reflection to those on the inside). Bernstein's concept of an 'elaborated code' is applied to the academic community by Gouldner, 1976 and 1979.

23. Training Agency/CNAA, 1989, *Towards a new Certificate in Management*, Section 4, London, HMSO.

24. See Chapter 2.

25. Gellner, E., 1969, The panther and the dove: Reflections on rebelliousness and its milieux, in D. Martin (ed.), *Anarchy and Culture: The Problem of the Contemporary University*, London, Routledge and Kegan Paul. See also Gellner, 1974, p. 192.

26. For example, Bourdieu's essays Intellectual field and creative project, and Systems of education and systems of thought, in Young (ed.) 1971; Bourdieu, P. and Boltanski, L., 1978, Changes in social structure and changes in the demand for education, in S. Giner and M. S. Archer (eds), *Contemporary Europe: Social and Cultural Patterns*, London, Routledge and Kegan Paul; Bourdieu, P. and Passeron, J. C., 1979.

27. See Giroux, 1983, p. 89, and Apple, 1979, pp. 32ff., for accounts of this concept in Bourdieu's thought.

28. 'Considerable difficulty [in securing full-time permanent employment] was reported by only 3% of Oxbridge graduates, rising to 29% in colleges': Boys, C. J., and Kirkland, J., 1988, *Degrees of Success*, p. 35, London, Jessica Kingsley; DES, 1989, *Economics Bulletin*, No. 1, fig. 4 and p. 4. Also see Roizen, J. and Jepson, M., 1985, *Degrees for Jobs*, Guildford, SRHE/NFER-Nelson, ch. 4, esp. pp. 90–91 for employers' views.

29. Ortega y Gasset, 1946, p. 44 and ch. V; Leavis, 1969, p. 59; Bantock, G. H., 1968, p. 179, op. cit., note 20.

Chapter 8   Rationality

1. See Habermas' essay, Technology and science as ideology, in his *Toward a Rational Society*, 1972; the essays by Grant, G., The university and the technological threat, and by Marx, L., Technology and the study of man, in Niblett (ed.), 1975; Feyerabend, 1978. ch. 10; Lyotard, 1984.

2. Feyerabend points to the way in which 'theoretical knowledge' and 'theoretical traditions' have supplanted 'empirical or historical traditions' of knowledge (1987, ch. 3, p. 118).

3. With a loss of the credibility of 'grand narrative' (Lyotard, 1984, p. 37).

4. Feyerabend (from within the philosophy of science) and post-structuralism share common ground in wanting to uphold and foster just these elements of anarchism and irrationality. For both parties, in anarchism and irrationality of thought and knowledge lies true liberation. The argument of this book is that (however super-ficially attractive) that position is ultimately untenable. If we are to talk to each other, there must be common ground rules of debate. That is why Habermas' framework is so valuable, in spelling out the minimal elements of a rational discourse while leaving open the content of any theory being offered within it.

5. The account of Habermas' analysis given here is taken from Roderick, 1986, ch. 4, pp. 108–114.

6. Kuhn, 1970. Though Masterman points out in her essay on *The nature of a paradigm* that Kuhn employs no less that 21 different senses of 'paradigm' (in Lakatos and Musgrave (eds), 1977).

7. On forms of life as rule-following, see Winch, P., 1958, *The Idea of a Social Science and its Relationship to Philosophy*, London, Routledge and Kegan Paul.

8. Cf. Feyerabend (1987, ch. 4), where he argues against understanding creativity as a kind of superhuman personal quality of extraordinary individuals. Quite apart from the fact that 'creativity' takes place within traditions and draws upon intellectual resources, the imagery of the lone 'creator' sponsors a view of man as separate from each other and (worse) from Nature.

9. For Habermas, knowledge built around critique is one of the fundamental forms of knowledge (alongside knowledge oriented towards control on the one hand, and towards communication on the other). He seems to me, though, to waver between seeing critical knowledge as an independent clustering of knowledge in its own right (including Marxism and pyschoanalysis), and seeing it as an intellectual resource that can be turned on to any form of knowledge to show up its assumptions and partial self-understanding (1978).

10. This point can be found in the work of both Gellner and Feyerabend. This is an unlikely pairing, for they have had little if anything to say that is complimentary about each other (Feyerabend, 1982, pp. 140ff.). Yet the fact remains that they both have a sense of the way thought has its home in traditions, and that it is possible to break through the confines of those traditions, even if only in turn to establish a new tradition.

11. And, partly for that reason, Feyerabend is against both (1978); and against Popper and Lakatos, who wish to defend both (1982).

12. See Moodie's own chapter in Moodie, G., 1986, *Standards and Quality in Higher Education*, Guildford, SRHE/NFER-Nelson.

13. Hirst, 1974, p. 30; Habermas, 1978, p. 302; Richard Bernstein, 1983, p. 54, where he offers an analysis of the Aristotelian concept of 'phronesis', or practical reasoning.

14. On groundedness, see Gouldner, 1976, pp. 42ff.

15. This is a key general feature of science, recognized from within the sociology of science: Barnes, B. and Edge, D. (eds), 1982, *Science in Context*, Milton Keynes, Open University Press, p. 5.

16. Lukes, S., 1970, *Some Problems about Rationality*, in Wilson (ed.).

17. Winch, P., 1970, *Understanding a Primitive Society*, in Wilson (ed.).

18. Peters, 1966, pp. 31ff.

19. Enlightenment is one of the key concepts of the Frankfurt School of Critical Theory. See Connerton, P., 1980, *The Tragedy of Enlightenment*.

20. I take this to be one of the central claims of Critical Theory, as represented especially but not only by Jurgen Habermas (1978, pp. 54, 287, 306 and 378). See also Connerton, ibid., p. 114; Held, D., 1983, *Introduction to Critical Theory*, London, Hutchinson; McCarthy, T., 1978, *The Critical Theory of Jurgen Habermas*, London, Hutchinson, pp. 88–95.

21. As Paulo Freire puts it, there is no such thing as personal self-empowerment, for 'liberation is always a social act' (Freire and Shor, 1987, p. 109).

22. MacIntyre, 1985, pp. 190–96.

23. Habermas, 1979, pp. 133ff., where he conceives of social evolution in terms of social learning, through the development of communicative action.

Chapter 9   Research

1. Gilman, the first President of Johns Hopkins University, observed that 'The term research . . . was presented to the English-speaking world in 1875, in a volume called The Endowment of Research . . .', quoted in Wegener (1978, p. 10). One of the contributors to the volume was Mark Pattison, and some inkling of the way in which

the meaning of the term has changed can be glimpsed in Pattison's view that 'the university . . . is a national institute for the preservation and tradition of useful knowledge. It is the common interest . . . that such knowledge should exist, should be guarded, treasured, cultivated, disseminated, expounded' (Sparrow, J., 1967, *Mark Pattison and the Idea of a University*, Cambridge, Cambridge University Press, p. 123). In other words, the nineteenth-century view was much more one of re-search, rather than today's conception of the systematic advancement and public demonstration of fresh knowledge.

2. Newman: we saw in Chapter 2 that Newman's idea of higher education centred on the enlargement of the individual mind. This had nothing to do with the acquisition of knowledge: indeed, 'Knowledge, in proportion as it tends more and more to be particular, ceases to be knowledge' (1976, p. 104).

   Ortega y Gasset, 1946, p. 58: 'scientific investigation has no place in any direct, constituent capacity among the primary functions of the university'.

   Moberly, 1949, p. 184: 'For God's sake, stop researching for a while and begin to think.'

   Jaspers (ed.), 1965, p. 55: 'the university is simultaneously a professional school, a cultural centre, and a research institute'.

   Phillips Griffiths, A deduction of universities, in R. D. Archambault (ed.), 1965, *Philosophical Analysis and Education*, London, Routledge and Kegan Paul, pp. 187–208, where he argues (pp. 192–3) that the university is essentially a centre for the pursuit of truth.

   Wegener, 1978, p. 75, where he picks out research as one of the diverse 'necessities inherent in the enterprise (of the liberal university)'.

3. Advisory Board for the Research Councils, 1987, *A Strategy for the Science Base*, London, HMSO. Also. Cm. 114, 1987, *Higher Education: Meeting the Challenge* (White Paper), London, HMSO, para. 3.18.

4. This is a worldwide phenomenon. See Burgess, T., 1977, *Education after School*, London, Victor Gollancz, pp. 31 *et seq.*

5. The 'customer-contract' principle was adumbrated by Lord Rothschild, 1971, and developed in subsequent Green and White Papers. See references in papers by S. Blume, R. J. H. Beverton and G. W. D. Findlay, and C. Smith, in G. Oldham (ed.), 1982, *The Future of Research*, Vol. 4, Leverhulme Programme of Study into the Future of Higher Education, Guildford, SRHE.

6. For Marx, 'the work is external to the worker . . . it is not his work but for someone else . . . the activity is not his spontaneous activity . . . his labour becomes an object, takes on its own existence, it exists outside him . . .'. Quoted in Bottomore, T. B. and Rubel, M., 1971, *Karl Marx: Selected Writings in Sociology and Social Philosophy*, Harmondsworth, Penguin, pp. 177–8.

   Herbst, P., in his essay Work, labour and university education, argues that the alienating character of universities is spreading, from research to teaching itself, in Peters (ed.), 1973.

7. Habermas, 1972, ch. 5, The scientization of politics and public opinion; Rose and Rose (eds), 1976, esp. chs 2, 3, 6 and 7; Maxwell, 1987.

8. Shaw, 1975, pp. 50–51.

9. Sklair, L., 1973, *Organized Knowledge*, St Albans, Paladin, p. 168. Sklair's book is a useful conventional analysis of science, from a sociological point of view. For example, it examines the value and rewards systems inherent in science.

10. Gellner, The crisis in the humanities and the mainstream of philosophy, in Plumb (ed.), 1964, op. cit., ch. 3, note 9.

11. Popper, 1975, pp. 121 and 185.

12. Popper makes a philosophical point out of this, in declaring that our sources of knowledge are irrelevant to our assessments of our theories; his essay, On the sources of knowledge and ignorance, in J. N. Findlay (ed.), 1966, *Studies in Philosophy*, Oxford, Oxford University Press.

13. For example, para. 3.15, Cm. 114, *Meeting the Challenge* (White Paper), London, HMSO, which talks of judging standards in higher education 'mainly by reference to students' achievements . . .'; it also talks of drawing on data on graduates' employment patterns and degree results.

14. Kogan, M. and Becher, T., 1980, *Process and Structure in Higher Education*, London, Heinemann, p. 12. (A new edition of this book is in press.)

15. This is the logic of Kuhn's analysis of the growth of science.

16. Peters, 1966, p. 62.

17. Elton says that there is little evidence of mutual linkages between teaching and research, but that is due to the limited way in which the investigations have been conducted. He goes on to argue for a link through scholarship, or the reinterpretation of existing knowledge. My argument is that it is possible to distinguish research and scholarship: the latter is a necessary obligation for the academic as teacher; the former is not. Elton, L., 1986, Research and teaching: symbiosis or conflict? *Higher Education*, 15, 299–304.

18. Cf. Minogue, 1973, p. 71: 'there is a certain crudeness about distinguishing the work of universities into teaching and research . . . teaching undergraduates is, in part, rethinking the fundamentals of a subject: it constitutes a kind of research'. In other words, the dialogue between the teacher and the students is parallel to the dialogue between the teacher and other fellow academics. Also, Freire and Shor (1987, p. 179), where the story is recounted of a liberating educator working with immigrant Spaniards in Germany. To do his work effectively, the educator had to conduct a kind of 'research' by working with the immigrants in order to understand them and to perceive the educational possibilities that could be realized by them: 'the teacher learnt how to read reality, changing his practice . . . the educator did not separate research from teaching'.

19. For example, at the levels of the system (its planning and resourcing); at the levels of the institution (which should develop appropriate staff development and staff appraisal policies, alongside internal 'research' policies which recognize the need for scholarship as a professional duty); and the level of the individual teacher, in recognizing the professional ethic implied by the analysis.

20. Op. cit., note 11, ch. 7.

Chapter 10   Academic Freedom

1. This 'principle' is also to be found in my contribution to the collection of papers edited by M. Tight, 1988, *Academic Freedom and Responsibility*, Milton Keynes, Open University Press where I explore academic freedom from a different perspective. The volume was published as precedings to the 1988 annual conference of the Society for Research into Higher Education. The papers presented to the conference are a useful additional resource, lengthy 'abstracts' of which were collected together for the conference programme, December 1988, University of Surrey.

2. For example, the debate on academic freedom, with key papers by Brown and Phillips Griffiths, in Brown, S. C., 1975, *Philosophers Discuss Education*, London, Macmillan.

3. For accounts of *Lernfreiheit*, see Searle, J., 1972, *The Campus War*, Harmondsworth,

Penguin; Hook, S., 1970, *Academic Freedom and Academic Anarchy*, New York, Cowles Book Co. Both these books were written in the context of the radical student movement of the 1960s, and offer a limited view of student freedom.

4. For Searle (ibid.), students are only justified 'academic freedom' in virtue of their civil rights on campus.

5. 'Wittingness and voluntariness' amounted to one of R. S. Peters' criteria under which a process could be termed educational (1966, p. 45). We may reflect that in practice the 'voluntariness and wittingness' of pupils and students varies in direct proportion to their age. Mature students in higher education are even more likely to be attending out of purer educational motives than the 18-year-old, whose presence includes a number of extrinsic motives.

6. See Magsino, R. E., 1978, Student academic freedom and the changing student/ university relationship, in Strike and Egan (eds).

7. The radical movement of the 1960s was notable for the strident and aggressive way in which some students confronted those on campus who were not of their persuasion. Today, we are perhaps seeing signs of a new aggressiveness, as some students – particularly 'mature' students, imbued with an exaggerated sense of their rights as consumers – exert unreasonable demands on their lecturers (to be available, to return scripts immediately, to allow them to insist on their point of view in seminars).

8. It may, of course, lead to action by the authorities which limits student freedom on campus, for example their opportunities to engage in discourse free from external constraint.

9. Berdahl, R., 1988, *Autonomy and Accountability*. Paper given to annual conference of Society for Research into Higher Education, December, University of Surrey.

10. This connection between infringements to institutional autonomy and academic freedoms is implicit in the paper by O'Hear, A., Academic freedom and responsibility, in M. Tight (ed.), op. cit., note 1. A test of the state's tolerance is whether, as O'Hear puts it, academic institutions are to be permitted to conduct 'useless conversations'. In so far as it is disinclined to do so, the range of academic discourse begins to close, and the academic freedom of academics is in effect curtailed.

11. Illich, I. D., 1971, *Deschooling Society*, London, Calder and Boyars.

12. For example, Dearden, R. F., 1970, *The Philosophy of Primary Education*, London, Routledge and Kegan Paul.

13. Witness the formation in 1988 of a pressure group, The Council for Academic Autonomy. See its inaugural statement, *The State and Higher Education: Restoring Academic Autonomy*, from Anthony Smith, London School of Economics.

14. The inquiries into alleged Marxist bias at the Open University and the Polytechnic of North London, initiated by government concerns, have suggested that these freedoms themselves should not be taken for granted in the UK.

15. Cf. Taylor, C., 1975, Neutrality in the university, p. 142, in A. Montefiore (ed.).

16. See my paper in Tight (ed.), op. cit. note 1.

Chapter 11   Beyond Teaching and Learning

1. Both the Robbins Report, 1963, and the Leverhulme/Society for Research into Higher Education Inquiry, 1983, gave explicit attention to teaching, teaching methods and the 'teaching function'; but virtually no attention to learning as such.

2. For example, Hutchins, R. M., 1936, *The Higher Learning in America*, New Haven, Yale University Press; Bok, D., 1986, *Higher Learning*, Cambridge, Mass., Harvard University Press.

3. Neufeld, V. and Chong, J. P., 1984, Problem-based professional education in medicine, in S. Goodlad (ed.), *Education for the Professions*, Guildford, SRHE/NFER-Nelson.

4. Handal, G. and Lauvas, P., 1987, *Promoting Reflective Teaching*, Milton Keynes, Open University Press.

5. To adapt the title of Allan Bloom's *The Closing of the American Mind* (1988, Harmondsworth, Penguin). Bloom observes many of the same features of higher education identified in this book (narrowing of intellectual culture; splitting off of the disciplines from each other; irrationalism of the radical movement). However, his general diagnosis (overdominance of relativism, and the university deserting its place of intellectual independence by succumbing to the general culture of modern society) and his prescription (return to the Great Books) run counter – it should be clear – to the argument of this book. Bloom's prescription is inadequate because his analyses are inadequate. Relativism is a set of philosophical perspectives which needs to be confronted seriously, that is philosophically. The relationship of higher education to society is a social matter which can only be understood sociologically. Polemic cannot deal with either issue. His 'return to the Great Books' demand represents the imposition of a question-begging belief in the great books, which it is the duty of a critical higher education to examine.

6. Ch. 1, The nature of authority, p. 17, in Peters, R. S., 1963, 2nd ed., *Authority, Responsibility and Education*, London, George Allen and Unwin. See also his debate with Peter Winch, pp. 83–111, in Quinton, A., *Political Philosophy*, Oxford, Oxford University Press.

7. Freire, 1972, p. 53.

8. Marjorie Reeves' book, *The Crisis in Higher Education*, 1988, provides perhaps the best available description of this 'personal knowledge' in higher education.

9. Bertrand Russell held this conception of the philosophic attitude. Asking philosophic questions will bring doubt and uncertainty, but can enable us to become 'citizens of the universe', p. 93 in Russell, 1967 (first published 1912), *The Problems of Philosophy*, Oxford, Oxford University Press.

10. Goodlad, 1976, p. 85.

11. Hallden, S., 1987, *Intellectual Maturity as an Educational Ideal*, Studies of Higher Education and Research, Stockholm, National Board of Universities and Colleges.

12. Perry, W. G., 1970, *Forms of Intellectual and Ethical Development in the College Years*, New York, Holt, Rinehart and Winston.

13. Kuhn, 1970, p. 80.

14. By productive, I mean conceptually productive. Research into the economics of higher education, and the relationships between higher education and the labour market, have perhaps constituted even larger research enterprises. But their theoretical insights seem surprisingly limited for the effort expended.

15. Marton, F. *et al.* (eds), 1984, *The Experience of Learning*. See also Richardson, J. T. *et al.* (eds), 1987, *Student Learning: Research in Education and Cognitive Psychology*, Milton Keynes, Open University Press.

16. See some of the descriptions of the first round of successful bids, *Enterprise in Higher Education 1988–89*, Sheffield, Training Agency.

17. Committee of Directors of Polytechnics, 1974, *Many Arts, Many Skills*, London.

18. For the application of this viewpoint in teacher education, see Hirst's paper, Educational theory, in his collection (1983).

19. Moodie, G. C., 1986, *Standards and Criteria in Higher Education*, Guildford, SRHE/NFER-Nelson.

20. Patrick Nuttgens recent book (ch. 1, note 3) has some pertinent things to say about student learning; but it is entitled *What Should We Teach and How Should We Teach It?* An exception is Brewer, I. M., 1985, *Learning More and Teaching Less*, SRHE/NFER-Nelson (an essay on group methods in plant anatomy, in the University of Sydney).

Chapter 12   A Critical Business

1. For example, the UK Government's White Paper, *Higher Education: Meeting the Challenge*, Cm. 114, London, HMSO, para. 2.11; although it is the areas of the arts, humanities and social studies that are seen as exercising critical abilities.
2. Roizen, J. and Jepson, M., 1985, *Degrees for Jobs: Employer Expectations of Higher Education*, Guildford, SRHE/NFER-Nelson, p. 45.
3. Introduction, in Goodlad, S. (ed.), 1984, *Education for the Professions*, Guildford, SRHE/NFER-Nelson.
4. See para. 3, Joint Statement by the National Advisory Body and the University Grants Committee, in UGC, 1984, Higher education and the needs of society, in *A Strategy for Higher Education into the 1990s*, London, HMSO.
5. Moberly, 1949, p. 127; Wegener, 1978, p. 92.
6. Cockburn, A. and Blackburn, R. (eds), 1970, *Student Power*, Harmondsworth, Penguin; Pateman, T. (ed.), 1972, *Counter Course*, Harmondsworth, Penguin; Rose, S., 1978, *What are Universities For?*, lecture given at University College, University of London, 11 May.
7. Peters, R. S., 1975, Subjectivity and standards, in Niblett (ed.).
8. Despite their differences, Popper, Lakatos, Kuhn and Feyerabend are all united in their belief in the importance of criticism. They differ, though, on the scope of permissible criticism, ranging from Popper's fairly restricted view to Feyerabend's belief that 'anything goes'. Feyerabend puts into practice what he preaches, giving numerous examples in his writings of external critique (drawn from disciplines outside philosophy of science) in his onslaughts against the rest.
9. Chomsky, N., 1968, *Language and Mind*, New York, Harcourt Brace.
10. Peters, R. S., 1966, p. 31.
11. Passmore, J., Teaching to care and to be careful, in his 1980, *The Philosophy of Teaching*, London, Duckworth; see also his essay in Niblett (ed.), 1975.
12. Hirst, Liberal education and the nature of knowledge, in his 1974.
13. This is one of the main planks of Critical Theory, as established in the 1930s, and developed by Habermas over the last 20 years. For example, Horkheimer, 1937, in his essay Traditional and Critical Theory: 'the [critical] theory never aims simply at an increase in knowledge as such. Its goal is man's emancipation from slavery', in P. Connerton (ed.), 1980, *Critical Sociology*, Harmondsworth, Penguin, p. 224.

    And Geuss, in his analysis of Habermas' formulation: 'By inducing . . . self-reflection . . . critical theory [brings] the agents to realize that the coercion from which they suffer is self-imposed, thereby dissolving the power or objectivity of that coercion and bringing them to a state of greater freedom' (1981, p. 70 *et seq.*).

14. The drive behind this chapter is indeed to show the cash value of that basic category of knowledge which Habermas (1978) terms 'critical' (alongside technical knowledge, and knowledge oriented towards understanding). For Habermas, the dominant interest behind critical knowledge is emancipation of the human subject. His key examples (Marxism and psychoanalysis), however, imply that the application of critical knowledge is confined to personal and social understanding. In this chapter, I try to show that critical perspectives with an emancipatory interest can and should be applied to all domains of first-order knowledge. (In fact, given his reflections

about the lack of self-understanding of the natural sciences, and their ideological character, the application of critical perspectives on to the natural sciences could be said to be entirely in keeping with Habermas' analytical framework.)

15. Gellner, E., 1968, *Words and Things*, Harmondsworth, Penguin.
16. Rose, S., Scientific racism and ideology: The IQ racket from Galton to Jensen, in Rose and Rose (eds), 1976.
17. Shaw, 1975, ch. 2.
18. Illich, I., 1976, *Medical Nemesis*, London, Calder and Boyars.
19. See Hatcher, D., 1985, A critique of critical thinking, in *Teaching Thinking and Problem-Solving*, 7(10) 14–16; McPeck, J., 1981, *Critical Thinking and Education*, Oxford, Martin Robertson. Also, in March 1988, an international conference on *Critical Thinking* was held at the University of East Anglia (organized by the Department of Philosophy).
20. Peters, R. S., 1966, p. 53.
21. McPeck, op. cit., note 19, p. 156.
22. Not necessarily to be used in the typical curriculum, but the work of Foucault shows just such a combination of philosophical and sociological investigations of the deep structure of knowledge (1974 and 1986).
23. 'Critique accepts the grammar of rationality calling for self-grounded, autonomous speech. On the other hand, in calling attention to the force of external influences, critique denies the very possibility of fully autonomous speech, and calls into question the norm requiring such autonomy' (Gouldner, 1976, p. 52).
24. It is through 'metacritique' that the project of Critical Theory gains its own epistemological legitimacy. See Habermas, 1978, p. 9. This is not a level of thought available only to intellectuals (Marx, Hegel, etc.), but is built into common forms of communication. 'Ordinary language permits communication only on condition that it is simultaneously metacommunication' (p. 357). In ordinary language, the hidden truth claims normally remain hidden. Higher education, on the other hand, has a duty to expose the hidden presuppositions, interests and ideologies of the knowledge corpuses to which it gives room.
25. Some of this phraseology comes from the work of Peters. I am, though, going further than Peters in suggesting the extent of possible cognitive transformation. For while he believes in the importance of breadth of understanding and seeing things in new ways, Peters also believes in the essential objectivity of forms of knowledge. On the argument here, however, the point of external critique is to free the student from dependence on *any* form of knowledge.
26. This may appear to be offering support for *The Homeless Mind* (Berger, P., Berger, B. and Kellner, H., 1974, New York, Random House/Harmondsworth, Penguin). But the argument also points to the value of intellectual and critical values as a worthwhile home in themselves.
27. The idea of 'critical dialogue' is central to Paulo Freire's conception of education (1972, pp. 53–4 and 60–65). See also Furedy, C. and Furedy, J. F., 1984, *On Strengthening the Socratic Dialogue in Higher Education*, unpublished paper, University of Toronto.
28. Boud, D., 1985, *Studies in Self-assessment*, Occasional Paper 26, Tertiary Education Research Centre, University of New South Wales, Kensington, Australia.
29. 'The university curriculum guarantees that there should be no serious criticism of itself, or of the society that it is shaped to serve', Grant, G., The university curriculum and the technological threat, in Niblett (ed.), 1975, p. 34.
30. As my comments show, I do not agree with those who argue that higher education should directly intervene in society's self-understanding and should seek to raise the

general consciousness of all citizens; or, as Birnbaum puts it, to 'reinvent a critical general consciousness' (Birnbuam, N., 1970, *The Crisis of Industrial Society*, Oxford, Oxford University Press, p. 157). The socio-critical role of higher education is less direct, less glamorous, less obvious and less immediate; but it may have just the same effect in the long run.

31. Thereby assisting the process whereby 'the self-consciousness of the species attain(s) the level of critique and free(s) itself from all ideological delusion' (Habermas, 1978, p. 55).

32. As Minogue remarks, 'there is an equivocation in the idea that universities are "critical institutions"' (1973, p. 180); but it is an equivocation not so much because universities might subject society to critical evaluation as such, but because they subject society's knowledge to critical assessment.

Chapter 13   Redrawing Interdisciplinarity

1. Lynne Chaney, Chairman, USA National Endowment for the Humanities, gives an example of a completely impenetrable sentence of over 100 words contained in an article on how to teach English! *Reflections on Higher Education*, No. 2, December 1988, Higher Education Foundation, Culham College Institute.

2. Asa Briggs, in Daiches, D. (ed.), 1964, *The Idea of a New University*, London, Deutsch.

3. Centre for Educational Research and Innovation, 1972, *Interdisciplinarity: Problems of Teaching and Research in Universities*, Paris, OECD; the series *Case-Studies in Interdisciplinarity*, produced by the Group for Research and Innovation in Higher Education during the 1970s, Nuffield Foundation, London; *Interdisciplinarity*, 1977 (proceedings of a European Symposium), Guildford, Society for Research into Higher Education: each of these publications contains working examples of interdisciplinarity within higher education.

4. Documented in, for example, Jago, W., 1981, The death of a contextual, *Studies in Higher Education*, **6**(1) 71–6; Thron, E. M. 1981, *The Adaptability of Interdisciplinarity at the University of Wisconsin-Green Bay: A Case Study*, University of Lancaster International Conference on Higher Education.

5. Squires, G., 1987, *The Curriculum Beyond School*, London, Hodder and Stoughton, pp. 150–53.

6. ' "Discipline", etymologically speaking, is rooted in a learning situation; it conveys the notion of submission to rules or some kind of order' (Peters, 1966, p. 267).

7. Gellner, op. cit., ch. 6, note 4.

8. Hirst, The forms of knowledge revisited, in his 1974, pp. 97–9.

9. Bernstein, B., 1971, On the classification and framing of educational knowledge, in Young (ed.), p. 53. Bernstein's paper shows sociologically some other reasons why moves towards an integrated code are likely to be resisted: they represent an attempt to challenge the dominant order and social structure within institutions of higher education. See also Edge, D., 1975, On the purity of science, in Niblett (ed.), which takes up Bernstein's analysis in the context of science.

10. Certain international groupings have been going down this path for some time, in the hope of producing a framework covering possible relationships between disciplines. The CERI volume (note 3) distinguishes four relationships, which it terms in ascending order of integration: *multidisciplinarity*; *pluridisciplinarity*; *interdisciplinarity*; and *transdisciplinarity* (establishing a common set of axioms for a set of disciplines).

The volume *Interdisciplinarity in Higher Education* follows this analysis, but adds *crossdisciplinarity* (where one discipline dominates another), European Centre for Higher Education (CEPES), 1983, Bucharest, UNESCO. These analyses are interesting so far as they go, but they are insufficiently sensitive to the epistemological issues (the different nature of 'disciplines') and the sociological issues connected with moving towards a common programme of interdisciplinarity.

11. Squires, G., in the SRHE volume (note 3): 'one of the motives behind ID may be an attempt to try and match the unity of the world as experienced with a unity of the world as known . . .' (p. 10).

12. Section A4.3, *Handbook, 1988*, London, CNAA, p. 18. (The emphases in the quotations are mine.)

13. In less technical terms, as we saw in Chapter 2, both Newman and Jaspers argued for a philosophical view of knowledge.

14. Lobkowicz, N., 1985, A new synthesis: Is it feasible?, *CRE-inform* **72**, 15–29.

15. A major initiative encouraging the use of computers in the university curriculum claims to cover 90 per cent of all subjects being taught, *Computers in Teaching Initiative Support Service*, Jonathan Darby, University of Oxford, 59 George Street, Oxford OX1 2BH.

16. Barnett, S. A. and Brown, 1981, Pull and push in educational innovation: Study of an interfaculty programme, *Studies in Higher Education*, **6**(1) 13–22.

17. *Towards a Partnership*, London, Council for Industry and Higher Education, 4.1 and 4.5.

18. Watson, in surveying the contemporary moves towards modular systems, mentions 'flexibility' as an attraction, including the possibilities for 'the deployment of staff' (p. 134). As he points out, in an 'era of retrenchment . . . the most powerful arguments surrounding modularity have to do with resources, rationalization . . .' (p. 133). Watson, D., 1989, *Managing the Modular Course: Perspectives from Oxford Polytechnic*, Milton Keynes, Open University Press.

19. Heyck, T. W., 1982, *The Transformation of Intellectual Life in Victorian England*, London, Croom Helm.

20. Edwards, E. G., 1974, *Interdisciplinarity: Learning and Purposes*, University of Bradford, unpublished paper.

21. Op. cit., note 3, p. 254.

22. Although it is commonly grouped within reviews of interdisciplinary work, I am not convinced that the University of Keele programme is genuinely interdisciplinary in this sense (see pp. 17–19 in the SRHE pamphlet, note 3).

23. Compare Horkheimer's conception of a critical interdisciplinary inquiry in the 1930s. He felt that social philosophy could play the part of a single or 'unifying questioner'. See Gray, W. N. and Wyatt, J. F., 1985, Justifying a curriculum and justifying an institution, *Journal of Applied Philosophy*, **2**(1) 63–8. In the previous chapter, I made clear that I believe philosophy and sociology are the most powerful tools of interdisciplinary critique; but other disciplines cannot be ruled out *a priori*. In principle, any discipline can be called on to critique another.

24. Analogously, Dennis Berry describes how he presented the topic of 'creativity' from the viewpoints of philosophy, psychology, neurophysiology and practical design to American arts students, and to British architecture and interior design students. In contrast to the British students, the American students brought all their previous studies to bear on the topic. 'The British students, once departed from the safety of their specialisms, were wide-eyed and lost.' Two-way street to a blind alley, *Times Higher Educational Supplement*, 7 July 1989.

25. See Gyarmati, G., 1986, The teaching of the professions: An interdisciplinary approach, *Higher Education Review*, **18**(2) 33–43.

26. Barnett, R. A., 1981, Integration in curriculum design in higher education, *Journal of Further and Higher Education*, **5**(3) 33–45.

Chapter 14   *A Liberal Higher Education Regained*

1. Peter Scott, 1981, The rediscovery of the liberal university, *Soundings*, **LXIV**(1) 5–28. (Another version of this essay is to be found in Bergendal, 1984.)
2. In approaching the idea of liberal education in the context of higher education, see Powell, J. P., 1965, The idea of a liberal education, *The Australian University*, **3**(1) 1–18 (essentially an analysis of liberal education in the university setting of Victorian England); Peters, R. S., Ambiguities in liberal education and the problem of its content, in both Peters (1980) and Strike and Egan (1978); Wegener, C., 1978, *Liberal Education and the Modern University*, Chicago; Muir, W. M., 1981, *The Classical Concept of Liberal Education and Today's Curriculum*, paper given to University of Lancaster conference on higher education, Canada, University of Regina, Department of Psychology.
3. For a parallel argument, see Wyatt, J., 1980, Accountability means more than coping: Renewing the justification of the liberal education tradition, *Oxford Review of Education*, **6**(1) 53–62.
4. As in Rousseau's *Emile*, for example, Book 2, p. 57 (1911; Everyman edition, London, Dent).
5. The conservative/radical concepts of this chapter have similarities with the Two Concepts of Liberty, identified by Isaiah Berlin. His key distinction, essentially freedom from interference, and freedom to be one's own master, is a helpful perspective on the discussion here (ch. III, in his 1979, *Four Essays on Liberty*, Oxford, Oxford University Press).
6. As in the work of Paulo Freire, for example his *Pedagogy of the Oppressed* (1972); and his discussion with Shor (1987); and Giroux (1983, ch. 5, pp. 190ff.). See also Edwards, E. G., 1982, *Higher Education for Everyone*, Nottingham, Spokesman, p. 163.
7. Many of the extracts in Tight (ed.), 1983, are apposite on this point, but see especially Jack Mezirow, A critical theory of adult learning and education, pp. 124–38.
8. This is the main drive behind the programme of Critical Theory, that in understanding the world, actors come to understand themselves and 'emancipate' themselves. Theories need to be not just descriptive, but critical; and in being critical, carry emancipatory power. See Geuss, 1981, p. 55–8; Gibson, 1986, ch. 1 and p. 100.
9. Tight, op. cit., note 7. Also, Jarvis, P., 1983, *Adult and Continuing Education: Theory and Practice*, London, Croom Helm, which contains emancipatory or radical dimensions in much of its discussion of the literature.
10. Mentioned, interestingly, as an example of independent learning by Michael Moore, The individual adult learner, p. 154, in Tight, op. cit., note 7.
11. Hirst, Liberal education and the nature of knowledge, in his 1974 collection; Blanshard, B., 1974, *The Uses of a Liberal Education*, London, Alcove/La Salle, Illinois, Open Court (ch. 2).
12. For Newman, the object of the cultivation of the intellect was 'to open the mind, to correct it, to refine it, to enable it to know . . .' (p. 112).
13. Both Hirst and Muir (op. cit.) refer to the Greek origins of this conception.
14. Gellert underlines the emphasis on character formation in his characterization of the nineteenth-century English idea of higher education (in comparison with the German conception), Gellert, C., 1981, *A Comparative Study of the Changing Functions of English and German Universities*, Cambridge, University of Cambridge, PhD thesis, unpublished.
15. Newman talked of liberal education 'making gentlemen' (not for gentlemen), by

which he meant the 'connatural qualities of a large knowledge' (1976 edition, p. 110).

16. Castles and Wustenberg, 1979; Small, R., 1984, The concept of polytechnical education, *British Journal of Educational Studies*. **XXXII**(1) 27–44.

17. As practised not only by Oxford and Cambridge, but also by the Civil Service.

18. Edwards, 1982, *Higher Education for Everyone*, Nottingham, Spokesman, ch. 11; Finch and Rustin (eds), 1986, in *A Degree of Choice? Higher Education and the Right to Learn*, Harmondsworth, Penguin.

19. Evans, N., 1980, *The Knowledge Revolution*, London, McIntyre Grant.

20. Percy, K. and Ramsden, P., 1980, *Independent Study: Two Examples from English Higher Education*, Guildford, SRHE.

21. Knowles, M., 1986, *Using Learning Contracts*, San Francisco, Jossey-Bass.

22. Robbins, D., 1988, *The Rise of Independent Study*, Milton Keynes, Open University Press.

23. Boyer, E. and Levine, A., 1981, *A Quest for Common Learning*, Washington, Carnegie Foundation for the Advancement of Teaching, p. 19. The essay is based on historical and empirical surveys, which show there has been successive waves of calls for general education in the USA, each connected with national and international crises.

24. Ibid., p. 35 *et seq.*

25. On 'general powers of the mind', Robbins Report, 1963, p. 6, para. 26.

26. Dearden, R. F., 1980, What is general about general education?, *Oxford Review of Education*, **6**(3) 279–88.

27. Cf. Derek Bok's suggestions in his *Higher Learning*, 1986, p. 54.

28. For example, Habermas, 1972, p. 113: 'The model of forces of production and relations of production would have to be replaced by the more abstract one of work and interaction.'

29. Cf. Barrett, W., 1979, *The Illusion of Technique*.

30. Cave, M. *et al.*, 1988, *The Use of Performance Indicators in Higher Education: A Critical Analysis of Developing Practice*, London, Jessica Kingsley, table 5, pp. 118–19.

31. Miller, C. and Parlett, M., 1974 (reprinted 1983), *Up to the Mark: A Study of the Exam Game*, Guildford, SRHE.

32. Herbst, P., 1973, Work, labour and university education, in R. S. Peters (ed.).

33. A line taken by Charles Wegener in his *Liberal Education and the Modern University*, 1978.

34. Silver, H. and Brennan, J., 1988, *A Liberal Vocationalism?* London, Methuen, ch. 14; Cheit, E. F. (ed.), 1975, *The Useful Arts and the Liberal Tradition*, California, Carnegie Commission on Higher Education and McGraw-Hill; papers by Sjostrom, Svensson and Wallen in Bergendal, 1984.

35. Birch, W., 1988, *The Challenge to Higher Education*.

Selective Bibliography

The titles in this list have been chosen so that collectively they map out the ground of this inquiry. The list is intended to constitute a usable resource for those wishing to do work in what might be termed the philosophy of higher education. The list includes key works of the main sources for this book, including Peters, Gellner, Habermas, Gouldner and Feyerabend. It also includes a number of secondary titles on Habermas and Critical Theory, which are a better way into that school of thought. For books having a USA publisher, I have given the location of the American office as well as the UK.

Where readers wish to go further into specific topics, they should turn to the references in the notes to the chapters concerned.

Althusser, L. (1969). Ideology and ideological state apparatuses, in B. Cosin (ed.), *School and Society*. London, Routledge and Kegan Paul.

Althusser, L. (1979). *For Marx*. Harmondsworth, Penguin.

Apple, M. (1979). *Ideology and Curriculum*. London, Routledge and Kegan Paul.

Apple, M. (1985). *Education and Power*. Boston and London, Ark.

Aronowitz, S. and Giroux, H. (1987). *Education under Siege*. London, Routledge and Kegan Paul.

Barnes, B. (1974). *Scientific Knowledge and Sociological Theory*. London, Routledge and Kegan Paul.

Barnes, B. (1977). *Interests and the Growth of Knowledge*. London, Routledge and Kegan Paul.

Barrett, W. (1979). *The Illusion of Technique*. London, William Kimber.

Becher, T. (1989). *Academic Tribes and Territories*. Milton Keynes, Open University Press.

Bell, D. (1976). *The Coming of Post-industrial Society*. Harmondsworth, Penguin.

Bergendal, G. (ed.) (1983). *Knowledge and Higher Education*. Stockholm, National Board of Universities and Colleges.

Bergendal, G. (ed.) (1984). *Knowledge Policies and the Traditions of Higher Education*. Stockholm, Almquist and Wiksell.

Berger, P. L. and Luckmann, T. (1971). *The Social Construction of Reality*. Harmondsworth, Penguin.

Bernstein, R. J. (1983). *Beyond Objectivism and Relativism*. Oxford, Blackwell.

Bernstein, R. J. (ed.) (1987). *Habermas and Modernity*. Cambridge, Polity.

Birch, W. (1988). *The Challenge to Higher Education: Reconciling Responsibilities to Scholarship and to Society*. Milton Keynes, Open University Press.

Bloor, D. (1976). *Knowledge and Social Imagery*. London, Routledge and Kegan Paul.

Bok, D. (1982). *Beyond the Ivory Tower*. Cambridge, Mass. and London, Harvard University Press.

Bok, D. (1986). *Higher Learning*. Cambridge, Mass. and London, Harvard University Press.

Bourdieu, P. and Passeron, J. C. (1979). *The Inheritors: French Students and their Relation to Culture*. Chicago and London, University of Chicago Press.

Brubacher, J. S. (1978). *On The Philosophy of Higher Education*. San Francisco and London, Jossey-Bass.

Cameron, J. M. (1978). *On the Idea of a University*. Toronto, University of Toronto Press.

Castles, S. and Wustenberg, W. (1979). *The Education of the Future: An Introduction to the Theory and Practice of Socialist Education*. London, Pluto.

Centre for Educational Research and Innovation (1972). *Interdisciplinarity: Problems of Teaching and Research in Universities*. Paris, Organization for Economic Co-operation and Development.

Chapman, J. W. (ed.) (1983). *The Western University on Trial*. Stanford, Calif. and London, University of California Press.

Connerton, P. (1980). *The Tragedy of Enlightenment: An Essay on the Frankfurt School*. Cambridge, Cambridge University Press.

Dickson, D. (1988). *The New Politics of Science*. Chicago and London, University of Chicago Press.

Feyerabend, P. (1978). *Against Method*. London, Verso.

Feyerabend, P. (1982). *Science in a Free Society*. London, Verso.

Feyerabend, P. (1987). *Farewell to Reason*. London, Verso.

Foucault, M. (1974). *The Archaeology of Knowledge*. London, Tavistock.

Foucault, M. (1986). In P. Rabinow (ed.), *The Foucault Reader*. Harmondsworth, Penguin.

Freire, P. (1972). *Pedagogy of the Oppressed*. Harmondsworth, Penguin.

Freire, P. and Shor, I. (1987). *A Pedagogy for Liberation*. London, Macmillan.

Gellner, E. (1969). *Thought and Change*. London, Weidenfeld and Nicolson.

Gellner, E. (1974). *Legitimation of Belief*. Cambridge, Cambridge University Press.

Geuss, R. (1981). *The Idea of a Critical Theory: Habermas and the Frankfurt School*. Cambridge, Cambridge University Press.

Gibson, R. (1986). *Critical Theory and Education*. London, Hodder and Stoughton.

Giroux, H. A. (1983). *Theory and Resistance in Education: A Pedagogy for the Opposition*. London, Heinemann.

Goodlad, S. (1976). *Conflict and Consensus in Higher Education*. London, Hodder and Stoughton.

Gouldner, A. (1976). *The Dialectic of Ideology and Technology*. London, Macmillan.

Gouldner, A. (1979). *The Future of Intellectuals and the Rise of the New Class*. London, Macmillan.

Habermas, J. (1972). *Toward a Rational Society*. London, Heinemann.

Habermas, J. (1976). *Legitimation Crisis*. London, Heinemann.

Habermas, J. (1978). *Knowledge and Human Interests*. London, Heinemann.

Habermas, J. (1979). *Communication and the Evolution of Society*. London, Heinemann.

(These titles of Habermas are now available from Polity Press.)

Hampshire, S. (1970). *Thought and Action*. London, Chatto and Windus.

Harris, K. (1979). *Education and Knowledge*. London, Routledge and Kegan Paul.

Hirst, P. (1974). *Knowledge and the Curriculum*. London, Routledge and Kegan Paul.

Hirst, P. (ed.) (1983). *Educational Theory and its Foundation Disciplines*. London, Routledge and Kegan Paul.

Hollis, M. and Lukes, S. (eds) (1982). *Rationality and Relativism*. Oxford, Blackwell.

Jaspers, K. (1965). *The Idea of the University*. London, Peter Owen (originally published 1946).

Jenks, C. (ed.) (1977). *Rationality, Education and the Social Organization of Knowledge*. London, Routledge and Kegan Paul.

Kerr, C. (1972). *The Uses of the University*. Cambridge, Mass., Harvard University Press.

Kuhn, T. S. (1970). *The Structure of Scientific Revolutions*. Chicago and London, University of Chicago Press.

Lakatos, I. and Musgrave, A. (eds) (1977). *Criticism and the Growth of Scientific Knowledge*. Cambridge, Cambridge University Press.

Larrain, J. (1979). *The Concept of Ideology*. London, Hutchinson.

Lawson, H. and Appignanesi, L. (eds) (1989). *Dismantling Truth: Reality in the Post-Modern World*. London, Weidenfeld and Nicolson.

Leavis, F. R. (1943). *Education and the University*. Cambridge, Cambridge University Press (reprinted 1979).

Leavis, F. R. (1969). *English Literature in our Time and the University*. London, Chatto and Windus.

Lyotard, J. (1984). *The Postmodern Condition: A Report on Knowledge*. Manchester, Manchester University Press.

MacIntyre, A. (1985). *After Virtue*. London, Duckworth.

Marcuse, H. (1968). *One Dimensional Man*. London, Sphere.

Marton, F. *et al.* (eds) (1984). *The Experience of Learning*. Edinburgh, Scottish Academic Press.

Maxwell, N. (1987). *From Knowledge to Wisdom*. Oxford, Blackwell.

Mepham, J. and Ruben, D.-H. (eds) (1978). *Issues in Marxist Philosophy. Volume 3: Epistemology, Science and Ideology*. Brighton, Harvester.

Minogue, K. (1973). *The Concept of a University*. London, Weidenfeld and Nicolson.

Moberly, W. (1949). *The Crisis in the University*. London, SCM Press.

Montefiore, A. (ed.) (1975). *Neutrality and Impartiality: The University and Political Commitment*. Cambridge, Cambridge University Press.

Moore, T. W. (1977). *Educational Theory: An Introduction*. London, Routledge and Kegan Paul.

Newman, J. H. (1976). *The Idea of a University* (ed. I. T. Ker). Oxford, Oxford University Press (originally published 1853).

Niblett, W. R. (1974). *Universities Between Two Worlds*. London, University of London Press.

Niblett, W. R. (ed.) (1975). *The Sciences, the Humanities, and the Technological Threat*. London, University of London Press.

Nisbet, R. (1971). *The Degradation of the Academic Dogma: The University in America, 1945–1970*. London, Heinemann.

Nuttgens, P. (1988). *What Should We Teach, and How Should We Teach It? Aims and Purposes of Higher Education*. Aldershot, Wildwood.

Ortega y Gasset (1946). *Mission of the University*. London, Kegan Paul.

Peacocke, A. (1985). *Reductionism in Academic Disciplines*. Guildford, SRHE/NFER-Nelson.

Peters, R. S. (1966). *Ethics and Education*. London, George Allen and Unwin.

Peters, R. S. (ed.) (1969). *The Concept of Education*, especially chs 1, 7–10 and 12. London, Routledge and Kegan Paul.

Peters, R. S. (ed.) (1973). *Philosophy of Education*, especially chs 1–4, 8 and 12. Oxford, Oxford University Press.

Peters, R. S. (1980). *Education and the Education of Teachers*, especially chs 3, 4 and 10. London, Routledge and Kegan Paul.

Phillipson, N. (ed.) (1983). *Universities, Society and the Future*. Edinburgh, Edinburgh University Press.

Plato (1971) *The Republic* (translated by F. M. Cornford). Oxford, Oxford University Press (first published 1945).

Polanyi, M. (1966). *The Tacit Dimension*. New York, Doubleday.

Poole, R. (1972). *Towards Deep Subjectivity*. London, Allen Lane.

Popper, K. R. (1975). *Objective Knowledge: An Evolutionary Approach*. Oxford, Oxford University Press.

Reeves, M. (1988). *The Crisis in Higher Education*. Milton Keynes, Open University Press.

Reid, L. and Reid, A. (1986). *Ways of Understanding and Education*. London, Heinemann.

Robbins, Lord (1963). *Higher Education: Report of the Committee*. London, HMSO, Cmnd. 2154.

Robinson, E. (1968). *The New Polytechnics*. Harmondsworth, Penguin.

Roderick, R. (1986). *Habermas and the Foundations of Critical Theory*. London, Macmillan.

Rorty, R. (1980). *Philosophy and the Mirror of Nature*. Oxford, Blackwell.

Rose, H. and Rose, S. (1976). *The Political Economy of Science: Ideology of/in the Natural Sciences*. London, Macmillan.

Ryle, G. (1949). *The Concept of Mind*. Harmondsworth, Penguin (reprinted 1968).

Schon, D. A. (1983). *The Reflective Practitioner: How Professionals Think in Action*. New York, Basic Books.

Scott, P. (1984). *The Crisis of the University*. London, Croom Helm.

Shaw, M. (1975). *Marxism and Social Science: The Roots of Social Knowledge*. London, Pluto.

Shils, E. (1984). *The Academic Ethic*. Chicago and London, University of Chicago Press.

Snow, C. P. (1964). *The Two Cultures and a Second Look*. Cambridge, Cambridge University Press (reprinted 1978).

Snyder, B. R. (1971). *The Hidden Curriculum*. Cambridge, Mass. and London, MIT Press.

Strike, K. A. and Egan, K. (eds) (1978). *Ethics and Educational Policy*, especially chs 1–3, 6 and 10. London, Routledge and Kegan Paul.

Taylor, W. (ed.) (1984). *Metaphors of Education*. London, Heinemann.

Tight, M. (ed.) (1983). *Adult Learning and Education*. London, Croom Helm.

Wegener, C. (1978). *Liberal Education and the Modern University*. Chicago and London, University of Chicago.

White, J. (1982). *The Aims of Education Restated*. London, Routledge and Kegan Paul.

Wilson, B. R. (ed.) (1970). *Rationality*. Oxford, Blackwell.

Wittgenstein, L. (1978). *Philosophical Investigations*. Oxford, Blackwell.

Young, M. F. D. (ed.) (1971). *Knowledge and Control*. London, Macmillan.

Young, M. and Whitty, G. (eds) (1978). *Society, State and Schooling*, especially chs 2.1, 2.3 and 2.4. Lewes, Falmer Press.

Index

Key references to the Notes (pp. 206–31) are included in this index and are shown in italics.

Benefits to members

Individual

Individual members receive:

* *SRHE News*, the Society's publications list, conference details and other material included in mailings.
* Greatly reduced rates for *Studies in Higher Education* and *Higher Education Quarterly*.
* A 35 per cent discount on all SRHE & Open University Press publications.
* Free copies of the Proceedings – commissioned papers on the theme of the Annual Conference.
* Free copies of *Research into Higher Education Abstracts*.
* Reduced rates for conferences.
* Extensive contacts and scope for facilitating initiatives.
* Reduced reciprocal memberships.
* Free copies of the *Register of Members' Research Interests*.

Corporate

Corporate members receive:

* All benefits of individual members, plus.
* Free copies of *Studies in Higher Education*.
* Unlimited copies of the Society's publications at reduced rates.
* Special rates for its members e.g. to the Annual Conference.
* The right to submit application for the Society's research grants.

Membership details: SRHE, 3 Devonshire Street, London W1N 2BA, UK. Tel: 0171 637 2766. Fax: 0171 637 2781. email: srhe@clus1.ulcc.ac.uk
Catalogue: SRHE & Open University Press, Celtic Court, 22 Ballmoor, Buckingham MK18 1XW. Tel: 01280 823388. Fax: 01280 823233. email: enquiries@openup.co.uk

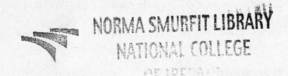

The Society for Research into Higher Education

The Society for Research into Higher Education exists to stimulate and coordinate research into all aspects of higher education. It aims to improve the quality of higher education through the encouragement of debate and publication on issues of policy, on the organization and management of higher education institutions, and on the curriculum and teaching methods.

The Society's income is derived from subscriptions, sales of its books and journals, conference fees and grants. It receives no subsidies, and is wholly independent. Its individual members include teachers, researchers, managers and students. Its corporate members are institutions of higher education, research institutes, professional, industrial and governmental bodies. Members are not only from the UK, but from elsewhere in Europe, from America, Canada and Australasia, and it regards its international work as among its most important activities.

Under the imprint *SRHE & Open University Press*, the Society is a specialist publisher of research, having some 60 titles in print. The Editorial Board of the Society's Imprint seeks authoritative research or study in the above fields. It offers competitive royalties, a highly recognizable format in both hardback and paperback and the worldwide reputation of the Open University Press.

The Society also publishes *Studies in Higher Education* (three times a year), which is mainly concerned with academic issues, *Higher Education Quarterly* (formerly *Universities Quarterly*), mainly concerned with policy issues, *Research into Higher Education Abstracts* (three times a year), and *SRHE News* (four times a year).

The Society holds a major annual conference in December, jointly with an institution of higher education. In 1994 the topic was 'The Student Experience' at the University of York. In 1995 it was 'The Changing University' at Heriot-Watt University in Edinburgh and in 1996, 'Working in Higher Education' at Cardiff Institute of Higher Education. Conferences in 1997 include 'Beyond the First Degree' at the University of Warwick.

The Society's committees, study groups and branches are run by the members. The groups at present include:

Teacher Education Study Group
Continuing Education Group
Staff Development Group
Excellence in Teaching and Learning